New Media Theory

Series Editor, Byron Hawk

New Media Theory

Series Editor, Byron Hawk

The New Media Theory series investigates both media and new media as a complex ecological and rhetorical context. The merger of media and new media creates a global social sphere that is changing the ways we work, play, write, teach, think, and connect. Because this new context operates through evolving arrangements, theories of new media have yet to establish a rhetorical and theoretical paradigm that fully articulates this emerging digital life.

The series includes books that combine social, cultural, political, textual, rhetorical, aesthetic, and material theories in order to understand moments in the lives that operate in these emerging contexts. Such works typically bring rhetorical and critical theories to bear on media and new media in a way that elaborates a burgeoning post-disciplinary "medial turn" as one further development of the rhetorical and visual turns that have already influenced scholarly work.

Other Books in the Series

The Two Virtuals: New Media and Composition, by Alexander Reid (2007). Honorable Mention, W. Ross Winterowd/*JAC* Award for Best Book in Composition Theory, 2007.

New Media/New Methods

The Academic Turn from Literacy to Electracy

Edited by
Jeff Rice and Marcel O'Gorman

Parlor Press
West Lafayette, Indiana
www.parlorpress.com

Parlor Press LLC, West Lafayette, Indiana 47906

S A N: 2 5 4 - 8 8 7 9

Library of Congress Cataloging-in-Publication Data

New media/new methods : the academic turn from literacy to electracy /
edited by Jeff Rice and Marcel O'Gorman.
p. cm. -- (New media theory)
Includes bibliographical references and index.
ISBN 978-1-60235-063-2 (pbk. : alk. paper) -- ISBN 978-1-60235-064-9
(hardcover : alk. paper) -- ISBN 978-1-60235-065-6 (adobe ebook)
1. Mass media--Study and teaching. 2. Mass media--Methodology. I.
Rice, Jeff. II. O'Gorman, Marcel.
P91.3.N49 2008
302.2301--dc22

2008020108

Cover design by David Blakesley.

Printed on acid-free paper.

Parlor Press, LLC is an independent publisher of scholarly and trade titles in print and multimedia formats. This book is available in paper, cloth and Adobe eBook formats from Parlor Press on the World Wide Web at http://www.parlorpress.com or through online and brick-and-mortar bookstores. For submission information or to find out about Parlor Press publications, write to Parlor Press, 816 Robinson St., West Lafayette, Indiana, 47906, or e-mail editor@parlorpress.com.

Contents

Acknowledgments

This collection could not have been completed without the support of Parlor Press. David Blakesley showed strong interest and support for our ideas and approaches towards new media where others may have flinched. We thank Byron Hawk for his support and enthusiasm in adding our collection to Parlor's New Media Series. And we thank Cynthia Haynes for her insightful comments and suggestions regarding the manuscript. We are grateful to our mentors and colleagues who patiently worked with us on this collection and contributed their work to this project.

—Jeff Rice and Marcel O'Gorman

New Media/New Methods

Getting Schooled: Introduction to the Florida School

Jeff Rice and Marcel O'Gorman

"The content of any medium is always just another medium. The content of writing is speech, just as the written word is the content of print, and print is the content of the telegraph."

—Marshall McLuhan, *Understanding Media*

"To invent an electronic academic writing the way Breton invented surrealism, or the way Plato invented dialectics: to do with 'Jacques Derrida' (and this name marks a slot, a passe-partout open to infinite substitution) what Breton did with Freud (or—why not?—what Plato did with Socrates)."

—Greg Ulmer, *Heuretics*

While assembling this collection, the editors got tangled up in the following question: What is new media? And why emphasize the concept of "newness" in the title of this book, as if we were attempting to market another flavor of soft drink or a more refreshing toothpaste? Indeed, the reference to the "new" in "new media" has become an obligatory gesture we find difficult to resist. As it turns out, the concept of "the new" is at the core of this project in which newness—in the form of *invention*—is posited as a generative link between media technology and critical theory. What this book has to offer is a school of critical theory that takes very seriously the implications of living in a culture driven by newness, and responds by placing invention at the center of a new form of academic writing.

For at least a decade now, the terms "new media" and "digital media" have been used interchangeably to identify everything from film and television to the Web and Virtual Reality. In *The Language of New Media,* Lev Manovich defines new media as a recent development: "graphics, moving images, sounds, shapes, spaces, and texts become computable, that is, simply sets of computer data. In short, media become new media" (25). Against this, scholars such as Lisa Gitelman and Geoffrey Pingree (*New Media, 1740–1915*) posit a more historical understanding of the term, emphasizing the cultural impact of specific technological inventions. From such a perspective, "All media were once new media" (12). "When we talk about new media," Scott Rettberg writes in the introduction to the *American Book Review's New Media* edition, "we're usually talking about art, literature, and other kinds of cultural 'objects' made for computer networks" (Rettberg). This collection enters the debate by focusing on newness as the process (one might even say, the continual state) of invention, which is the essence of contemporary technological being. Whether or not "new media" means "computable media," what matters for us is that new technologies are the result of an unrelenting drive toward invention, evidence perhaps, of our immersion in "late capitalism" or even in what Martin Heidegger called the "challenging-forth" that is characteristic of a technological way of being. What mode of critical theory is appropriate in such an environment? In this situation of relentless technological invention we offer a school of relentless methodological invention.

Where this collection meets the work of Manovich, Gitelman and Pingree, and others, is in our understanding of how new media are invented and how they take shape. Drawing on the term coined by Jay Bolter and Richard Grusin, we see new media arising out of a process of "remediation," whereby new technological apparatuses appropriate the forms of earlier apparatuses, and vice versa, through a gradual process of invention. But this collection differs greatly from other new media texts in that it sees remediation not only as the process of media invention, but also as a way of inventing a new scholarly poetics. The contributors to *New Media/New Methods* remediate terms, concepts, and systems from all levels of discourse, transforming them into critical methodologies suitable to a culture of computing. In this collection, funk music provides the theory for teaching English composition, Elvis collaborates with Godard to teach us film criticism,

William Blake offers a method for new media production, and music videos provide a formal paradigm for conducting academic research. Rather than transposing traditional print-oriented machinery (5-paragraph essay, canon, etc.) into the critique of new media, the contributors in this book draw their methods from the media itself, and from its practitioners. As Greg Ulmer writes in his contribution, "Florida Out of Sorts," members of the Florida School treat "theory not as a content or object of study but as a creative or generative poetics." How we generate a poetics of new media plays out in this volume's divergent contributions.

Even Gainesville, Florida, site of the University of Florida, is not immune from this logic of remediation. Gainesville (in specific, the Devil's Millhopper sink-hole), Gregory Ulmer has written, signifies one of the four imagined places of Xanadu in Samuel Taylor Coledridge's poem "Kubla Khan." Ulmer includes this observation in a larger heuristic designed as a remake in his essay "Kubla Honky Tonk: Voice in Cyber-Pidgin." Ulmer utilizes the coincidental overlap of William Bartram's travels to North Central Florida (Gainesville) and Coledridge's later usage of that moment in order to explore how Xanadu's various meanings—including Ted Nelson's vision of the Xanadu hypertext system—can produce a design practice for Internet writing. One by one, each of the contributors to this collection encountered his or her own Xanadu in Gainesville, more specifically in the English department at the University of Florida, under the counsel of Gregory Ulmer and Robert Ray. Ulmer and Ray's teachings situate the very specific ways we have come to understand digital media. Digital media encompasses the complex and intersecting paths of rhetoric, technology, and film; their overlaps and juxtapositions form an emerging apparatus. Following Ulmer and Ray's work, we attempt to invent practices for that apparatus. The result of Ulmer and Ray's teachings, as well as our shaping of those teachings, is a series of methodologies, theories, and neologisms invented for the purpose of rendering scholarly research more suitable to an age of digital media.

This collection is meant to demonstrate as well how we have come to adopt Ulmer's notion of *electracy,* the consequent shift in meaning-making which follows—and integrates—orality and literacy. "All the practices used to conduct schooling are relative to the apparatus of literacy. In the history of human culture there are but three apparatuses: orality, literacy, and now electracy. We live in the moment of the emergence of electracy, comparable to the two principal moments of literacy (The Greece of Plato, and the Europe of Galileo)" ("What is Electracy?"). Typically, scholarly collections on literacy in the age of digital media position the emerging apparatus in terms of literacy and literary conventions. Such studies—triumphed by Harvey Graff, Deborah Brandt, Cynthia Selfe, and Mike Rose—reflect how we are coming to terms with media's relationship to literate practices. Even the erstwhile avant-garde anthologies known today as "hypertext theory" posited the emerging apparatus in terms of conventional print practices. Hypertext was viewed either as "super-literacy," a more efficient mode of archiving and thus interpreting literary texts, or as "anti-literacy," a non-sequential, multi-linear fulfillment of such deconstructive mainstays as "intertextuality" and "the death of the author." Rather than interpreting or positioning the electronic apparatus within the terms of print, or even within the terms of critical theory, members of the Florida School seek to jump right in and *shape* the electronic apparatus by inventing new modes of discourse that take both critical theory and digital media for granted.

As Terry Eagleton argues in *After Theory,* literary scholarship in the past forty or so years has made us experts in literacy, to the point of establishing a highly technical jargon—critical theory—with which texts (including books, films, and other forms of mass media) can be dissected. But the end result of this specialization seems to be nothing more than *hyper-hermeneutics,* a more efficient production of interpretive essays which rely on critical theory as the software in a sort of post-literate writing machine. As Robert Ray asserts, in the past several decades, what we have come to call film and media studies has

> constructed an enormously powerful theoretical machine for exposing the ideological abuse hidden by the apparently natural stories and images of popular culture. That machine, however, now runs on automatic pilot, producing predictable essays and books on individual cases. (*Avant-Garde* 7)

The "machine" in this case, what Eagleton calls "high theory," is nothing more than the apotheosis of the apparatus of literacy. To resist this machine, members of the Florida School are attempting, out of necessity, to construct another apparatus by focusing on heuretics (the logic of invention) rather than on hermeneutics (interpretation). As

Eagleton suggests, "those who can, think up feminism or structuralism; those who can't, apply such insights to *Moby Dick* or *The Cat in the Hat*" (2).

The term "Florida School" itself was invented as a way of identifying this new approach to criticism characterized by methodological invention. The process of self-naming may seem counter to how other schools of thought have been named by outside forces or long after their inception (Birmingham School of Cultural Studies, Yale School of Deconstruction). As many of the essays in this volume show, self-naming is itself a new media practice. Encountered in the neologism, the signature, the remake, the alter ego, and other types of media-oriented rhetorical gestures embraced by the contributors, this desire to name one's self is perhaps a reflection of today's cyber-structured identities. More to the point, the Florida School's act of self-naming is a form of pattern recognition, a strategy for organizing information in the otherwise overwhelming infoscape of new media studies and critical theory.

As a way of illustrating this strategy, and also as a strategy for presenting a simultaneous manifesto and book introduction, the remainder of this section outlines key concepts and terms that give shape to the Florida School. By presenting keywords rather than narrative, we embrace the fragment as a rhetorical gesture found in poststructuralism and in new media work. In this way, this introduction may function as a manual or how-to guide for new modes of writing and critique. The reader, then, might view this list as a series of "commonplaces," such as those used in classical rhetoric to locate an appropriate argument (*inventio*) for an appropriate situation. It would be more appropriate from the perspective of the Florida School, however, if the reader would view these terms only as a scant, provisional, and tantalizingly nonsensical list of ingredients. In the words of Paul Feyerabend, "the inventor of a new world view must be able to talk nonsense until the amount of nonsense created by him and his friends is big enough to give sense to all its parts" (256–257). With this in mind, readers are invited to be Friends of the Florida School, to contribute to this list, and to generate their own methods towards giving shape to the nascent apparatus of electracy.

ABC

Definition. Recognizing the need to simultaneously step outside of alphabetic categorization (exemplified by the topoi) while reshaping discursive functionality, Robert Ray borrows (remixes) Roland Barthes' ABC method as another new media strategy seldom appropriated. Ray applies Barthes' ABC breakdown most notably in *The Avant-Garde Finds Andy Hardy*, where he asks, "Is there an alternative to criticism?" (10). The ABC method attempts to forge such an alternative by reapplying the logic of categorization through fragmented observations, most of which are not meant to follow or complement one another in hierarchical fashion. "This approach," Ray writes, "seems ideally suited for film studies. Indeed, it anticipates the notion of cyberspace, which assumes that we are always operating 'within information'" (*Avant-Garde* 122). Ray's approach destabilizes the hierarchies print establishes by remediating the alphabet so that it functions associatively. While Ray's contribution to this volume is not an ABC, it suggests the ABC as one way writers can work with the "ruffles" and "wind in the trees" conducive to a 21st century film studies that requires writers to focus on details and memories in place of narrative structure, explication, or analysis. "How can academic film scholars devise a 'narrative synthesis' that will propagate professional knowledge about the cinema?" Ray asks. His question, which fuses history with imagination, disruption with recognition, attempts to spark a new media-based film theory.

Instruction. To compose an ABC, one must isolate details, fragments of interest, and construct around the pleasure one experiences from such moments (what Barthes calls *jouissance*). When writing the ABC method, think associatively in place of syllogistically. Expose, don't explain. Always keep in mind that the ABC method is a performance of a text (or series of texts) which, in turn, yields an entirely new text reflective of how new media shapes alphabetic literacy. Follow Ray's advice by composing through epigrammatic, metaphorical, anecdotal, playful, lyrical, and analytical fragments (*Avant-Garde* 120–21). Your goal, as Ray notes in his contribution, is to generate a "hallucinatory quality," an imagistic reasoning as much filmic as it is about film.

Chora

Definition. For many of the contributors to this volume, the Aristotelian topoi, places of argumentation typically associated with invention, yield to chora, what Ulmer defines as based on "pattern making, pattern recognition, pattern generation. It is not that memory is no longer thought of as 'place,' but that the notion itself of spatiality has changed" (*Heuretics* 36). The topoi of new media, which often focus on access, race, community, and other terms, have become canonized into repeated tropes which dictate new media study. These topoi allow for what Robert Scholes has called the impossible task of literary coverage; their selections function as canonized entries. Familiarity serves canonical work by establishing common grounds which tend to override the practice of invention. Imagining new media in terms of familiarity, Marshall McLuhan wrote, is an ideological push to establish uniformity, to fashion an unwavering topos from which we can discuss or critique the practices we associate with this idea. When we depend too strongly on topoi, we are interpellated to see familiarity as the sole basis of the emerging media.

Instruction. To write with chora, you will need to work outside the limitations of restricted meaning that print requires (i.e. definition and categorization). The chorographer, Ulmer notes, uses multiple meanings at once, writes with patterns, allows place to do more than hold ideas. What the essayist or the anthologist was to the topoi, the chorographer is to chora. Rethink the topoi of new media by inventing new methods for research, writing, and teaching (as opposed to canonical replication of established disciplinary practice: explication and thesis driven work). Chora signifies a new media (electracy) approach to discourse. Consider Ulmer's contribution to this volume, which demonstrates chorography in terms of the Florida Research Ensemble's mapping of the Miami River. "The theory guiding the experiment," Ulmer writes, "dictated that the image capable of grasping the zone as a whole would not be a 'universal' in the mode of a literate concept, but would be a singularity, a 'third meaning,' expressing the electrate mode of categorization—chora."

The Fragment

Definition. The writers in this collection draw heavily and frequently from avant-garde art in the search for a poetics more suitable to new media. While this book is about making methods and not art (as Greg Ulmer reminds his students on a regular basis), avant-garde artists serve as ideal exemplars in the invention of new modes of discourse.

In *The Language of New Media,* Lev Manovich suggests that by looking at the history of visual culture and media, in particular, cinema, we can find many strategies and techniques relevant to new media design. Put differently, to develop a new aesthetics of new media, we should pay as much attention to cultural history as to the computer's unique new possibilities to generate, organize, manipulate, and distribute data. (314)

Roland Barthes, in *A Lover's Discourse,* borrowed the *fragment* of avant-garde art and film to integrate portions of his own life with scenes from Goethe's *Young Werther.* Whereas Barthes was designing for book production, Barry Mauer and his students are designing for digital media, as evidenced in Mauer's essay "Clipography." Rather than focusing on the term "fragment," Mauer points specifically to "the clip," an essential part of music and video production (editing), but also, as Mauer notes, the dominating poetics of a generation raised on music videos. Clipography, as a pedagogical exercise, "borrows from rock'n'roll to offer polyvocality, discourse crossing, fragmentation, and pattern formation in a collage form of writing." The clipographer selects a specific problem to solve, and creates a collage of clips from the discursive levels of family, entertainment, school, and discipline (Ulmer's "popcycle"), thereby locating herself within the matrix of that problem. Like many of the Florida School methodologies, the result of clipography is not a sequential set of arguments leading to an inevitable logical conclusion, but "a performance of discourses" that sheds light on a problem by means of complexification rather than simplification.

Instruction. From the history of visual culture, borrow an image-making or narrative technique that seems suitable for "remediation" in a new media environment. Once a specific technique has been identified, use it to generate a broader poetics by turning it into a *puncept,* a pun that generates a concept. Mauer, for example, notes that the word clip can mean an extract, a news story cut out of a print publication, any of numerous devices that grip or clasp loose things together, and a container for bullets, slotted directly into an automatic firearm. The implications of these terms resonate with clipography by emphasizing the collage nature of the work as well as its striking effects.

The puncept echoes the visual logic of film editing and of hypertext production. Allow your puncept to not only generate a new mode of knowledge production, but also to justify its form and content, thereby replacing the reductive or abductive logic of traditional research with a new conductive logic that is characteristic of electracy.

Hypericon

Definition. Is it necessary any longer to insist that western culture is dominated by a pictorial aesthetic, that we are bombarded by images on a daily basis, from billboards and magazine ads to television and graphical user interfaces? If this is an acceptable conclusion, a cliché even, then why is humanities scholarship still stubbornly rooted in text-based communication? This observation is central to W. J. T. Mitchell's thesis in the book *Picture Theory,* where he also suggests that western philosophy has undergone a "pictorial turn," as evidenced in the Frankfurt School's obsession with mass media, Foucault's study of the power networks in scopic regimes, and Derrida's grammatology, a turn from logocentrism to the visible traces of writing (12). But none of these can compete with the rhetorical power mobilized in a single Hollywood movie or magazine ad, whose complex interweaving of image and text, what Mitchell calls "imagetexts," dominate the living patterns and imaginations of millions of North Americans. As Marcel O'Gorman argues, to compete with this onslaught of visual information, critics of contemporary culture must not only learn how pictures work (picture theory), but also how to work more effectively with pictures (picturing theory). O'Gorman proposes "a mode of picture theory, a form of meta-discourse that produces knowledge while calling into question the techniques of that production." Whereas the philosophers and rhetoricians of the 15th century planted the roots of literacy, their contemporaries must scatter the rhizomes of electracy.

Instruction. Learn not only how to write about images, but also to write *with* images. Turn your texts into imagetexts and make careful use of what Mitchell has called "the hypericon." According to Mitchell, Michel Foucault's essay "Ceci n'est pas une pipe," demonstrates an excellent use of "the hypericon." Whether Magritte likes it or not, his painting, *La trahison des images,* is transformed by Foucault into "a kind of summary image [that] . . . encapsulates an entire episteme, a theory of knowledge" (49). Like Foucault, learn to turn a picture into a theory, and find images that encapsulate your theories. Hypericons, as O'Gorman suggests serve not only for persuasion, but also as mnemonic devices, which can be equally useful for the purposes of pedagogy and propaganda. Draw deep from the well of visual culture and, like the typical digital artist or graphic designer, don't be squeamish about re-purposing images for your own devices.

Legacy

Definition. The legacy, as Craig Saper writes in this volume, is complicated by the nexus of theory, pedagogy, and personal influence. The association's writers forge between these areas lead to theoretical and productive output. "The Florida School simply recognizes that its legacy, its meanings and methods, depends on ana-logic and a responsibility to those overdetermined associative strings" (Saper). In this sense, Florida School writers juxtapose theory, pedagogy, and the personal in order to develop instructions or guides for other researchers, teachers, and students (in order, therefore, to forge legacies). Our legacy, in the words of Greg Ulmer, is to use new media in order to "teach students to make stuff." Saper's musings over the Florida School legacy consider how legacy plays out in Ulmer's work while simultaneously playing out in Saper's own work (and, in turn, the new media researcher's). Such a legacy differs from the typical English studies paradigm of analysis and interpretation, what Robert Scholes (Ulmer's dissertation director at Brown University) calls the "pursuit of a humanistic education that is its own reward" (144). In this sense, also following Scholes, Saper is trying to push English studies away from a "canon of texts" and towards a legacy-oriented "canon of methods" (Scholes 145).

Instruction. Identify the intersection of your personal life, media and theoretical influences, and pedagogy or research practices. Forge associations among these areas based on discovered patterns (often highlighting the less obvious or the detail in place of the general or obvious). Use puns, allusions, neologisms, and other less typical rhetorical strategies to demonstrate how your various "legacies" come together and shape your work. The patterns can be demonstrated in any variety of media: video, film, website, or other not yet invented (and still without legacy).

Mapping

Definition. Frederic Jameson proposed cognitive mapping as a method for making sense of the world in a global information economy. Denise Cummings, on the other hand, produces an alternative mapping, one which juxtaposes geographical exploration, film history, and film writing as means towards creating another kind of filmic text. Visiting the never completed Picture City Studios in Picture City, Florida, Cummings generates an imaginary reading of the film company which never made a film. Her fragmented citations and entries reflect the overall fragmented history of filmic production. Cummings' proposal for film studies crosses Ray's call for a new kind of filmic reading and writing practice with Walter Benjamin's Arcades Project; her observations are fragmentary, material, and imaginative. While Benjamin wrote about film, he was too early in film's receptive history to alter how we read film. Cummings attempts to change our reading and writing practices of film history so that the writing itself reflects the structure of film. "Like the pieces that make up a film," Cummings writes, "history is ordered, sorted, and spliced into in an even continuum." Cummings demonstrates that if film is to be perceived as new media, the ways we write with and about film must change.

Instruction. Locate a site of media work that never reached its potential or was never completed. Like Cummings' interest in Picture City, focus on the not-yet-created. Map your visitation and recreation of that site. Your objective is not historical revelation ("what was here"), but speculation ("what could have occurred"). Cummings chooses her immediate surroundings, North Central Florida; choose the area you live in, work in, or recreate in order to generate your own map. Your map should reconstruct history through the anecdote, historical fact, speculation, and media. Structure your work with citations, accounts, and the imaginary simultaneously. The rhetoric of your work will come from these "ruins" you find; unfinished projects, speculative reports, photographs long forgotten.

Remix

Definition. Digital technology dictates the remix as a new media method of knowledge production. "You have to look at yourself as a machine programmed, as a biocomputer programmed by the decks," music theorist Kodwo Eshun writes of the mix's effect on new media composition. Michael Jarrett acknowledges as such in his remix of Elvis and Godard films. The remake, Greg Ulmer writes, "has no standard form of its own, but calls for the sampling of an existing practice immanent within the object of study" ("Kubla" 252). The object of new media study is the production of media. Thus, Jarrett's point that remixed and remade texts circulate in new media environments for us to remix further resonates within much of Florida School thought. The challenge, as Jarrett's essay demonstrates, is not how we read these texts, but rather how we create them on our own. "Elvis is a text; he is new media," Jarrett tells us, noting that the replication and remixing of Elvis already exists in the singer's film oeuvre—a body of work in which Elvis reappears as Elvis no matter the role. "No wonder film studies—oriented toward interpretation and critique—has not figured out what to do with Presley's cinematic *oeuvre:* multiple remakes of remakes" (Jarrett). Jarrett's essay deals with the pedagogical implications of the remix (how to teach students to remix filmic texts as opposed to how to read such texts), yet his method can be applied to research and theoretical work with other media as well. Indeed, one can imagine his essay or any combination of essays in this collection, remixed and remade for further inventive work on the Web or elsewhere.

Instruction. Stop thinking of media in terms of permanent and stable production. In addition, stop thinking of media in terms of authorial creations. Place yourself outside of the authorial concept and allow yourself to become a media-being, one who is a remix as well as remixes. Instead of producing "true" texts, consider the alternative, the out-take, the remake, and the remix as new media divergences. When you construct or read a media composition, remix it so that other versions emerge and juxtapose with the one you began with. Find the content of your work in other work (online, in print, in film) as well as in various versions of any single composition (film, video, Web) you have produced.

Transparency

Definition. Members of the Florida School, it's safe to say, all learned to develop web sites by coding in raw HTML, even in the late 1990s when Web development software with WYSIWYG interfaces was introduced. This form of digital ascetics (not to be confused with digital aesthetics) might be considered as a modernist appeal to depth, a hermeneutic desire to peer beneath the veil and reveal "the truth." As Sherry Turkle has argued,

> the transparent early IBM PC modeled a modernist technological aesthetic, the Macintosh-style interface was consistent with a postmodern one whose theorists suggest that the search for depth and mechanism is futile, and that it is more realistic to explore the world of shifting surfaces than to embark on a search for origins and structure. (36)

Like geeked-out programmers and neurotic MUD (Multi-User Dungeon) dwellers, members of the Florida School advocate the openness and transparency of code. The purpose of this, however, is not rooted in a self-deluded search for objective truth, nor in a self-righteous, geeky denial of graphical user interfaces, but in a desire to showcase complexity, to make information visible and accessible, open to the multiple concatenations required for invention to take place. Most of all, this openness to the complexity and messiness of code is an outright refusal to make things easy, which is precisely what both consumer technologies and literacy prescribe. As Bradley Dilger explains, "for writing and technology, transparency is a pragmatic erasure of code: the goal is to make the technological status of an object or an utterance disappear, in order that the code can invisibly do its work, or deliver its message." As an antidote to the all-pervasive drive toward user-friendliness, ease, and transparency, Dilger prescribes "translucence."

Instruction. Don't strive for opacity for opacity's sake, but at the same time, don't make things easy. Learn to do some basic programming or HTML coding, and tinker with the innards of your computer. Take steps to reveal the materiality of production. Click on "view source" in your web browser and lift the lid on the box. Rather than vacillating between transparency and opaqueness, strive for translucence. According to Dilger, "the choice between transparent and opaque forbids the interaction of multiple objects or practices, whereas translucence would permit much more complex relationships: the programmability of new media [Lev] Manovich proposes." Create a hybrid by combining the postmodern "world of shifting surfaces" with modernist origins and structures of your own invention.

Schizophrenia

Definition. Although the Florida School focuses primarily on media criticism and theory, this does not mean that it is relevant only to students, instructors and aficionados of Film and Media Studies departments. Both critical theory and new media know no disciplinary boundaries. For this reason, it should not be surprising to find in this collection Ron Broglio's schizophrenic, MUD-mediated re-purposing of the Romantic poet William Wordsworth. Following Gilles Deleuze and Felix Guattari, Fredric Jameson describes schizophrenia as definitive of postmodern being, a condition in which a person is "reduced to an experience of pure material signifiers, or, in other words, a series of pure and unrelated presents in time" (27). Broglio's inventiveness lies not in his recognition of schizophrenia as the penultimate way of being in a digital culture (this formula has become a standby of postmodern theory), but in his desire to invent a pedagogy by "translating a Deleuzian stroll into an online environment, . . . [providing] an open system of play as a heuristic strategy for understanding literature." Broglio's students learn about Wordsworth's high-literary work in a schizo-inspired MOO space (Object Oriented Multi-User Dungeon). The instruction of literature then, even the study of the most canonical of poets, can be radically enhanced through the use of new media. In Broglio's classroom, "the text becomes a textual and textured environment where players work from within the literary object itself. Inside the text, players orient themselves by creating paths of meaning with steps and missteps, dead ends and long rambling journeys." This rambling charts a path towards the future of humanities research in the age of electracy.

Instruction.

> Write to the *n*th power, the *n*-1 power, write with slogans. Make rhizomes, not roots, never plant! Don't sow, grow offshoots! Don't be one or multiple, be multiplicities! Run lines, never plot a point! Speed turns the point into a line! Be quick, even when standing still! Line of chance, line of hips, line of flight. Don't

> bring out the General in you! Don't have just ideas, just have an idea (Godard). Have short-term ideas. Make maps, not photos or drawings" (Deleuze and Guattari 24–25).

Writing

Definition. "The age of writing has passed," Marshall McLuhan wrote. "We must invent a new metaphor, restructure our thoughts and feelings" (*Probes* 17). Jeff Rice's proposal that funk serves digital writing echoes McLuhan's concerns. The limitations of new media become obvious when we reduce our work to that of print. Mood, feeling, and the groove are particular aspects of the digital lost when we cling only to the print-based paradigms we have grown comfortable with. With this in mind, Rice proposes that the alphabet as metaphor for writing be replaced by funk. Funk's interests in expression and technology position it as a metaphor worth appropriating for digital production. Rice calls this appropriation of funk for composition purposes "funkcomp," a method which allows new media writers to utilize funk's usage of ambiguity, identity, and technology for rhetorical output. Rice's claim is that outrageousness and ambiguity have been overlooked as tropes for digital writing. By foregrounding funk's usage of such tropes and how they translate for new media, Rice concludes the collection with a call for a different kind of digital writing practice, what he names the "What the . . ." The ambiguity of how such a practice might look in HTML, Flash, or any other new media-based writing is intentional, for that very ambiguity is what Rice sees central to funk's contribution to electracy.

Instruction. Compose with the outrageous. Allow both your alter ego and the work you produce to provoke response through non-clear and non-coherent channels. Use code as you would use the alphabet to structure arguments, generate narrative, or disseminate information. But instead of proposing claims, make it funky. Worry less about being understood when you compose digitally and be more concerned with provocation, with evoking a "What the . . ." response in your readers so that they must devote attention and effort towards comprehending how you are working with identity, technology, and rhetoric at once.

Works Cited

Bolter, Jay David, and Richard Grusin. *Remediation: Understanding New Media.* Cambridge: MIT Press, 2000.

Deleuze, Gilles, and Felix Guattari. *A Thousand Plateaus: Capitalism and Schizophrenia.* Minneapolis: U of Minnesota P, 1987.

Eagleton, Terry. *After Theory.* New York: Basic Books, 2003.

Feyerabend, Paul. *Against Method.* London: New Left Books, 1975.

Foucault, Michel. *This Is Not a Pipe.* Translated by James Harkness. Berkeley: U of California P, 1982.

Gitelman, Lisa and Geoffrey B. Pingree, eds. *New Media, 1740-1915.* Cambridge, Mass: M.I.T. Press, 2003.

Jameson, Fredric. *Postmodernism, Or, The Cutural Logic of Late Capitalism.* Durham: Duke UP, 1991.

Manovich, Lev. *The Language of New Media.* Cambridge: MIT Press, 2000.

McLuhan, Marshall. *The Book of Probes.* Corte Madera, CA: Gingko Press, 2003.

Mitchell, W. J. T. *Picture Theory.* Chicago: U of Chicago P, 1994.

Ray, Robert. *The Avant-Garde Finds Andy Hardy.* Cambridge, MA: Harvard UP, 2002.

Rettberg, Scott. "Focus: New Media Studies." *American Book Review.* 24.3 (March/April 2003). 24 June 2004. <http://www.litline.org/ABR/Issues/Volume24/Issue%203/Rettberg.pdf>.

Turkle, Sherry. *Life on the Screen: Identity in the Age of the Internet.* New York: Touchstone, 1995.

Ulmer, Gregory. *Heuretics: The Logic of Invention.* Baltimore: Johns Hopkins UP, 1994.

—. "What is Electracy?" 24 June 2003. <http://web.nwe.ufl.edu/elf/electracy.html>.

Part 1

Origins: What Is the Florida School and Where Does It Come From?

1 Florida out of Sorts

Gregory L. Ulmer

The EmerAgency is a virtual consultancy whose purpose is to deconstruct instrumental consulting by using the Internet to bring to bear arts and letters knowledge and method on public policy formation. For its contribution to the consultancy, The Florida Research Ensemble (FRE—a faculty group at the University of Florida) selected Miami in general, and the Miami River in particular, as the community "wound" to address in its experimentation with a new mode of inquiry called "choragraphy" (Ulmer 1994). The following entries represent an introduction to and sample of the archive of working papers, memos, notes, lecture outlines and related materials produced as part of the theoretical elaboration of the project.

The Florida School

Part of this documentation should include a genealogy of the FRE itself as an example of collaborative inquiry. There are two threads to this story, one concerning rationale and the other concerning events. The rationale goes back to my encounter with the work of Joseph Beuys and his Free International University (FIU), which was a conceptual institution. Beuys' version of the avant-garde commitment to the merger of art and life took the form of a consultancy that existed in part as an art performance, and in part as information. He used the publicity generated by his provocative installations and performances as a means to disseminate his ideas about the practical relevance of art to politics and policy formation. He and his loosely organized group once made an official proposal to the European Union to establish a branch of the FIU in Ireland to bring art to bear on "the Irish Question." The FRE in Miami is in homage to the FIU.

Between the encounter with Beuys in the 1970s and today exists several decades worth of activity at the University of Florida, the most important of which was the arrival of Robert Ray in 1980. Our discussions of "heuretics" (treating theory not as a content or object of study but as a creative or generative poetics) influenced our seminars as well as our research. This collaboration took various institutional forms as well, working with a diverse group of colleagues and students, including the formation of an Institute for European and Comparative Studies, a media studies institute, and finally the FRE itself. Students noticed the difference between our seminars and the rest of the curriculum (not always approvingly), and this sense of difference resulted eventually in a feeling of identity. Our students returned from conferences to report that ideas and methods that seemed obvious in Gainesville were news elsewhere (whether good or bad was in the mind of the beholder). Having used the phrase "Florida School" as a shorthand among ourselves, we began to use it in public, to which the objection was made that "schools" do not have a right to declare themselves, but exist only when they have been observed from "elsewhere."

Modesty is a pre-industrial virtue, no doubt, ill-suited to the information age. In any case, an epiphany that confirmed our declaration of existence (modest in not being shouted from the rooftops), was my discovery that I lived in Xanadu. At least I lived in one of the four regions of the world that inspired Coleridge, through his reading of travel books, to write "Kubla Kahn." William Bartram's descriptions of the underground rivers, springs, and prairies of North Central Florida in his "Travels" found their way into this poem whose legendary city lent its name to the visionary network of the man who invented the term "hypertext" (Ted Nelson), not to mention the homes of the real Bill Gates and the fictional Citizen Kane. The lesson that the "exotic" is local (or "glocal") found its aphoristic expression in the Japanese poet Basho's admonishment not to follow in the footsteps of the masters, but to seek what they sought. The Florida School does not want to follow in the footsteps of Plato and Aristotle, the inventors of literacy, but to seek the equivalent of literacy for digital technology—electracy. The proof of the value of this effort, now taken up by a second generation of grammatologists, is in the interest of the work produced. The documents that follow represent a work-in-progress by the FRE, developing out of Miami a prototype of an electrate category called "Miautre." The collaborators include Barbara Jo Revelle (creative photography), William Tilson (architecture), John Craig Freeman (digital arts), Will Pappenheimer (videography and performance), and Gregory Ulmer (theory).

Tourism

There are a number of versions of the Miami River zone that need to be taken into account. One way to imagine the consultation is as an unpacking of the tourist guide description, or as a tour of that part of downtown considered irrelevant to the guide.

> *Michelin Guide to Florida: Downtown, Miami.* A vibrant 1.5 sq mi surrounded on three sides by the warm waters of Biscayne Bay and the Miami River, Miami's downtown exudes the bustling atmosphere of a Latin city. Here, retailers purveying electronic goods, jewelry, clothing and fragrances in Spanish and Portuguese draw visitors from Cuba, Puerto Rico and Latin America. The site of the city's first wooden commercial structures now features a dense array of government and office buildings in a host of architectural styles including Neoclassical, Art Deco, Mediterranean Revival and the stark contemporary design of the skyscrapers that illuminate Miami's night skyline.

The Caribbean Code

An example of an instrumental approach to the Miami River is the annual report of the Miami River Quality Action Team. The report is organized as a series of statements formulated as problem and solution, dealing with a broad range of public policy issues such as drug smuggling, crime, pollution, economic development, port facilities, immigration, and the like. Some thirty-four separate government agencies have responsibility for and authority over some aspect of river management. As it turned out, the policy issue foregrounded by the FRE inquiry concerned vessel maintenance and safety.

> Miami River Quality Action Team: Annual Report 1996–97.
>
> Problem: Substandard vessels operating on the River.

> The Miami River is vulnerable to the potential safety and environmental consequences posed by substandard foreign flag shipping. In general, a ship is regarded to be substandard if the hull, crew, machinery or equipment used for lifesaving, fire fighting, and pollution prevention is substantially below the standards required by U.S. laws or international conventions.
>
> Solution: Targeting of high risk vessels—OPERATION SAFETY NET.
>
> In April 1994 in response to a Congressional mandate, the Coast Guard implemented an initiative to eliminate substandard commercial ships from U.S. waters. The Seventh Coast Guard District, which includes the Miami River, instituted a three-year interim boarding program for foreign flag vessels under 500 gross tons. Many of these smaller freight vessels routinely operate between the Caribbean, Central America, and the Southeast United Sates.

The Quantum Zone

For instrumental consultants, for whom the river is a problem to be solved, the intractability of the problems afflicting the river is assumed to be a temporary obstacle to progress; the problems are anomalies in an otherwise coherent world whose difficulties eventually will give way before the powers of method (analysis and synthesis) and technology. The FRE premise, however, is that "problems" are emergent phenomena in a quantum world picture, such that they must be addressed holistically: to analyze the river into its "elements" is to make "problem" disappear, its qualities being not "parts" (the "properties" of a conceptual description) but a localized manifestation of a global condition. The Marxists, who asserted that no one problem may be solved unless all problems are solved, had a point, except that they still thought in terms of solutions, their final solution being "revolution." The EmerAgency attempts not to confuse holism with totalization. The river itself, as it flowed around the hull of a barge pushing upstream, provided an image of what was needed to grasp the zone as a whole (a strange attractor).

> As stated in John Briggs' and F. David Peat's, TURBULENT MIRROR. *Turbulent Mirror:*
>
> When the speed of the river is low, its motion is well described by a point attractor, but as the speed increases a limit cycle attractor applies. Clearly there must be some critical point at which the description of the river's behavior jumps over from one attractor to the other. . . . Ruelle, who was the first to dub the attractor for turbulence and chaos with the name "strange," agrees with Landau and Hofp that in the convection current the smooth flow gives way to a first oscillation in which the point attractor jumps into a limit cycle. After this the limit cycle transforms into the surface of a torus. But Ruelle argues that at the third bifurcation something almost science fictional begins to happen. Instead of a system jumping from the two-dimensional surface of the torus onto the three-dimensional surface of a torus in four-dimensional space. It is the torus itself which begins to break apart! Its surface enters a space of fractional dimension. Put another way, the surface of the torus attractor is actually caught between the dimensions of a plane and a solid.

Cultural Turbulence

The newspapers in Florida carry reports from Miami, monitored by the FRE, to form a profile of a mediated "Miami" (called "Myami"). This item on the Rose-Marie Express became a catalyst for a consultation.

> As reported by Evan Perez (Associated Press), and published in the *Sun*(Gainesville, Florida) on May 13, 1998. MIAMI
>
> More than 150 undocumented Haitians jumped from a freighter into the Miami River Tuesday and were

> chased into and around river front businesses by U.S. immigration agents and police. "We had a lot of policemen running in and out with their guns drawn," said Este Garcia, owner of Garcia's Seafood Grill. "They were in the restaurant, jumping into the water. It was a madhouse. A couple of them hid in trash cans." At least 86 people were captured and many were ordered to sit against the wall of a warehouse near the river, which is frequented by small freighters from the Caribbean and the Bahamas. Forty teenagers were among the Haitians who jumped from the green-and-white freighter named Rose-Marie Express as it pulled into dock, police said. Some of the passengers ducked into waiting cars and escaped while others hid under the docks. . . . Garcia said some immigrants were stumbling around as they tried to escape. "They were disoriented. They've been on the water for three or four days" The freighter set out from Cap Haitian on Haiti's northwest coast about four days ago, according to a volunteer from the Haitian Refugee Center. The U.S. Coast Guard in July began banning wooden freighters such as the Rose-Marie Express from entering the Miami River because they are not considered safe.

Poetic Encounter

The FRE constituted itself as a "theoria"—after the institution created by ancient city-states: a group of citizens sent to the site of a rumored disturbance in order to determine what had happened, whose task was to render a true account. The challenge was to find a holistic approach to the river, beginning with a way to bring the zone into representation. This representation, given our commitment to finding a specifically "electrate" mode of reason, had to be an image: a photograph in this case. Barbara Jo Revelle, a creative photographer, lived at a bed and breakfast beside the river for six weeks during the summer of 1998. Her goal was, by means of the "poetic encounter," to make an image capturing the attunement (the mood, atmosphere) of the river. The poetic encounter as a method is derived from the experience and practice of poets and artists living and working in Paris from Baudelaire to the situationist Guy Debord. In her practice of the encounter, Revelle toured the zone every day, recording with her still and video cameras whatever attracted her attention. Out of thirty rolls of film and twenty hours of videotape, a pattern emerged that, through group work, produced an illumination (epiphany). This fragment of a June 1998 interview with Simon Lubin, a Haitian owner of one of the boats caught in Operation Safety Net, is a metonym for the condition of Haitians working in the zone. After eighteen months under impoundment, the boat was seized for nonpayment of fees.

> You see, look at de carpet, mattress, ole bicycle, whole thing; we just come in here to get de junk. We go over dere, okay, make a little money, help de poor people. But now we can't do the same thing anymore because American people say; not, not even American people—like de Coast guard. Immigration. If they give you a job to do for like $60,000 to do de job on de boat, what de job? De paint, de boat very, de paint . . . When dey come in every day dey come and dey say do that. You do it. tomorrow dey come and dey say do dat again, you do it. But so whats, how about me, I'm not gonna get no dollar to pay de people, to take care of my muddah, to take care of myself, to take care of my family. Don't think about color. We're de same. if it white, if it black, we same. Only one God is above us. See, white American people just kick all, kick de Haitians' ass. But dey don't kick de Cubans, dey don't kick de other people, de Venezuela—only de Haitian people. Why? They told me to get a Belize flag before you get out. Okay, if you don't have the $10,000 it cost, den stay docked over dere all year until you get de $10,000. They pay dock $100 day. Where da money come from? Dey don't know how to tell you, okay, get out of here. But dey put sometin in da middle. If you can't do it, just get out. So, what you want me to do? So, God, dey supposed to know one day God is gonna come down. He's not comin' to get me, to get you. He's comin' to get everybody. Dat's it. I don't have no money to pay it so I come

> here. Pay $100 every day. So, when I can't pay, the dockman say okay, I'm gonna get your boat.

Misrecognition

The method of encounter involves a physical experience of recognition on the part of the agent. "Recognition" in the encounter names a particular kind of experience whose base mode is that of ideological "misrecognition"—the effect of identification with images that flatter the ego (everything from favorite entertainment stars to role models). The ironic or paradoxical insight of the encounter is that the flash of insight in the eureka of creative invention, or even of mystical satori for that matter, is made possible by the identifications that interpellatea subject into the hegemonic order of a specific culture and society. Movement out of interpellation toward illumination begins with that surprising repetition of the familiar in the unfamiliar known as the "uncanny" (Unheimlich). Epiphany and illumination were religious experiences of revelation secularized in modern letters from Wordsworth through Joyce. Greek tragedy explored this same dimension of experience in terms of "anagnorisis" and "peripeteia."

In the encounter, the agent (egent) tunes the zone by finding the point of correspondence between the material place and the inner state of mind. The egent apprehends the attunement of the zone by creating an image with the inner-outer quality that the poet Rainer Marie Rilke termed "Weltinnenraum." Other relative aesthetic terms would include T. S. Eliot's "objective correlative," Wordsworth's "spots of time," Keats' "negative capability," or even Brecht's social "gest." The point of testing "epiphany" as the arts method for grasping the zone whole, in an image, is to adapt a device perfected within modernism for general use as a practice of electracy (electracy is to the digital apparatus what literacy is to the civilization of print technology). This grammatological framing approaches the historical arts not in terms of periods, but as an experimental laboratory in which the forms and practices needed for general electracy already exist in an aesthetic version.

The river for an egent (consultant for the EmerAgency) is not addressed as an object of study, and certainly not as a problem to be solved, but as a "chora" or sacred space (the usage based on Derrida's reading of Plato's *Timaeus*) within which may be experienced the agent's "situation." The agent does not explain the zone; on the contrary, the zone explains the agent, which is why the motto of the EmerAgency is "Problems B Us." The intractability of problems is due to the fact that the conditions manifested in the social breakdowns are in us as well, not external but "extimate" (outside within, figured in Lacan's topology as a moebius strip). The zone is not so much a site of disorder and breakdown, but precisely a materialization of our metaphysics (chora as a place of classification, of category formation). Chora contains the sorting principles of a civilization (how that society sorts chaos into the kinds of being). In the Miami River (as in any such wound), the American metaphysics comes into appearance. An image of a "zone" in this mode is found in *Stalker,* the film by Tarkovsky (a title that suggests "stalker" as an analogy for the egent).

As discussed in Andrey Tarkovsky's, *Sculpting in Time*:

> What then is the main theme that had to sound through *Stalker?* In the most general terms, it is the theme of human dignity; of what that dignity is, and of how a [person] suffers if [s/he] has no self-respect. Let me remind the reader that when the characters in the film set out on their journey into the Zone, their destination is a certain room in which, we are told, everybody's most secret wish will be granted And while the Writer and the Scientist, led by Stalker, are making their hazardous way over the strange expanse of the Zone, their guide tells them at one point either a true story, or else a legend, about another Stalker, nicknamed Diko-obraz. He had gone to the secret place in order to ask for his brother, who had been killed through his fault, to be brought back to life. When Diko returned home, however, he discovered that he had become fabulously wealthy. The Zone had granted what was in reality his most heartfelt desire, and not the wish that he had wanted to imagine was most precious to him. And Diko-obraz hanged himself. And so the two men reach their objective. They have been through a great deal, thought about themselves, reassessed themselves; and they haven't the courage to step across the threshold into the room which they have risked their lives to reach.

Mystory Popcycle

The method used to tune the river is "mystory" (Ulmer 1989)—a group mystory in which Barbara Jo Revelle provided the family discourse for the ensemble (the way Spalding Gray's anguish over the madness and suicide of his mother provided the personal problems for improvisatory elaboration by the Wooster Group in *The Rhode Island Trilogy*). The mystory is a genre created to write holistically or simultaneously with all the discourses into which an individual has been interpellated, the core discourses being those of family, entertainment, school (community history), and career (disciplinary field). The entry into each discourse/institution is called in psychoanalysis "mourning" (introjection of authority figures to produce a superego), and in Althusser's ideological critique "interpellation." In medieval culture (manuscript apparatus) the discourses were integrated by means of a metaphysics of correspondences—the famous four-fold Christian allegory linking the believer's mortality to the stories of Israel coming out of Egypt, Christ's crucifixion, and the anagogic theology of world historical redemption at the end of time. Modern alienation is the story of the dissolution of this religious world picture.

Mystory assumes that alienation as an experience of dissociation and reification may be overcome in electracy by a practice adapted to the digital capacities of multimedia. This practice is fundamentally "aesthetic." Following Lacan's reading of Joyce, mystory brings the discourses into correspondence (uniting them into a "popcycle") by means of "signifiance" ("signifierness")—the repetition of a signifier through the details of each discourse, the circulating prop that organizes any well-made narrative, like the letter that passes from character to character in Poe's "Purloined Letter." Using an archaic spelling of "symptom"—"sinthome"—to name this signifier without a signified (what Barthes called the "obtuse" or "third" meaning of a photograph), Lacan located the coherence principle of a civilization at the opposite end of the scale of order from that of medieval cosmology. Constituting the loosest possible framing condition, the "sinthome" has no meaning, or has the meaning of a proper name: it sutures together for an individual subject the registers that Lacan termed the imaginary, symbolic, and real, in the way that an artist's singular style holds together her oeuvre (for example, the way the "sponge" is the "sinthome" for the oeuvre of Francis Ponge [Jacques Derrida, *Signep-*

onge]). The prop that circulated through Barbara Jo Revelle's popcycle was a mattress.

As Revelle chronicled in her journal during the summer of 1998:

> Linda McDonald's house, with the basement where her daddy did upholstering when he wasn't drunk, and where the kids from Skeeversville [the contemptuous name assigned to the bad side of town by Barbara's father, who forbid her to go there] played sexual and scary games in the dark amidst the mattresses, old chairs, and moldering upholstering material. Two brothers from Skeeversville, Ricky and Bobby Eason, were often in on those games. There was one we called Perfume in the Black Hole. We divided into two groups, boys and girls and went to parts of the basement where we couldn't see the other group. The girls had passed around a perfume bottle, and put some on in turn, and the idea was that where you put the perfume was related to the secret you were required to remember and tell to the rest of the group. We went around the circle, and when a player couldn't think of any more secrets to tell, she "lost" and the punishment was that she had to crawl into a mildewed and spider-infested space created by a folded-over and broken open mattress. This was the Black Hole. Then someone from the boys' side of the basement, chosen through some more manly ritual we never got to witness but were told had to do with their "privates," would crawl inside and try to guess the losing girl's identity by feeling her body.

Correspondences

The story of Skeeversville in the family discourse (childhood memory) produced a flash of correspondence with two other discourses—what Walter Benjamin called a "dialectical image." The FRE theoria had determined in advance that the target of witnessing was the Haitian arrival in Miami. The attunement of the zone, however, had to occur at the level of sinthome, specific to the stalker/agent (Barbara). The theory guiding the experiment, that is, dictated that the image capable of grasping the zone as a whole would not be a "universal" in the mode of a literate concept, but would be a singularity, a "third meaning," expressing the electrate mode of categorization—chora. The detail that repeated across the discourses was the mattress, with the mattresses in the Skeeversville basement resonating with the piles and heaps of used mattresses that constituted one of the principle items of the cargoes bound for Haiti, stacked on the decks of the boats and in the warehouses along the docks of the river. This cargo existed within the discourse of Miami, the community history recording the story of the "Floribbean."

This repetition located the relevant theory in the disciplinary discourse as Lacan's "point de capiton" or quilting point: "The French term 'point de capiton' is variously translated in English editions of Lacan's work as 'quilting point' or 'anchoring point.' It literally designates an upholstery button, the analogy being that just as upholstery buttons are places where 'the mattress-maker's needle has worked hard to prevent a shapeless mass of stuffing from moving too freely about,' so the 'points de capiton' are points at which 'signified and signifier are knotted together'" (Evans 149). Slavoj Žižek extended the term to a collective ideology from its original application to the discourse of a "normal" subject (for whom the endless play of signification is halted by means of a number of fundamental "attachment points"). The quilting points for a collective order are embodied in certain scapegoat figures, whose exclusion sutures the gap in the mythological system, fills the hole of incompleteness that prevents any identity from coinciding with itself. The quilting point for America, at least as manifested in the river zone, is the Haitian. This "uncanny" repetition across the family and discipline discourses indicated that what could be grasped by the image was not the "whole" but a "hole" in this psychoanalytic sense.

> From Žižek's *The Sublime Object of Ideology*: This then is the fundamental paradox of the "point de capiton: the "rigid designator,'" which totalizes an ideology by bringing to a halt the metonymic sliding of its signified, is not a point of supreme density of Meaning, a kind of guarantee which, by being itself excepted from the differential interplay of elements, would serve as a stable and fixed point of reference. On the contrary, it is the element which represents the agency of the signifier within the field of the sig-

> nified. In itself it is nothing but a "pure difference": its role is purely structural, its nature is purely performative—its signification coincides with its own act of enunciation; in short, it is a "signifier without the signified." The crucial step in the analysis of an ideological edifice is thus to detect, behind the dazzling splendor of the element which holds it together ("God," "Country," "Party," "Class" . . .) this self-referential, tautological, performative operation. A ["Haitian"], for example, is in the last resort one who is stigmatized with the signifier ["Haitian"]; all the phantasmic richness of the traits supposed to characterize [Haitians, (disease, voodoo, and so on)] is here to conceal not the fact that ["Haitians] really are not like that," not the empirical reality of [Haitians], but the fact that in the [bigoted] construction of a ["Haitian"], we are concerned with a purely structural function (99).

Critical Divination Studies

The other methodological consequence of constituting the theoria as a response to the call of the Haitians arriving on the Rose-Marie Express was the decision to deconstruct "consulting" by syncretizing the Western scientific sense with its usage in Afro-Caribbean divination practices. The point of connection from the side of poststructuralism was the theory of "fetish" in general, and specifically a metaphor used by Roland Barthes to characterize his method of reading: "The text, in its mass, is comparable to a sky, at once flat and smooth, deep, without edges and without landmarks; like the soothsayer drawing on it with the tip of his staff an imaginary rectangle wherein to consult, according to certain principles, the flight of birds, the commentator traces through the text certain zones of reading, in order to observe therein the migration of meanings, the outcropping of codes, the passage of citations" (*S/Z* 13–14). The river was to be treated as this "text/sky." From the side of divination proper was borrowed the attitude of the "querent" who comes to the diviner with a "burning question"—a personal problem that has resisted all other forms of resolution, and that constitutes for the querent a dilemma.

The poetic encounter, in other words, was practiced more as a divining device, with Revelle in the position of querent, and the river zone as the divination system. Her burning question concerned her relationship with her partner. The bed and breakfast residence where she was staying, situated within the discourse of entertainment as part of the tourism infrastructure of Miami, constituted the data for the fourth institution of the popcycle in the group mystory (entertainment). The rented room became the setting for a lover's discourse at those times when the partner visited Revelle, such that she recognized this bed as belonging to the set of mattresses materializing her sinthome. The rhyming beds conjured a further recognition, that the answer the river gave to her burning question was the story of Simon Lubin's boat, impounded by the Coast Guard, caught in Operation Safety Net, as authorized by the Caribbean Code, leading to confiscation and forfeiture of possession. This image, while specific to Revelle, also serves as a "cognitive map" (Jameson) tracing the connections between an individual and the collective order that may be recognized in turn by others.

> As stated in Eugenio Matibag's *IFA and Interpretation: An Afro-Caribbean Literary Practice*: African divination is a self-validating system of thought offering "strategies for handling problems in daily life" and therefore must be understood as mediating between the client's misfortunes and the social structure. Divination may mediate between individual desire and the social context, although its "misuse" can also work against the interests of the collectivity. Among the "consensual community," the words of the oracle are considered sacred because they come directly from Ifa. They demand belief. The faith in the Ifa system and probably its efficacy are based on the related belief that each of us chooses a personal destiny, determining future success or failure, when we kneel before Olodumare prior to birth. . . . The Ifa itself is a vast information-retrieval system that preserves, accesses, and processes the texts of mythological, naturalist, medicinal, and spiritual knowledge. At the heart of the Ifa system lie the thousands of narratives that the babalao has memorized as part of

his training and that he recites to clients in consultations.

Miami River Blues

The image tuning the zone in the FRE consultation was that of an impounded Haitian boat, piled high with its cargo of used mattresses. What this image meant as an answer to a burning question only Revelle could decide. The larger question concerned the goal of the experiment, which was to use whatever image was produced by the theoria as the basis for an electrate mode of category formation (or "metaphysics"). The intention was to use the image to put the river zone online, to represent it holistically and make it intelligible, or intuitable, for the community. The image worked categorically by means of emotion in the profound sense of atmosphere or mood ("Stimmung," to use Heidegger's term for an attunement in this metaphysical sense). The querent/egent/stalker functioned as a kind of "divining rod" to locate through recognition a point of impasse in the zone. The imaged "Weltinnenraum" (what Lacan called "extimacy") expressed the correspondence between an inner and outer "aporia" (the feeling of "no-way," "I'm stuck," the impossible). The first function of this image is to interrupt and supplement the instrumental mood of "anomaly" and "solution." The mood of critical divination—of the syncretic consultancy—rather, is that of "the blues."

To bring the "problem" out of empirical science and into the realm of arts and letters in this syncretic frame is to integrate the practical politics of public policy formation with the emotional wisdom of the Afro-Caribbean musical and dance traditions (related with the syncretic religious traditions of the black Atlantic) whose different names in different regions and nations reflect the different nuances of creolization that have occurred historically. In the United States, that creolization of the Judeo-Christian-Greco-Roman West with the black Atlantic has developed in the mood of blues (the related mood in Brazil, for example, is the samba feeling of "saudade," and in Argentina it is the tango feeling of "mufarse"). The EmerAgency goal is to fashion a consulting practice from the lessons of "blutopia," combining the two major impulses of African-American music: "a utopian impulse, evident in the creation of imagined places (Promised Lands), and the impulse to remember, to bear witness, which James Baldwin relates to the particular history of slavery" (Lock 3).

As Stephen Diggs explains in *Alchemy of the Blues*

> I have built a cultural narrative about the transformation of Western consciousness through African-American music by focusing on color and alchemy. In *Shadow Dancing in the USA* (1985), Michael Ventura arrived at many of the same conclusions by constructing a historical narrative about jazz and rock 'n 'roll that focused on a return to the body through the 'loa' or spirit possession of the musician and listener/dancer. The bluesmen are the secular carriers of the hoodoo or voodoo religion which is a hybrid of traditional West African religions and Christianity. As such, bluesmen and women tend to spirit and psyche in a manner handed down from Africa to hoodoo; spirit possession. Where the Northern soul, from shaman to Christian priest, operates dissociatively, leaving the body to travel the spirit world, the African priest, the hoodoo conjurer, and the bluesmen ask the 'loa' to enter bodies and possess them. It is through this possession that the 'loa' is known and expressed. . . . Blues lyrics have tremendous breadth, within which are two core streams, depression and libido. The depressive quality of the blues is the most recognizable to the majority of people, an example of which is the lament for being 'done wrong' by a lover. But the blues is also highly sexual and at times exuberant. There are many 'happy' blues about good time fun, including the joys of food and dance. The blues is about the passions of the flesh. Where the pathological Western mind tended to create dirty movies out of this blue, blacks turned these libidinous hurricanes into the huge body of art called the blues. . . . It is fascinating to note that in addition to the lyric content of the blues, its music and performance practices also worked to transform the dissociative consciousness. Harmonically, the blues is based on the tritone interval, which is considered the

> most dissonant of all intervals and thus full of tension. In Renaissance times, this interval was known as the "Diabolus en musica" and for a time, its use in performance was actually illegal. In the blues, almost every chord contains the tritone, even the tonic. The problem of union of the opposites is managed in the blues by permeating the music with the tension of the tritone. The Christian Devil is everywhere, the dream of salvation nowhere.

Cyberchora

The FRE theoria consultation of the Miami River—the poetic encounter with the Haitians—may be understood as a continuation in digital media of the syncretism that began with the coming of Haitians to New Orleans that led eventually to the invention of jazz (Ventura). To say that Miami will be to hypermedia what New Orleans is to music gives an idea of the ambition, the larger scope of the experiment with choramancy. The relevance of Vodou in particular to the invention of cyberspace is confirmed by the novels of William Gibson, who invented the term "cyberspace" in the prototype of cyberpunk fiction, *Neuromancer.* While working on the next book in what became his trilogy, Gibson read in his doctor's waiting room a *National Geographic* article about Haitian religion. He recognized at once the value of spirit possession as a metaphor for the experience of "jacking-in." What is it like to think with the total knowledge of "the matrix," the unconscious, the symbolic order, which is extimate for me? It is like spirit possession. Michael Benedikt edited the collection entitled *Cyberspace,* crediting Gibson's vision in *Neuromancer* (without discussing the vodun metaphor in the other volumes), however much it might be tainted by its origins as an adolescent male fantasy, as a motivation for serious research aimed at inventing the institutional practices for the new technologies.

The article in *Cyberspace* closest to the FRE intention to use the mood or "Stimmung" of blues, attuned specifically by the image produced through the theoria consultation with the river, was Marcos Novak's "Liquid Architectures in Cyberspace." Agreeing with some of the other commentators that the virtual character of cyberspace has most in common with the omnipotence of thought already thoroughly worked out in the traditions of magic, Novak asserted the essentially poetic nature of the logic organizing this dimension of inhabitable patterns. The metonym he chose to convey the nature of this poetry was the quality of "duende," the soul of authentic art performance in any culture, and of Andalusian (gypsy) folk arts in particular, as articulated in the literature of Federico Garcia Lorca. Novak's insight clarifies what is at stake in framing public policy problems in the atmosphere of the blues (American duende). An apparatus, that is, includes not only a technology institutionalized in its practices formed to manage the technology in a civilization, but also the identity (subject) formation of the people experiencing that lifeworld. Oral people experience their being as "spirit" in religion; literate people experience their being as "self" within a scientific framing. And electrate people? Electrate subjectivation is emerging in relation to "soul" ("ashe") in the institution of entertainment, including the embodied quality of "funk" that is part of the Afro-Caribbean addition to the new syncretic postcolonial civilization. The attunement of postmodernity is no longer angst (Heidegger's diagnosis of the mood of modernity), but funk.

From William Gibson's, *Count Zero*:

> "Bobby, do you know what a metaphor is?"
>
> "A component? Like a capacitor?"
>
> "No. Never mind metaphor, then. When Beauvoir or I talk to you about the loa and their horses, as we call those few the loa choose to ride, you should pretend that we are talking two languages at once. one of them, you already understand. That's the language of street tech, as you call it. We may be using different words, but we're talking tech. Maybe we call something Ougou Feray that you might call an icebreaker, you understand? But at the same time, with the same words, we are talking about other things, and that you don't understand. You don't need to." He put his toothpick away.
>
> Bobby took a deep breath. "Beauvoir said that Jackie's a horse for a snake, a snake called Danbala. You run that by me in street tech?"

"Certainly. Think of Jackie as a deck, Bobby, a cyberspace deck, a very pretty one with nice ankles." Lucas grinned and Bobby blushed. "Think of Danbala, who some people call the snake, as a program. Say as an icebreaker. Danbala slots into the Jackie deck, Jackie cuts ice. That's all."

"Okay," Bobby said, getting the hang of it, "then what's the matrix? If she's a deck, and Danbala's a program, what's cyberspace?"

"The world," Lucas said.

Miautre

The next phase of the theoria experiment is to put the river zone online, in a site named "Miautre." This name for virtual Miami is a result of further table-work by the FRE. The principle from the beginning was that the political process of policy formation (the action target of the consultation) has as much to do with "Myami" (a term for the media representations of the city) as with the actual Miami. Choragraphy originated as a hyperrhetoric by replacing the invention practices of literate (Aristotelian) rhetoric (creating "topoi" or abstract themed categories for the storage and retrieval of the best arguments) with another notion of space or place also available in ancient Greek culture—"chora," used to name sacred and hence particular or specific places (Ulmer 1994). Methodologically, hyperrhetoric is invented out of rhetoric by deconstructing the topoi of a given discourse, which is rewritten (remade) in the register of its grounding in images of its choral places. Myami, in these terms, consists of topoi established in such discourses as the neo-noir TV series, *Miami Vice,* the advertising campaigns that promote the city to tourists, and the journalism that circulates an endless series of reports of crime, drugs, immigrant aliens, corruption, and other disasters.

The FRE theoria site is intended to use the Internet to allow netizens another understanding of Miami-Myami, to attend to it and bear witness in an electrate public or civic sphere in a way that changes the political and ethical environment of policy making. In brainstorming the design for the virtual zone (conceived at this point as a divination interface to access a database of materials related to the river), the FRE turned to the work of Jacques Derrida for at least two reasons:

first, the image of impasse in Revelle's mystory tuning lent itself to Derrida's reformulation of "problem-solution" as "aporia" (impossible impasse). Second, the title of Derrida's book, *The Politics of Friendship,* analyzing the failures of the history of political theory based on the scene of "friend-enemy," rhymed in a macaronic way with the creole of the zone. Miami, in this linguistic play, is "my friend" (mon ami, mi amigo), and that is its dilemma, since this friendship depends upon making enemies. Derrida proposes as an alternative a politics of host and guest, well-suited one might think to the tourist economy of Florida, except that the theory situates the "restricted economy" (to use Bataille's terms) of capitalist profit and accumulation in relation to the "general economy" of expenditure and loss: the gift in short. The general guest is not my friend, but my other (mi otro, mon autre): Mi-autre. This other is welcome without restriction, and the impossibility of this welcome shows us our border, our chora.

Crossroads

This photograph, taken in June, 1998 by Barbara Jo Revelle on the Miami River, entitled "Crossroads," answered the burning question, and tuned the river zone. This scene marked the site of the hole that made the handle by which we grasped the place as chora.

In an online consultation the querent/egent forms a dialectical image by entering along with the burning question ("what is my situation with regard to X?") an anecdote expressing a childhood memory—or childhood block (as in Revelle's memory of Skeeversville). The database simulates for the online querent the accident-match in Revelle's prototype between the mattress of her childhood memory and the mattress-objects within several policy problems. The querent "recognizes" one of the circumstances as an objective correlative showing her relative position in a process. Here is a summary of the procedure used to generate the Miautre attunement.

> Mystory is transferable. The counterintuitive claim of choragraphy is that one individual's consultation of a zone attunes a region into a category (chora). Miami chora = Miautre (the terms are macaronic puns, or perhaps Creole—my friend, my other). Miautre = one situation of an American Book of Changes (from *I Ching* to Cha-Ching). The parts of the attunement include:
>
> 1—The river zone (Miami River and everything found there: water, police, warehouses, Cubans, Haitians, tourists, oil drums, mattresses, dogs, boats . . .).
>
> 2—A querent (Revelle).
>
> 3—The querent's burning question, related to a personal problem ("what is my situation with my partner?").
>
> 4—A chance procedure (the mystory popcycle juxtaposing signifiers from several discourses).
>
> 4—A diviner (the FRE). The diviner makes decisions about which elements of the archive (the zone) are most relevant to the question.
>
> How did we arrive at the photograph entitled "Crossroads" as the categorical image? The chance mystorical procedure produced the mattress as a sinthome, a vinculum repeating across four discourses:
>
> Family = Skeeversville ("perfume in the black hole" = Revelle childhood memory);

> Entertainment = *Miami Vice,* the role of the femme fatale (the seductive woman uses the bedroom strategically);
>
> Career = poststructural theory, Lacan's quilting point metaphor for ideology and the Symbolic order (ideology is like the stuffing in a mattress that requires upholstery tacks to be kept in place).
>
> History = the community story of the Miami River (here is a significant modification for applying group mystory to EmerAgency consulting: community history is not the one motivated by the querent's biography but by the disaster addressed in the consultation).
>
> The FRE, as diviner, sees the patterns in the materials produced by the querent's encounter with the river (the querent cannot be expected to see these patterns for herself; she is the blind spot in the field of light). She remembers a childhood game involving a mattress. The mattress repeats, persists through a number of circumstances in the zone: Jose Marti Park (homeless); the ruins of the apartment house under demolition (immigrants displaced by gentrification); cargo for Haitian traders (older boats being forced off the river). Each of these circumstances represents a different social issue, and at the same time each contributes to the larger ecology of the river as a dilemma. The querent recognizes one of the possibilities as an answer to her question.

The "table work" of the FRE resulted in selecting an impounded Haitian trader (Simon Lubin's impounded boat) as the answer to the burning question. The consultation constitutes a structural portrait: Barbara Jo + Ron = impounded Haitian + Coast Guard. The querent's situation served in turn as an attunement, measuring the "Stimmung" or categorical mood of the scene, constituting one hexagram or archetype of American wisdom. The genre of these choragrams remains to be defined. Working with the hexagram relay, we named this configuration "Aporia" (impoundment, impasse). The idea of contemporary divination as a way to add attraction to the civic sphere, to interest netizens, even school children, in public policy formation, addresses the Miami River zone as at once in its multiple elements a "tarot" system and, as a whole, one "situation" in a contemporary oracle. One consequence of this insight is the need to produce up to eight choras, which through permutation and combination generate 64 archetypal situations of contemporary American life.

ASSIGNMENT: PRODUCE A CHORA IN YOUR REGION.

Diagram

In his dismissive description of self-help astrology, Adorno mentioned the tendency of such journalism to reinforce the common sense of the culture. A purpose of an online oracle (the cha-ching) is in fact to rehabilitate common sense, to revise and update it rather than to confirm it. Specifically in the case of Miautre the goal is to revise the frontier myth, to include a jazz state of mind (embodying a mood of the blues life) in the scenario that guides public policy and entertainment production alike. This revised scenario is embodied in a composite scene, the creative geography made possible by digital technology that visualizes the vortex of default moods determining the propensity of things in Miami. Every visible feature of the scene opens onto a genealogy of events and forms directing the forces that converge and interact to create the zone (what Foucault calls a "diagram"). The riverscape is mapped into a chora with the help of the allegorical mystory that sets up the correlations, the correspondences across the institutional discourses constituting the imagined community. The protagonists of each discourse register are linked to their respective histories.

PRESENT	PAST
Family	
Ron and Barbara Jo Revelle	Pleasant Lake and Skeeversville
Entertainment	
Miami Vice, Crockett and Tubbs	from the Western to film noir
Community History	
Coast Guard and Creoles	Teddy Roosevelt, Buddy Bolden
Career, Discipline	
Conventional Consulting and the FRE	Progress, Melancholia

The design principle is that of the memory palace: Miautre remembers the genealogy, the "etymology" of the images and places. Everything in the scene is a potential emblem. The unsafe Haitian boats link to the history of the philosophical topos "shipwreck with spectator" traced by Hans Blumenberg, that expressed the ascetic state of mind—ataraxy—associated with the ancient sages. A storm at sea, such as the ones commonly observed in Biscayne Bay, is a traditional image of fortune. The lightning flash in the storm links to Heidegger's clearing, Benjamin's historiography, and the other philosophies of suddenness and epiphany associated with the epistemology of the encounter. The port as such is a crossroads. The drawbridges over the Miami River recall the semiotics of bricolage operating in jazz improvisational compositions.

> The enunciative praxis exemplified by bricolage corresponds to a 'lowering' of the paradigmatic with respect to the syntagmatic—a movement which, according to Jakobson, is characteristic of the poetic. Therefore bricolage, as an enunciative praxis, must be seen as an event in two movements, where the second movement presupposes the first.
>
> The first movement is the integration of facts of usage into the linguistic system or, more generally, into the cultural system: it is a creation of fixed types spoken and non-spoken conventions. This integration can be visualized as a 'lifting' of the syntagmatic over the paradigmatic, remembering that, in linguistics and semiotics, the conventional representation of the paradigmatic axis is a vertical line and that of the syntagmatic axis is a horizontal line. The second movement is the selection and use, in whole or part, of facts of usage with a view to creating a signifying structure such as a myth, a poem or a painting. This invocation and contextualization can now be seen as a 'lowering' of the paradigmatic against the syntagmatic.
>
> In the process of defining bricolage in terms of 'drawbridge' (raising and lowering) movements we should note here that, were bricolage actually to be-

> come established as a style, it could be interpreted as the effect of a third movement, as a new 'lifting' of the syntagmatic over the paradigmatic. All this may seem rather empty; but my purpose here is only to account in the simplest way possible for the perfectly normal layering by which cultural phenomena are constituted. (Floch 139)

A digital medium (website, DVD) facilitates a seamless, immediate movement between the visible and invisible (material, cultural, theoretical) registers of the chora. The propensity or directionality of the category supplies the predictive power signaled by the divination interface: the genealogy of the throughline suggests how "things" are likely to develop in the situation, given their present positions as measured by the attunement. The trajectory or trend, the propensity of things in Miami, once mapped in Miautre, becomes accessible to democratic revision. Miautre is just the beginning of this mapping, one "choragram" in an Internet oracle whose wisdom remains to be invented.

Works Cited

Barthes, Roland, *S/Z: An Essay.* Trans. Richard Miller. New York: Hill and Wang, 1974.

Benedikt, Michael, Ed. *Cyberspace: First Steps.* Cambridge, MA: MIT, 1991.

Briggs, John, and F. David Peat. *Turbulent Mirror: An Illustrated Guide to Chaos Theory and the Science of Wholeness.* Grand Rapids, MI: Harper & Row, 1989.

Derrida, Jacques. *Signeponge/Signsponge.* Trans. Richard Rand. New York: Columbia, 1984.

—. *Politics of Friendship.* Trans. George Collins. New York: Verso, 1997.

Diggs, Stephen. "Alchemy of the Blues." *Spring: A Journal Of Archetypes and Culture.* 61 (1997).

Evans, Dylan. *An Introductory Dictionary of Lacanian Psychoanalysis.* New York: Routledge, 1996.

Floch, Jean-Marie. *Visual Identities.* Trans. Pierre Van Osselaer and Alec McHoul. New York: Continuum, 2000.

Gibson, William. *Count Zero.* New York: Ace, 1987.

Jameson, Fredric. "Cognitive Mapping." *Marxism And the Interpretation of Culture.* Ed. C. Nelson and L. Grossberg. Urbana, IL: U of Illinois P, 1988.

Lock, Graham. *Blutopia: Visions of the Future and Revisions of the Past in the Work of Sun Ra, Duke Ellington, and Anthony Braxton.* Durham: Duke UP, 1999.

Matibag, Eugenio. "Ifa and Interpretation: An Afro-Caribbean Literary Practice," in Sacred Possessions: Vodou, Santeria, Obeah, and the Caribbean. Ed. Margarite Fernandez Olmos and Lizabeth Paravisini-Gebert. New Brunswick, NJ: Rutgers UP, 1997.

Tarkovsky, Andrey. *Sculpting In Time: Reflections on the Cinema.* Trans. Kitty Hunter-Blair, Austin: U of Texas P, 1986.

Ulmer, Gregory L. *Teletheory: Grammatology in the Age of Video.* New York: Routledge, 1989.

—. *Heuretics: The Logic of Invention.* Baltimore: Johns Hopkins UP, 1994.

Ventura, Michael. *Shadow Dancing in the USA.* Los Angeles: Tarcher, 1985.

Žižek, Slavoj. *The Sublime Object Of Ideology.* New York: Verso, 1989.

2 Eight Film Studies Problems for the Twenty-First Century

Robert Ray

In 1900, at the Second International Congress of Mathematicians in Paris, the famous Göttingen professor David Hilbert gave a talk innocently titled, "Mathematical Problems." It was August, the room was hot, and Hilbert's conference was only one of 200 academic meetings held in Paris that year to promote the World's Fair. Hilbert was 38, already past the age when many mathematicians do their best work. He was not a particularly compelling speaker, often allowing a formal presentation to dissolve into fitful self-questioning and backtracking. For this speech, however, he had prepared a lecture, which he simply read. Departing from the convention dictating that mathematical papers report on work already done, Hilbert addressed what he called "The Future of Mathematics." Despite the title, which seems to promise the kind of generalities so often encountered in that peculiarly American form, the commencement address, Hilbert had something different in mind. "The future of mathematics," he argued was inextricably linked to specific *problems* that focus research and attract researchers. "As long as a branch of science offers an abundance of problems," Hilbert observed, "so long is it alive" (Gray 241).

With that idea in mind, Hilbert took it upon himself to define mathematics' future by proposing ten problems for the century to come. (The published lecture expanded his list to 23. All but one have now been solved.) These problems, Hilbert insisted, "should be difficult in order to entice us, yet not completely inaccessible" (241). They should offer "a signpost on the torturous paths to hidden truths" (241). In fact, Hilbert had anticipated the twentieth-century concern with the relationship between theory and problem (see Thomas Kuhn), realizing, as one commentator has put it, that the two operate in "a to-and-fro process whereby theories are created to solve problems and then problems bring the theories into focus" (Gray 237).[1] Hilbert was arguing that *problems come first,* even if, as we now understand, problems become visible only in particular contexts at least partially determined by theories.

Although we tend to associate Hilbert's emphasis on problems with the scientific disciplines, this method has a tradition within the humanities. Philosophy, after all, has one of its origins in Socrates's problems: what is justice? what is virtue? And Wittgenstein's later career demonstrates how the move from theory to particular questions (how do you teach a word to a child? what is involved when someone says, "I have a pain in my arm"?) can reanimate an entire field. What would happen if we applied Hilbert's example to film studies? What are the film studies problems for the twenty-first century.

Simply asking this question might stir things up. Hilbert insisted that with mathematics, problems come first, but with film studies, theory has usually had the upper hand. From Eisenstein to Bazin to post-1968 semiotic critique, the dominant ways of thinking about the cinema have come from theory. Even when, as in Eisenstein's case, general propositions seemed to have emerged from technical matters, the resulting theory soon gained the upper hand: as Jean-Marie Straub once observed, everyone thinks of Eisenstein as a great editor because he had so many *theories* about it (Rosenbaum). The one major exception to this rule, *auteurism,* may owe its long life to its origins in a particular problem: the young Turks at the *Cahiers du Cinéma* were, after all, trying to figure out how to break into the French film industry.

For twenty years, Gregory Ulmer has organized his research around a problem: how do the new technologies of photography, film, video, and computers transform what we call "thinking"? It's a big question, one for the next century, and it has informed much of the Florida work in film and media studies. (But not all: see Nora Alter, Mark Reid, and Maureen Turim.) In Brecht's sense, Ulmer is a *messingkauf,* someone who buys a trumpet not for its music but for its brass; he approaches the arts not as objects of study but as implicit solutions to the problem at hand.[2] That project involves one irony: despite Ulmer's recent emphasis on digital media, his method remains analogical, using Walter Ong's analysis of the orality-literacy transition as a model for what happens when literacy gives way to what Ulmer calls "electracy."

Although I remain compelled by Ulmer's work (no one has influenced me more), I am interested in the movies themselves. Thus, Hilbert's example prompts me to try to formulate the problems that might guide film studies into the twenty-first century. At the end of the cinema's own century (in 1995, dating from the Lumière Brothers' first projections in 1895), all sorts of articles appeared summing up the last hundred years of film and film criticism. If we want to start thinking about the next hundred, we have to imagine the problems that will guide us. I will try to make a start here, noting that my problems (1) are concerned with film criticism, not filmmaking and (2) are both small and large. I hope that others will add to this list.

1. The Problem of Attribution, or Who's Responsible for This Shot?

Let's take a simple moment from a representative classical Hollywood movie, *Grand Hotel* (1932). Returning to her room after an aborted performance, the fading ballerina Grusinskaya, played by Greta Garbo, slumps to the floor and begins undressing. As she slips her arms from the straps of her white tutu, the camera films her from above, making her image resemble a flower petal opening in a bowl. Who's responsible for this shot?

In many ways, the history of film studies has amounted to attempts to answer this question. From roughly 1920 to 1960, the average viewer would have assigned responsibility for this shot to Garbo; even if their makers knew better, movies were marketed, after all, as star vehicles. Irene Dunne once complained, "If it's bad, they will say 'Irene Dunne's latest picture is bad'" (Davis 115). Although the *auteur* theory would seek to correct this sense of a movie's provenance, prior to 1950 only a handful of directors' names would have been able to attract an audience: DeMille and Hitchcock, certainly; Capra and Welles, probably; Ford and Hawks, maybe. After *auteurism* taught us to think about Ray and Walsh, Wilder and Mann, Thomas Schatz's *The Genius of the System* (1988) reminded us that the American cinema issued from a studio system modeled on Henry Ford's factories, committed to an extreme division of labor. Schatz made heads of production Irving Thalberg, Darryl Zanuck, and Hal Wallis his heroes, but his title suggested filmmaking's intensely collaborative nature, its reliance on scores of specialists writing the scripts, doctoring the dialogue, running the camera, positioning the lights, dressing the actors, designing the sets, recording the sound. And yet, more than ten years into the cinema's second century, we still don't know how to talk about these things. Who, after all, *is* responsible for the *Grand Hotel* shot I've mentioned? We could start with a list: the producer (Thalberg), the director (Edmund Goulding), the cameraman (William Daniels), the set designer (Cedric Gibbons), the costumer (Adrian), the star (Garbo). But we have probably only scratched the surface. This is a relatively simple problem, but it gets at something essential to filmmaking.

2. The Problem of the Wind in the Trees

"What's missing from movies nowadays," D.W. Griffith said as he lay dying, "is the beauty of the moving wind in the trees." [3] He was referring, of course, to the kind of incidental, unforeseen details that, when noticed in a shot's margins, so excited the first film spectators. The most famous example of Griffith's wind occurs in the background of Lumière's *Le Déjeuner de bébé,* whose effect Dai Vaughan has explained:

> Audiences had hitherto been familiar only with the painted backdrops of the theatre. . . . people were startled not so much by the phenomenon of the moving photograph, which inventors had struggled long to achieve, as by the ability of this to portray spontaneities of which the theatre was not capable. The movements of photographed people were accepted without demur because they were perceived as performance, as simply a new mode of self-projection; but that the inanimate should participate in self-projection was astonishing. (Vaughan 5)

André Bazin would found a whole cinematic theory on such moments: an actor's unrehearsed gesture, the dust on Boudu's country road. For Bazin, the wind in the trees amounted to the real shining through; it resulted from the camera's *automatic* recording of the world before it, and on that automatism rested the cinema's ontology. Dai Vaughan again: "The evangelical function of cinema," at least in Bazin's eyes, rested on "the promise of a language purged of authoritarian impositions" (184). "*Film material,*" Noël Burch reminds us, "*is always refractory to some degree,*" but as Burch warns, "over the last fifty years or so [Burch was writing in 1969], film directors essentially attempted to eliminate, as much as possible, any intrusion of mere chance, of the contingencies of everyday reality" (Burch 115). This project has accelerated with the invasion of computer-generated-imagery and digital effects, which have encouraged twenty-first-century filmmaking to drift towards animation.

Here's how to think about what has happened. In *Of Grammatology,* Derrida described Western culture's denigration of writing as a technology that alienates us from the presence implicit in speech. If orality seems to offer untrammeled contact with the thing itself, writing inevitably removes us to a realm of codes, conventions, and articulation. Cinema's history, however, suggests exactly the opposite of Derrida's argument. Filmmaking's first century amounts to a steady retreat from the implications of automatism, from the presence offered by the camera lens. From Eisenstein's metaphor of shots as words to Astruc's "*la caméra stylo*" to contemporary cgi, the road leads straight to writing. Although Lumière's first movies demonstrated, as Burch puts it, that "the aleatory is quite at home in film and always has been" (109), Lumière himself, with his careful framing, "had already begun that *struggle against the accidental* that was to characterize nearly all filmmaking" (109) for the next century.

Where are we now? Roland Barthes once identified incidentals like the wind in the trees (his "third meanings") with "the filmic" itself, which he maintained lies "outside (articulated) language":

> The filmic is what, in the film, cannot be described. . . . The filmic begins only where language and articulated meta-language cease. Everything we can *say* about *Ivan* or *Potemkin* can be said about a certain written text (which would be called *Ivan the Terrible* or *The Battleship Potemkin*), except this. . . . The filmic is precisely here, at this point where articulated language is no more than approximative and where another language begins. . . . (*Responsibility* 58–59)

Film history is a record of the resistance to this other language, and recently, that resistance has become nearly complete. Dai Vaughan has argued that "From Today, Cinema Is Dead" (181), suggesting that because film's authority rests on our knowledge of its automatic production, it cannot survive our awareness of its images' manipulation. The movies, Vaughan maintains, have always been a faith, "and once we have lost it, we will never get it back" (189). Can the cinema survive losing the wind in the trees? That's a problem for the century if there ever was one.

3. The Problem of the Blown Veil, or Contingency

In *How Green Was My Valley* (1941), as Maureen O'Hara walked out of the church on her wedding day, a sudden gust of wind caught her veil, billowing it in the air as it trailed behind her. The actor playing her husband reached out to catch it. John Ford, the movie's scriptwriter Philip Dunne later said, had just experienced "one of the greatest strokes of luck a director ever had. . . . The man shouldn't have *touched* it when the veil spiraled up. My God, what a shot! Luckily, Joe LaShelle, who was the operator, just gave it a little tilt with the camera." One cameraman admitted that he had been so taken by this shot that he had tried to reproduce it in subsequent films, "but it never quite looked right." While O'Hara derided Dunne's story as apocryphal, claiming that the blown veil had resulted from wind machines, the story might stand for the accidents that enter the filmmaking process at every stage.[4]

With moviemaking, there is "instability at *every* point," and changing anything resembles "giving an extra shuffle to an already well-shuffled pack of cards. You know it will change your luck, but you don't know whether for better or for worse" (Gleick 19, 21). The quotations come from James Gleick's *Chaos: The Making of a New Science,* one of the first books to make chaos theory a term that now circulates in what Sherry Turkle has called the discourse of "superficial knowledge" (8). Like the weather, chaos theory's first object of study, filmmaking's outcome resists prediction. Thus despite classic Hollywood's determined efforts to rationalize production and its devotion to Taylorist efficiency, no one has ever been able to *guarantee* a hit or make a star. "Nobody knows anything," says Art De Vany, an industrial economist who has studied filmmaking. "None of them know what they are doing. There is no formula, no way of predicting how a film will do" (Cassidy 36–37).

De Vany's work attends primarily to the cinema-as-investment. We should recall, however, that François Truffaut launched *La Nouvelle Vague* by insisting that only the director, the person *on the set,* could readily take advantage of filmmaking's contingencies. In arguing for this *disponibilité,* Truffaut was following his mentor, André Bazin, who had consistently championed a cinema that regards accidents like

O'Hara's blown veil as opportunities. The shooting script, invented in 1920s Hollywood precisely to police directors like Von Stroheim, had become what it was intended to be all along, a straitjacket.

But even Truffaut's corrective is slightly off. Talking about moviemaking only in terms of directors resembles analyzing battles only in terms of generals. Writing about the First Minnesota regiment's efforts on Gettysburg's second day, when its 82 percent casualty rate bought the Union army the ten minutes it needed to save Little Round Top, Kent Gramm has argued that despite all the plans of Lee, Longstreet, Hancock, and Meade, "sometimes it simply comes down to a fight" (84). That fight, Gramm goes on, is "subject to accident or intention or chance or absurdity," and "the essence of war is one step beyond the whole duty of generals, as it is one step beyond the knowledge of planners or analysts" (86). Filmmaking, of course, isn't a battle (well, sometimes it is), but it often lies beyond the control of its generals, the producers, writers, directors, and technicians at the top of its command chain. Sometimes it simply comes down to the wind blowing a veil.

Jean-Luc Godard once composed a mini-cinematic essay about the kinds of contingencies that intrude into even the most planned moviemaking. In *2 or 3 Things I Know about Her,* when his heroine visits her husband's garage, Godard's own voiceover questioned his shot selection:

> how do you describe an event? How do you show or tell that on that afternoon, at about ten past four, Juliette and Marianne went to a garage near the Porte des Ternes where Juliette's husband worked? . . . Do you really have to use these words and these images? Are they the only ones possible? Are there no others? . . . For example . . ., there's another young woman there, and we don't know a thing about her. And, in all honesty, we don't even know how to talk about it. (Godard)

Nearly four decades after *2 or 3 Things,* we still don't know how to talk about the contingencies that affect filmmaking.

4. The Problem of Timbre. In *Rhythm and Noise: An Aesthetics of Rock,* Theodore Gracyk poses an important question: how can a song like "Louie Louie," which "shuns compositional complexity," enable hundreds of pleasurable listenings? Given its repetitive, predictable melody, rhythm, and harmony, how does the song retain its impact? Gracyk's answer is the song's *timbre,* precisely that aspect of music most difficult to remember.

We can certainly remember the basic differences between the timbre of a saxophone and a trumpet, or identify the voice of a favorite singer, and we can summon them at will into "the mind's ear." . . . but auditory memories seem to be restricted to *species* of timbre. We can *hear* minute differences between similar timbres while listening, but those nuances begin to be forgotten about a second after the sounds cease. . . . memories of timbre "fade" after a moment, becoming more precise with the passage of time. (57) The more that a particular kind of music forgoes melodic or harmonic richness, the more it will rely on timbre for its expressive qualities: the mere *sound* of a guitar or snare drum or human voice. Because we cannot remember exactly how the Kingsmen's recording of "Louie Louie" sounds, its timbre keeps seeming fresh.

The cinema's exact equivalent of timbre is what the *Cahiers* critics called *mise-en-scène,* and like pop music's timbre, *mise-en-scène* grows in importance as a film's obvious formal complexities decline. Timbre is crucial to the experience of "Louie Louie" because the song itself is so simple. *Mise-en-scène* is more important to *The Maltese Falcon* than to *The Seventh Seal.* In many ways, *mise-en-scène* is another term for Barthes's "filmic," something simultaneously crucial and elusive. Take, for example, Andrew Sarris's provocative uses:

> For me, *mise-en-scène* is not merely the gap between what we see and feel on the screen and what we can express in words, but is also the gap between the intention of the director and his effect upon the spectator. . . . To read all sorts of poignant profundities in Preminger's inscrutable urbanity would seem to be the last word in idiocy, and yet there are moments in his films when the evidence on the screen is inconsistent with one's deepest instincts about the director as a man. *It is during these moments that one feels the magical power of mise-en-scène.* . . . ("Preminger's" 13)

Or, Sarris again, writing about Preminger's *Bunny Lake Is Missing:* "Although the plot collapses. . . . and there are really no characters to consider. . . . Preminger's *mise-en-scène* is the most brilliant I have seen all year" (*Confessions* 213–14).

Students asked to describe the café scenes in *Grand Hotel* and *Casablanca,* even after recent viewings, will typically prove unable to distinguish them. And yet when the comparable sequences appear on two monitors placed side-by-side, the differences could hardly be more obvious. Those differences amount to cinematic *timbre,* and although Classical Hollywood's technicians were its masters, film studies has never been very good at accounting for it.

5. The Problem of the Uninvited Visitor

Here is a scene from Hitchcock's 1955 version of *The Man Who Knew Too Much.* While entertaining their new friend, Louis Bernard, Doris Day and Jimmy Stewart respond to a knock on the door. In what we will call Shot 1 of this sequence, Day walks quickly towards the door, brushing past her husband. Shot 2 begins with a bust shot of Day from behind as she opens the door, revealing a mid-shot of a man obscured by shadows. A light suddenly comes on, accompanied by a quick dolly-in to a medium-close-up of the man's face as he shifts his gaze from Day (now out of the shot) to the room behind her. Shot 3, the object of his look, provides a deep-focus look at the hotel room, with its three figures arrayed in distinct planes, Day in the right foreground and Stewart in the left middle, turning their heads to follow the uninvited visitor's scrutiny of Bernard, on the balcony in the deep center. They turn back to look at the stranger, motivating the reverse Shot 4 of him still at the door.

How can we account for this sequence's chilling effect? Christian Keathley has pointed out that although we have the analytical tools to do so, the exigencies of teaching (the fifty-minute periods, the film-a-week schedule) make it far easier to discuss topics like "the Orientalism of Hitchcock's Marrakesh." Nevertheless, as an academic discipline, film studies needs to figure out ways of talking about sequences like this one.[5]

6. The Problem of Benjamin's Ruffles

"To someone looking through piles of old letters," Walter Benjamin once wrote in a kind of note to himself, "a stamp that has long been out of circulation on a torn envelope often says more than a reading of dozens of pages" (*One-Way Street,* 91). And in a letter: "the eternal would be the ruffles on a dress rather than an idea" (Wolin 130). What would it mean for film studies to learn to write with Benjamin's ruffles?

Wittgenstein kept a notebook, where he once described his own method: "If I am thinking about a topic just for myself, and not with a view to writing a book, I jump all around it; that is the only way of thinking that comes naturally to me" (28). Jumping all around Benjamin's ruffles leads me to the following remarks:

> I think I summed up my attitude toward philosophy when I said: philosophy ought really to be written as a *poetic composition.* (Wittgenstein 24)

> The Lacanian subject (for instance) never makes him think of Tokyo, but Tokyo makes him think of the Lacanian subject. This procedure is a constant one: he rarely starts from the idea in order to invent an image for it subsequently; he starts from a sensuous object, and then hopes to meet in his work with the possibility of finding an *abstraction* for it, levied on the intellectual culture of the moment. . . . he finds the gesture first . . . then the idea. (Barthes *Barthes*)

> Let us not underrate the value of a fact; it will one day flower in a truth. (Thoreau)

Ezra Pound once named this approach "the method of the Luminous Detail" (15). To develop a film studies based on Benjamin's ruffles will involve working closely with the movies' details, its concrete objects, its particular gestures. Historian Carlo Ginzburg has suggested that his own approach involves "squeezing the evidence," looking at something closely until it yields some precious information that has been hidden (Kandell 48). What have Hollywood movies hidden from us? The work that went into them. The movies were all made bit by bit, in increments that piled up in the developing rooms, on the sound stages and in the editing suites. The details in these fragments, in those shots and images, contain the record of the work and ideas that produced them. In our unconscious memories, we recognize something there, tantalizing and just beyond reach. The problem for film studies is to unlock those memories, to make them conscious and explicit so that they will help us understand the most powerful and important storytelling system ever seen.

In my own courses at Florida, I have asked students to spend an entire semester on a single movie, with the goal of writing a paper composed of twenty-six entries (one for each letter of the alphabet) triggered by a particular cinematic detail. Here is an example concerning *The Maltese Falcon:*

> *(P)oster:* As they look down at Archer's murder scene, Spade and Polhaus stand in front of a battered apartment building plastered with a tattered poster for *Swing Your Lady,* an actual 1938 Humphrey Bogart musical (?!), widely regarded as his worst film. The sign, of course, functions first as the kind of insider joke that prompted Huston and Bogart to make 1954's *Beat the Devil,* a parody of movies like *The Maltese Falcon.* It also plays with notions of "the trap," for just as *Swing Your Lady* stands for the kind of trap late-1930s Bogart-the-actor had fallen into, it also provides a clue to the movie's enigma and its villain's probable fate: Archer has not been killed at random, but led into a trap by Brigid, who will probably "swing" for her crime.

But the poster raises other questions, too. What, for example, is the status of a real object in a fictional world? If we imagine the hermetically-sealed space of *The Maltese Falcon* as one large theater set, the *Swing Your Lady* poster seems like a door in the stage's rear wall, suddenly flung open to reveal the actual world. The very lack of attention accorded the poster achieves another effect. As Barthes points out, when real historical characters (or objects) get introduced into a novel *obliquely, in passing,* "their modesty, like a lock between two levels of water, equalizes novel and history." After *The Maltese Falcon*'s success, Warners would exploit such "locks," casting Bogart in a series of WW II adventures (*Across the Pacific, Casablanca, Action in the North Atlantic, Sahara, Passage to Marseilles, To Have and Have Not*), the first of which, 1941's *Across the Pacific,* concerns the Panama Canal.[6]

7. The Problem of the Hallucinatory Spell

Seventy years ago, struggling to devise a means of writing that would work as powerfully as the cinema, Walter Benjamin made a cryptic proposal:

> Uprising of the anecdotes. . . . The constructions of history are comparable to instructions that commandeer the true life and confine it to barracks. On the other hand: the street insurgence of the anecdote. The anecdote brings things near to us spatially, lets them enter our life. It represents the strict antithesis to the sort of history . . . that makes everything abstract. (*Arcades* 846)

Benjamin's championing of the anecdote's mysterious specificity, its disabling of history's generalizations, contradicted his own previous insistence on photographic *captions.* In "A Small History of Photography," he had cited Brecht's insistence that "a photograph of the Krupp works or A.E.G. tells us next to nothing about these institutions. . . . So something must in fact be *built up,* something artificial, posed" (*One-Way,* 255). In the face of photographs whose "fleeting and secret moments" "paralyse the associative mechanisms in the beholder," "the caption," Benjamin argued in 1931, would "become the most important part of the photograph" (*One-Way* 256).

In effect, film studies has amounted to the movies' captions. Florida student Brian Doan argues that in the academic community, the captions have displaced the films themselves, as students are taught to approach every movie with the powerful explanatory systems developed since 1968. In their *Practicing New Historicism,* Catherine Gallagher and Stephen Greenblatt have made a case for the anecdote as a means for redressing this imbalance:

> [B]oth of us were and remain deeply skeptical of the notion that we should formulate an abstract system and then apply it to literary works (2).
>
> The task of understanding then depends not on the extraction of an abstract set of principles, and still less on the application of a theoretical model, but rather on an encounter with the singular, the specific, and the individual (6).
>
> [The anecdote] functions . . . to subvert a programmatic analytical response. . . . but also to arouse the bafflement, the intense curiosity and interest, that necessitates the interpretation of cultures. (22)

In writing history or film criticism, part of the problem simply involves the vividness of the thing studied. "I'm not talking about making it livelier than it was," said Shelby Foote about the Civil War, in a remark that could easily apply to film history; "I'm just talking about some attempt to make it as lively as it was" (70). Foote's solution was the novelistic detail, Lee at Fredericksburg, looking through his binoculars over the battlefield to the house, with a tree in its front yard and a seat under it, where he had proposed to his wife.

Here is what Benjamin might have called a "dialectical anecdote" about the cinema. One morning in 1933, MGM's story editor Samuel Marx arrived at his office to find scriptwriter F. Hugh Herbert waiting for him. Herbert had worked in Hollywood since the silent days, and loved MGM so much that he had been married in a church set on the back lot. But with the coming of sound, his career had waned, and although still on salary, he was used less often. Marx tried to brush him off, but Herbert said that Irving Thalberg himself had told him to come for an assignment. "When did Thalberg say that?" Marx asked skeptically. "Last night. He dropped in to see me at my house." Convinced that Herbert was inventing an excuse, Marx persisted: "How was he dressed?" "In a tuxedo." "And does he usually dress like that when he drops in on you?" Admitting that Thalberg had never paid him a visit before, Herbert nevertheless insisted that Irving had come calling around 10 o'clock the previous night, and that after drinking some brandy, had asked whether Herbert was working. Told that he wasn't, Thalberg suggested he go to Marx for a job. "When I woke up the next morning," Herbert confessed, "I thought I had dreamed it, so I went downstairs and there was the brandy bottle, with two glasses on the dining room table." Still incredulous, Marx saw Thalberg later that day and asked him about Herbert's story, which, surprisingly, Thalberg confirmed. "I went to see someone who lives on the same street, but I rang the wrong doorbell. He asked me in, and I couldn't refuse." "It seemed odd," Marx remembered, "he didn't explain what had happened and go on to his planned destination." "Hughie's not a bad writer," Thalberg added. "See if you find something for him." Marx bought a story from Herbert that became a B-movie, *Women in His Life,* the first picture at MGM for George B. Seitz, the director of the Andy Hardy series that made Mickey Rooney a star (Marx 75–76).The contradictory elements seem almost allegorical: an abandoned party, implied but not described; a Fitzgeraldian Hollywood night long ago;

filmmaking's supreme rationalizer, lost on a suddenly strange street; a chance encounter, prolonged out of politeness; a coincidence leading to a new routine of perfectly planned serial production. When Benjamin proposed a historical method based on such images, Theodor Adorno could only reply: "Your study is located at the crossroads of magic and positivism. That spot is bewitched. Only theory could break the spell" (129).

Adorno meant to be dismissive. In fact, he had produced the perfect definition of the cinema ("the crossroads of magic and positivism") and of film studies' traditional project (to "break the spell"). As a technologically based, capital-intensive medium, filmmaking quickly developed into an industry attracted by positivism's applications: the Taylorist-Fordist models of rationalized production. And yet, as Thalberg realized, the movies succeeded commercially to the extent that they *enchanted.* Hence the inevitable question: could enchantment be mass-produced? Yes, as Godard once told Colin MacCabe, "the cinema is all money" (McCabe 27). But at any moment, it can also become as Godard wrote of Renoir's *La Nuit du carrefour (Night at the Crossroads*), "the air of confusion . . . the smell of rain and of fields bathed in mist" (Godard 63).

In the 1920s, the Surrealists and French Impressionists focused almost exclusively on magic, offering the idea of *photogénie* as the essence of cinema. After 1968, magic became the problem, the source of the movies' ideological menace. Thus, breaking the spell became film studies' object, a goal explicitly announced by Laura Mulvey in her brilliant "Visual Pleasure and Narrative Cinema," the 1975 *Screen* essay that became the breviary for two decades of theory. "It is said that analyzing pleasure, or beauty, destroys it," Mulvey wrote. "That is the intention of this article" (16).

The anecdote about Thalberg, however, suggests that film studies errs whenever it forgets either of the cinema's two elements. If surrealism settled for mystification, *Screen* theory often ignored the reasons why people went to the movies in the first place. Where do we go from here? Trying to formulate a new way of writing about the past, Walter Benjamin once asked "[M]ust the . . . understanding of history necessarily come at the cost of graphicness?" (*N* 6) Although he never completed what has become known as *The Arcades Project,* his dream of a different critical writing, "exact fantasy," as he called it, still provokes questions. For example, when Peter Wollen tells us that *couturier* Paul

Poiret celebrated the 1925 Art Deco exhibition with three show barges named *Amours, Délices,* and *Orgues,* the three words in the French language that are masculine in the singular and feminine in the plural, why does his explanatory gloss ("Thus Poiret translated the economy of fashion into that of the singular masculine phallus and Leporello's endless list of women's names") seem so much less interesting than the story itself (7)?[7]

I don't mean to single out Wollen for blame: he is, in my opinion, one of the three or four best living writers about the movies. But if even Wollen can at times seem overmatched by his object of study, then we must acknowledge that Benjamin's problem of "graphicness" is even more acute for film studies. In his famous study of imperialist terror, *Shaminism, Colonialism, and the Wild Man,* Michael Taussig suggests that the task of understanding "calls neither for demystification nor remystification but for a quite different poetics of destruction and revelation" (369). Hence,

> Conrad's way of dealing with the terror of the rubber boom in the Congo was *Heart of Darkness.* There were three realities there, comments Frederick Karl: King Leopold's, made out of intricate disguises and deceptions, Roger Casement's studied realism [in his official reports], and Conrad's, which, to quote Karl, "fell midway between the other two, as he attempted to penetrate the veil and yet was anxious to retain its hallucinatory quality. This formulation is sharp and important: *to penetrate the veil while retaining its hallucinatory quality*"(10).

Here is the proposition: the goal of a twenty-first-century film studies should be to penetrate the movies' veil while retaining their hallucinatory quality. The problem is inventing a method that will achieve this balance.

8. The Problem of the Three Audiences

In a 1995 essay, Princeton professor James McPherson addressed the inability of professional historians to reach a general readership. The question "What's the Matter with History," McPherson's title, recurs every generation, leading to periodic attempts, like the creation in 1954 of *American Heritage,* to bridge the great divide the academic and lay audiences. By the mid-1980s, the problem had aroused even the professionals, and one of them, Thomas Bender, famously called for a "narrative synthesis"—"an incorporation of the findings and interpretations of specialized subfields [McPherson sites race, class, gender and ethnicity studies] into a new synthesis written in a narrative format that would be accessible and interesting to a lay public" (McPherson 235-36).

McPherson wrote that his own specialty, the Civil War, had this problem in spades because, in fact, it has *three* distinct audiences. The first consists of "professional historians," academics concerned with big questions, the causes and effects of the war. This audience reads the work of other professionals, and while it attends to such sweeping events as America's "great transformation" from a rural, pre-capitalist society to an urban, wage-labor economy, this audience's writers have, typically "neglected the military dimensions of the Civil War" (239–40).

The second Civil War audience consists of buffs, non-academics, interested "mainly, often exclusively, in the military campaigns and battles. This audience is "overwhelmingly male," and it prefers non-academic authors whose massive volumes on individual battles strain the shelves of every Borders, crowding out other kinds of history (243). The third audience, the "general reader," is the one that has largely abandoned professional historians. It prefers Bender's "narrative synthesis," but tends to find it in the work of amateurs like Douglas Southall Freeman, Bruce Catton, Shelby Foote, and, more recently, Ken Burns (244–45).

Burns has said that in college "I was never taught what happened in the Civil War. I was taught causes, and then I was taught effects. And [yet] this happens to be a war in which the outcome of battles mattered." As McPherson summarizes it,

> Burns consciously set out to provide the kind of narrative synthesis that neither the "old school" (as he termed it) nor the "new history" offered—the old school because while narrative in approach, it did not incorporate material on "women, labor, minorities, and the social transformation" accomplished by the war; the new history because it "often abandoned narrative completely." (238, 245)

Of the other major academic fields, film studies most resembles the Civil War in having distinct audiences. The first, the professional, reads the books and articles written by other academics, and like the Civil War monographs concentrating on causes and effects, these studies have often lost touch with the movies themselves. The second audience of film buffs, like the Civil War audience interested in generals, cares largely about stars, and its preferred books dominate mass-market bookstores. Film studies' third audience, that mythical "general reader," seems less established. It almost certainly constitutes the main buyers of books by non-academics like James Harvey (*Romantic Comedy)* and Otto Friedrich (*City of Nets*), and it used to read Pauline Kael and Andrew Sarris. But professionals rarely write for this audience, although Thomas Schatz's *The Genius of the System* seems a model work: an academic analysis of Hollywood's Studio Era, extracting its thesis from case-studies of how individual movies were made. I would also say that my own *A Certain Tendency of the Hollywood Cinema, 1930–1980* has surprised me by its appeal to lay readers who have, from time to time, pleased me with their letters.

Here then is the problem: how can academic film scholars devise a "narrative synthesis" that will propagate professional knowledge about the cinema? This is already happening on DVD.

These are my eight problems for twenty-first century film studies. I know, of course, that there are others. I would list, for example, the following:

—What happens to the cinema when its consumption shifts from theatrical exhibition to home viewing, from programmed screenings in large public spaces to intermittent appearances on small monitors, started and stopped at the viewer's discretion?

—What happens to the movies when the cinema dissolves into the larger, more amorphous world of "visual culture": television, video games, Internet imagery?

—Can the cinema survive the inevitable demystification effected by DVDs?

These problems already have plenty of people on the case.[8] The ones I have raised seem as consequential as their solutions have remained elusive. Hilbert asked his listeners to go to work on his problems. I would do the same with mine.

Notes

1. For more information about Hilbert and his problems, see Ben H. Yandell, *The Honors Class: Hilbert's Problems and Their Solvers* (Natick, Mass.: A.K. Peters, 2002) and Constance Reid, *Hilbert* (New York: Copernicus, 1996).

2. Brecht's metaphor of the *Messingkauf,* the purchaser of brass, comes from his own *Messingkauf Dialogues,* imaginary backstage conversations among the Actor, the Actress, the Dramaturg, the Electrician, and the Philosopher (Brecht himself). Here is the Philosopher's crucial passage:

> I can only compare myself with a man, say, who deals in scrap metal and goes up to a brass band to buy, not a trumpet, let's say, but simply brass. The trumpeter's trumpet is made of brass, but he'll hardly want to sell it as such, by its value as brass, as so many ounces of brass. All the same, that's how I ransack your theatre for events between people, such as you do more or less imitate even if your imitations are for a very different purpose than my satisfaction. To put it in a nutshell: I'm looking for a way of getting incidents between people imitated for certain purposes; I've heard that you supply such imitations; and now I hope to find out if they are actually the kind of imitations I can use. (Brecht 15-16)

3. For the definitive summary of this problem, see Christian Keathley, *The Wind in the Trees: Cinephilia and History* (Bloomington: Indiana UP, 2006).

4. For a brief summary of Hollywood's Taylorist/Fordist attempts to rationalize production, see my "How a Film Theory Got Lost," in *How a Film Theory Got Lost and Other Mysteries in Cultural Studies* (Bloomington: Indiana UP, 2001), pp. 1–3.

5. I am grateful to Christian Keathley for this problem. The example from *The Man Who Knew Too Much* also comes from him.

6. I am grateful to Florida student Ashley Bowen for pointing out the *Swing Your Lady* poster, something I had never noticed, despite having seen *The Maltese Falcon* scores of times.

7. The problem here resembles one described by Roland Barthes in *The Pleasure of the Text,* trans. Richard Miller (New York: Hill & Wang, 1975), pp. 53–54: "Why do some people, including myself, enjoy in certain novels, biographies, and historical works the representation of the "daily life" of an epoch, of a character? Why the curiosity about petty details: schedules, habits, meals, lodging, clothing, etc.?"

Thus, impossible to imagine a more tenuous, a more insignificant notation than that of "today's weather" (or yesterday's); and yet, the other day, reading, trying to read Amiel, irritation that the well-meaning editor (another person foreclosing pleasure) had seen fit to omit from this Journal the everyday details, what the weather was like on the shores of Lake Geneva, and retain only the insipid moral musing: yet it is this weather that has not aged, not Amiel's philosophy.

8. I would especially single out for praise Sylvia Harvey's "What Is Cinema? The Sensuous, the Abstract and the Political," in *Cinema: The Beginnings and the Future,* ed. Christopher Williams (London: U of Westminster P, 1996), pp. 228–252. Three works by University of Florida students also have great promise. Christian Keathley's *The Wind in the Trees: Cinephilia and History* (forthcoming from Indiana University Press), I have cited in note 7: it works towards a new film criticism based on the contingent detail. David Johnson's recently completed dissertation, *The Accidental Extra,* explores the relationship between contingency and the cinema's ontology. And Brian Doan's dissertation-in-progress uses the anecdote itself as a potential vehicle for film criticism.

Works Cited

Adorno, Theodor. *Aesthetics and Politics.* London: Verso, 1980.

Barthes, Roland. *Roland Barthes.* Trans Richard Howard. New York: Hill & Wang, 1977.

—. *The Responsibility of Forms: Critical Essays on Music, Art, and Representation.* Trans. Richard Howard. New York: Hill & Wang, 1985.

—. *Roland Barthes.* Trans Richard Howard. New York: Hill & Wang, 1977.

Benjamin, Walter. *One-Way Street.* Trans. Edmund Jephcott and Kingsley Shorter. London: New Left Books, 1979.

—. *The Arcades Project.* Trans. Howard Eiland and Kevin McLaughlin. Cambridge: Harvard University Press, 1999.

—. "N [Theoretics of Knowledge; Theory of Progress]." *The Philosophical Forum.* 15.1-2 (Fall-Winter 1983–84).

Brecht, Bertolt. *The Messingkauf Dialogues.* Trans. John Willett. London: Methuen, 1965.

Burch, Noël. *Theory of Film Practice.* Trans. Helen R. Lane. Princeton: Princeton U P, 1973.

Cassidy, John. "Chaos in Hollywood." *The New Yorker.* 31 March 1997.

Davis, Ronald L. *The Glamour Factory: Inside Hollywood's Big Studio System.* Dallas: Southern Methodist UP, 1993.

Foote, Shelby. *Conversations with Shelby Foote.* Ed. William C. Carter. Jackson: UP of Mississippi, 1989.

Gleick, James. *Chaos: Making a New Science.* New York: Penguin Books, 1987.

Godard, Jean-Luc. *Godard on Godard.* Trans. Tom Milne. New York: Viking Press, 1972.

Gracyk, Theodore. *Rhythm and Noise: An Aesthetics of Rock.* Durham: Duke UP, 1996.

Gramm, Kent. "The Chances of War: Lee, Longstreet, Sickles, and the First Minnesota Volunteers" *The Gettysburg Nobody Knows.* Ed. Gabor S. Boritt. New York: Oxford UP, 1997 .

Gray, Jeremy J. *The Hilbert Challenge* . New York: Oxford UP, 2000.

Kandell, Jonathan. "Was the World Made out of Cheese?" *The New York Times Sunday Magazine,* 17 November 1991.

Karl, Fredrick. *Joseph Conrad: The Three Lives.* New York: Farrar, Straus and Giroux, 1979.

MacCabe, Colin. *Godard: Images, Sounds, Politics.* Bloomington: Indiana UP, 1980.

Marx, Samuel. *A Gaudy Spree: Literary Hollywood When the West Was Fun.* New York: Franklin Watts, 1987.

McPherson, James M. *Drawn with the Sword: reflections on the American Civil War* (New York: Oxford UP, 1996).

Mulvey, Laura. *Visual and Other Pleasures.* Bloomington: Indiana UP, 1989.

Ong, Walter J. *Orality and Literacy: The Technologizing of the Word.* New York: Methuen, 1982.

Pound, Ezra. "I Gather the Limbs of Osiris." *New Age* (1911–12). Rpt. Catherine Gallagher and Stephen Greenblatt, *Practicing New Historicism* Chicago: U of Chicago P, 2000.

Ray, Robert. *How a Film Theory Got Lost and Other Mysteries in Cultural Studies.* Bloomington: Indiana UP, 2001.

Rosenbaum, Jonathan. "The Films of Jean-Marie Straub and Danielle Huillet," in *Film at the Public: Program for a Film Series* (New York: Public Theater, 1982).

Sarris, Andrew. "Preminger's Two Periods: Studio and Solo." *Film Comment.* Summer 1965.

—. *Confessions of a Cultist: On the Cinema, 1955/1969* (New York: Simon and Schuster, 1970).

Taussig, Michael. *Shaminism, Colonialism, and the Wild Man: A Study in Terror and Healing* Chicago: U of Chicago P, 1987.

Thoreau, Henry David. "Natural History of Massachusetts," in Henry David Thoreau, Collected Essays and Poems. New York: The Library of America, 2001.

Wittgenstein, Ludwig. *Culture and Value.* Trans. Peter Winch. Chicago: U of Chicago P, 1980.

Wollen, Peter. *Raiding the Icebox: Reflections on Twentieth-Century Culture.* Bloomington: Indiana UP, 1993.

3 The Florida School's Legacy, or The Devil's Millhopper Joke Revisited

Craig Saper

No avant-garde group has ever achieved major acceptance without a catchy name: think of Futurism, Structuralism, Situationism, the Yale School, Fauvism, La Nouvell Vague, and even Dada, a parody of such names, meaningless, or at least intended to be. The name provides a group identity . . . The final stage of this group identity generally results in the formation of some official institute or association. . . .

—Robert B. Ray,
How a Film Theory Got Lost

If Saper hadn't met the Florida Research Ensemble (FRE), he would have had to invent it. Just as Hamlet invented his Father's ghost for the sake of Shakespeare's adaptation of the old myth, Saper's projective, or FRE associated, reading gives birth to the legacy he inherits.

—Richard Burt, performing in the film,
The Florida School's Legacy

Not entirely without merit!

—Greg Ulmer, a blurb for the film,
The Florida School's Legacy

What tiresome and laborious folly it is to write lengthy tomes, to expound in five hundred pages on an idea that one could easily propound orally in a few minutes. Better is pretending that the books [or films] exist already and offering a summary or commentary.

—Jorge Luis Borges

When you come to a conference on APPLIED YOU, it is **as if** *you're dead. I would like to see what it is like when I am dead. That's why I came.*

—Jacques Derrida

Writing has been bottled up in books since the start. It is time to pull out the stopper.

—Bob Brown

Devil's Millhopper gets its unique name from its funnel-like shape. During the 1880's, farmers used to grind grain in gristmills. On the top of the mill was a funnel-shaped container called a "hopper" that held the grain as it was fed into the grinder. Because fossilized bones and teeth from early life forms have been found at the bottom of the sink, legend has it that the millhopper was used to feed bodies to the devil. Hence, Devil's Millhopper.

—Florida Park Service

Nobody ever tells jokes for the first time.

—G. Legman

In the late 1980s, Greg Ulmer produced a video, *Ulmer Reads Reading on TV*, with Paper Tiger TV, a group of media makers and critics who produced television programs for public access channels. In each program, a media critic analyzed mass media in almost funny and sometimes insightful ways. For example, one program, *Joan Does Dynasty*, included hilarious rants, mixing sophisticated Marxist analysis with catty snipes about the characters' make-up and costumes. That critic,

Joan Braderman, used low budget blue-screen technology to insert her face into the actual scenes. In that context, Ulmer's program was one of the most elaborate productions, including multiple settings, a cast of actors, many clips, and an ambitious argument. The video was framed as an episode of *Believe It or Not,* and appeared to claim that a wacky Professor believed that a sinkhole in Florida (called the Devil's Millhopper) was the meaning of (Shakespeare's play) *Hamlet.* When it first appeared on pubic access stations, the audience share was unusually high for Paper Tiger TV. Public Access, first mandated by governments allowing cable companies to carve out territories as monopolies in most markets, was a fleeting space for low-rent diversity and experimentation that *Wayne's World* lovingly parodied. Ulmer's video, and Paper Tiger in general, tried to use that liberating low budget sense of expression, and its atmosphere also attempts to recreate a Freudian joke-logic. One could not financially live up to broadcast quality standards; so humor, montage sequences of clips, and using the stuff available for the audience-member-as-critic-host made the do-it-yourself programs inspiring. For example, Herb Shiller, in his Paper Tiger TV series of programs simply read the New York Times and, like someone sitting at the breakfast table, literally yelled at the paper his criticism of the editors' biased and surreal associative connections. Paper Tiger wanted to help broadcast programs that intelligently criticized particular programs and series. Ulmer took up the challenge. Although his published books and essays on his theories of *heuretics* and tele-theory are well known, the promise of a genre of video theory (i.e., theory-on-video, in new media, or online) is only now emerging.

Ulmer's video examined, and parodied, the Annenberg/CPB (Corporation for Public Broadcasting) Project's "Voices and Visions," an attempt to televise how to read (poetry) on television. Ulmer's video suggested that the well-intentioned and ambitious reading on TV project depended exclusively on one discredited model of interpretation: the only meaning of a poem was a product of the author's life and place. These psychobiographies, common in PBS documentaries on authors especially, have a neat and tidy melodramatic tautology: author's meaning completely explained by personal childhood strife, trauma, and nostalgia (for a fleeting happiness). Over and over again, the programs focused on places, like where Emily Dickinson lived, to explain the meaning of poems. The PBS project even attempted this stunt with poets, like Wallace Stevens, widely regarded as producing works tangled in metonymic analogies eluding any singular reference. The visual track of the "Voices and Visions" programs made the poem's meaning a literal interpretation of the poet's surroundings. Ulmer's video offered an alternative model of interpretation: to pull the (Mill's) stopper and let writing out of the logocentric book-logic. One could appreciate the meaning of even a masterpiece of literature and drama in terms of the reader's setting and situation. This was not a "reader response" version that sees a particular reader's interpretation as a window on to a singular (and usually neurotic) psychic formation. This was not simply a "cultural studies" version that contextualizes the meaning in terms of the situation of consumption and production. Rather, Ulmer suggested that the meaning of *Hamlet* in terms of a reader's geographical location also suggested ways to solve disciplinary problems. That is, readers could use literature to help solve social, cultural, and even specialized scholarly problems. Of course, the rhetoric of literary and humanistic disciplines has always claimed that the importance of great works resides in their ability to help readers solve these problems, but projective readings (using literature to solve problems) also finds itself mythologized as dangerous. Ulmer's video cites the case of Mark David Chapman, who assassinated John Lennon, as an example of the warnings media teach us about projective readings: they lead to murder and death. The non-projective readers usually find meaning in a process that discounts theoretical (or re-contextualization in terms of a reading) in favor of the theatrical (interpreting the author's intention and performing the author's meaning). Critics, like Joan Braderman, could talk over the media they study making the production something like video art or experimental media itself. Ulmer tells a visio-verba-semantic joke in the style of Freud's Marriage Broker joke.

The cinematic essays of Robert Ray, the videos and writing primers of Greg Ulmer, and the essays of many others associated with the Florida Research Ensemble did not merely talk about, but through and with, media. As Ray asks if "film theory can imitate filmmaking and recognize that, at its best, the cinema requires . . . a subtle mixture of logical structure and untranslatable allure. . . . Can film theory . . . write differently, to stage its research in the form of a spectacle? " He goes on to connect this new media theory to Ulmer's work and suggests that it can "provide a complement to critique"(Ray 13), and later that these new types of reading associated with the Florida School, "show us how we might use them to think" (54). The first published discussion of the Florida School was in the late 1980s in the introduction to a special issue of *Visible Language* on "Instant Theory" (). Since its publication, the School's shift away from traditional media studies toward new institutional practices (e.g., pedagogy, scholarship, publication, curriculum, and cultural change) continued and intensified. In that shift in ground, a variant of poststructuralism marked the emergence of *infrastructuralism.* ()

In speculating about ways to teach reading and interpretation using television, Ulmer's video also hinted at ways to construct pedagogical infrastructures and delivery systems as well as deal with theoretical legacies. Like Ray's work (and many of the contributors to this volume), Ulmer has couched his investigations of film and media in terms of pedagogical innovation. Specifically, Ulmer and Ray have suggested that one can simulate the invention process found in both the achievements of creative geniuses (e.g., Darwin) and vanguard artists (e.g., Picasso, the Surrealists, etcetera). As Ray explains, "Surrealist film-watching tactics, for example, were designed to reassert the autonomy and ambiguity of images: think, for example, of Man Ray's habit of watching the screen through his fingers, spread to isolate certain parts of the screen"(Ray 4). Robert Ray goes on to connect the invention process to Ulmer's *theory joke,* whose "prototypes are Duchamp's readymades" and "in fact, all radically new knowledge seems like a joke (think of Darwin and the monkeys). As Freud saw, the joke is a denial that also functions as a means of access, a channel capable of being confronted directly"(Ray 49). The joke and vanguardist experiment are played out on something Ulmer calls a *mystory.* Others in this volume will, no doubt, discuss in great detail these strategies (the use of personal memories, entertainment citations, and problem solving strategies to solve social and disciplinary problems). They do not ask one to solve personal problems by voicing personal memories. Instead, Ulmer and Ray describe in great detail how artists and other significant cultural innovators use personal stories, neologisms, coincidences, and details drawn from areas apparently unrelated to specific disciplinary problems. They then go on to demonstrate that process themselves in *mystories* on, for example, Ray's widely respected examination of the emergence and disappearance of the cinema's (unrecognized) inventor. Ray uses his own personal trauma, a friend and mentor's disappearance, to connect to a way to understand the future of media theory in its (missing) crucial precursor in the work of Walter Benjamin. He later uses that idea of a film theory lost as the basis, and title, for his third book of experimental film theory in which he wonders why the theory of "photogenie" (photogenia) had long ago vanished from most serious writing about film, and how we can construct a new legacy built on that lost theory. To follow the "cinematic detail whose insistent appeal eludes precise explanation," and to "follow this detail wherever it leads and report your findings,"(13) forms the method of this theory. It is based on Roland Barthes' notion of the *punctum,* the photographic detail that points to a lost Kierkegaardian absurd residue of existence precisely because it resists social or aesthetic explanations and captures a reality that is now gone. Barthes describes and invents the punctum in an extended essay, *Camera Lucida,* that examines how to build a theory from these contingencies of loss and mourning that the *punctum* marks. These details (images, words, phrases), for Ray, are "precisely not yet ideas, but rather maps for which the territory must be, not found, but invented; incomplete allegories, clues . . . swiveling back and forth between the desire to know and the desire to remain ignorant" (51). As the citations from Ray above demonstrate, loss and the effort to use loss (of ego, mentors, life, and even a firm ground of denotation) are the themes that flow through the Florida School's work. In fact, the titles of my own earliest essays express in condensed form this angst of loss and pedagogical redemption: "Learning From Being Lost" and "A Nervous Theory." Much of Ulmer's work concerns mourning, memorialization, and specifically the memories of his late literal father Walter Ulmer and figurative father of media theory Walter Benjamin. Because the Florida School presents these allegories of loss in terms of the surrealist jokes described above, many will miss the Devil's Millhopper aspect of the School's legacy.

To simulate innovation, one needs to use personal analogies, popular icons and stories, and specific strategies. Once personal analogies, especially traumatic childhood memories, enter the scene, the issue of (and the suggestive mana-word) legacy becomes paramount. Of course, *Hamlet* is the story of a vexed legacy, a theme common in many of Shakespeare's plays. It is even the crucial issue surrounding the on-again off-again controversies about who actually authored the plays, and Ulmer's video, on reading, jokes suggestively that it was Edward DeVere; whose legacy? The sinkhole, a literal part of Ulmer's setting. The countless millions of sinkholes in Florida are waiting to sink catastrophically or already mark the shifting ground. My relatively new Florida University is in a sinkhole zip code: built on a sinkhole literally and perhaps, in terms of its uncertain future, figuratively as well.

Sinkholes also function as an analogy for legacies. In Ulmer's case, it references working in his father Walter's gravel plant in Montana as well as the Norse myth about Hamlet's Mill being built on a plug (or sinkhole). It is time, to borrow Bob Brown's phrase, to pull out the stopper that has kept writing bottled up in books and to televise reading. Walter Annenberg of Philadelphia, wanting to legitimize his father's legacy (his father made a fortune as a bookie), invested heavily in improving education in America, including sponsoring the "Voices and Visions" series on reading on television. In a series of similar surreal connections, his video also includes Marie Osmond reading a Hugo Ball Dada sound poem (for a *Believe It or Not* segment) as a symptom of her own literalism. She finds the meaning (it is nonsense) in a literal interpretation of the poem ("it doesn't make any sense"). This literalism appears throughout contemporary culture, not just in the "Voices and Visions" program, and finds itself entangled in narcissistic fantasies where one goes beyond taking responsibility for one's actions to take a paranoid responsibility for self-invention as in Osmond playing her own mother in the "Osmond Story," in which no meaning escapes the desire of an ego (giving birth to itself). The metaphoric or analogistic sensibility allows for a leakage. In psychoanalytic and surrealist terms, that which exceeds the ego, the unconscious or the Symbolic realm, appears in everyday discourse as a startling association, an odd unintended pun, and in the logic of a joke. While self-invention, along the lines of Osmond's role playing her own mother, depends on effacing any (analogistic) leakage, one could see it also as a model for a theory joke on a School's legacy. Legacy suggests that the myth of self-invention and pulling yourself up by your own bootstraps always depends on someone else's legs to hold you up as in Jacques Lacan's image of the metaphorically suggestive mirror stage. We see ourselves as complete and standing up on our own only as a parent figures hold us up: self-reflection and the formation of the ego depend on a projection, a fantasy, of a moment in the future when one walks without strings attached. Collaboration and group identity depend on recognizing strings of associations; in Ulmer's case, using the stories about Walter Ulmer's stone mill to examine Walter Benjamin's theory of historical progress, and to use that string to re-open Hamlet's mythic connections to the Norse Water Mill that drains through a sinkhole near Ulmer's home. One could dismiss these associative strings as absurd residues of an absolutely particular reading, a surrealist joke that never rises to the truths of literal attribution, legacy, and empirical fact, or a legacy that seems to willfully resist, in its ever spreading webs of associations, progress toward, for example, efficient use of media technology for assessed learning. The Florida School simply recognizes that its legacy, its meanings and methods, depends on ana-logic and a responsibility to those overdetermined associative strings.

Ulmer's video begins and ends with Laurie Anderson's music video, broadcast on the PBS program "Alive, From Off Center," in which she sings the words to Walter Benjamin's (another Walter) "Thesis on History." The poetic thesis describes how an angel wants to "go back and fix things, but there is a storm blowing from paradise pushing the angel backward into the future and that storm is called progress" (257). It is a thesis on the tension between responsibility to a historical legacy and the destructive forces marching on into the future in the name of progress. Layers of meaning, trauma, monumentality, and the puzzling question of what to do with great literature and literary analogies (sinkholes, legacies, etcetera) all circulate in that ecology. There is a sinking feeling pondering how to sift the rubble of the past and build on a legacy.

Although all the commentaries on the Florida School, and the work of its affiliates, discuss the ways that the poststructuralist legacy has left its mark on their work, no one has as of yet mentioned a more personal legacy especially for Ulmer's work: Leslie Fiedler. Fiedler, recognized as a leader and innovator of the literary and cultural essay form, had long ago used personal analogies about his life as a Montanan to examine literary and cultural issues: "one becomes a Montanan in strange ways,"(331). His essays, widely regarded as the epitome of insightful and lively literary analysis, debunk the myths of innocence in American literature and culture. His most famous essay, "Come Back to the Raft Ag'n, Huck Honey," (*Partisan Review,* 1948; written when he was 31), did not claim that Mark Twain had written this line or that Tom and Huck were even flirting with gay sexual encounters. Rather, Fiedler showed how the myth of 19th century American innocence made the suggestion of a sexual encounter particularly unpalatable and scandalous. His somewhat parodical posturing also took aim at the stuffy sanctimoniousness of mainstream literary and cultural criticism. Likewise, his three controversial essays on Montana attacked the myth of white Montanans as the protectors of a naïve American innocence. He worried that the "Montana face," blank and friendly, actually expressed xenophobia, and that his own "dark, nervous, over expressive" "New York face" (euphemism for Jewish) was distrusted by Montanans who demanded a more grounded, literal interpretation of the world, and expressed this in their faces. Fiedler later wondered (after many loud complaints from Montanan's about his attack) if he should have called it the "Gary Cooper Face," as Ulmer (unwittingly?) alludes to in his use of the *Beau Geste* film (and Gary Cooper as that movie's star) as an analogy to unpack his own legacy of Montanan's knightly honor and smug simpleness. Montana was for Fielder, instead, "a by-product of European letters, and invention of the Romantic movement in literature" with a past "artificially contrived for commercial purposes" as a tourist's Frontier (131). Ulmer inherits Fiedler's deMon(tana)s and haunting devils. Ulmer does not express an innocent nostalgia for a Montana of his rock-pile youth or the literal demands of his father's generation to do the honorable thing and get a real job, but Fiedler's demythologized Montana. For example, Ulmer spoofs, and is spoofed by, a "community pageant" that presents in "dramatic form" the perverse identification with the Indians' predicament (Fiedler 138–139). Ulmer, who writes about finding his way to Jacques Derrida through his research on Rousseau, knows that in the mythic-Montana the "corpse of Rousseau is still twitching"(Fiedler 139). The other Montana, the *artificial myth* where the Noble Savage is a lie and Huck Finn went to die, came from the East. It came not from Gary Cooper's face, but from Fiedler, who died in 2003 at the age of 85, and was "the last—or rather the first—of the wild-man literary critics . . . the original chest-thumping extrovert of American criticism, and no one ever did it better"(Tanenhaus, n.p.). Fiedler, credited by the OED with the first instance of someone applying the term "postmodernist" to literature, celebrated the demise of modernism. In that sense, he is closely aligned with the Florida School, and, in fact, Fiedler visited Florida in the 1980s as part of a lecture series organized (as I recall) by Ulmer that also included Harold Bloom, Hayden White, and (later) Jacques Derrida. Fiedler wallowed in hyperbole and his most famous pronouncement that the classic white male American writers return "in a compulsive way to a limited world of experience, usually associated with childhood, writing the same book over and over again until he lapses into silence or self-parody"(Tanenhaus n.p.). At around the same time in the 1980s, Ulmer gave one of his best public lectures, in which he talked about innovative forms of writing essays about architectural theory and legacies. During the entire talk he held a concrete block on his shoulder. He talked about working at his father Walter's gravel and cement mill and about key issues in architecture. The block, a central image in most modern and contemporary buildings, sat there weighing on his shoulder. Finally, at the end of the talk, he talked about what to do with a legacy and he put the old block down.

Fiedlerian deMon(tana)s of paranoid hostility toward otherness and outsiders migrated on the highways throughout the United States since the 1950s as transience became a generalizeable condition. In fact, Ulmer's sinkhole is called the "devil's millhopper." That wandering created the context for another aspect of the Florida School. In the context of central Florida, Aileen Wuornos's story about her life and execution as a serial killer suggests that the tragedy—the particularly central Florida tragedy—appears when family and community connections break down. When one lives in a transient place, characterized by shifting ground, truckers and travelers, grifters and drifters, orchid thieves and hanging chads, and the newly arrived (and soon to depart) resident aliens, then tragic consequences find opportunities. Oddly, the traditional notion of tragedy, based on ancient Greek drama, and a cornerstone of the Western philosophical tradition, suggested that the strangle hold of tradition and family ties led to tragic results. The code of tribal blood vengeance, the revenge of the son for wrongs done to the father, has led so many tragic heroes to their demise. Hamlet is a particularly apt example. He is a serial killer caught-up in seeking vengeance for his haunting family ties. Wuornos is the Florida Hamlet.

In this version, Florida tragedy becomes a marker, an analogy, for a shift in philosophical traditions away from the cathartic model of Greek tragedy. The Florida or floral philosophical tradition depends on the Greeks recruited to live here by the British (because the Brits thought Florida was the new Greece). And, names like New Smyrna Beach or the sponge divers of Tarpon Springs, constantly remind visitors of that link. Instead of catharsis, closure, and conclusion, the floral tradition produces enervation, enigmas, and exceptions. It is a theory more suited to understanding the Florida hamlet, the notion of community and an electronic village, and the tragic consequences of its dissolution. The Florida philosophy uses the phrase, "it takes a village," a hamlet, a *sociopoetic* network, to appreciate a new terrain for cognition, thought, and what Ulmer calls "mentality" in general.

In his video, *Mr. Mentality,* Ulmer once again produced a work of video conceptual art that crossed over becoming theory; that is, it demonstrated how the false opposition (or at least distinction) between art, as conceived as an academic discipline, and theory prevents theory from incorporating vanguard problem-solving strategies and art from experimenting with conceptual issues. Like the Paper Tiger TV video, *Mr. Mentality* borrowed a popular culture format, in this case a corny teaching video in which kids visit the teacher who explains some issue. Ulmer plays the role of Mr. Mentality and explains theoretical issues to two young boys. The three sit down and talk over the problem of why people have pets, and Ulmer explains that it has to do with monumentality that pets dying "teaches you about how to mourn: how to deal with the loss of something you love and identify with." On a more general level, a nation has to learn this same lesson: how to deal with the loss of one generation after another. That is, we use monumentality as part of national identity to remember that although the "founding fathers are long dead," we still have national identity. Ulmer explains that he's been working on a monument that "recognizes the contribution our pets make to our American national identity." We need a surplus of available animals to allow for everyone to have a pet and to practice mourning. In a version of a Bataillian analysis (with a mix of Derrida's work on archive fever and memorialization), Ulmer explains patiently that the left over has to be wasted (1 pet is euthanized every 1.5 seconds or 8 million a year). The pets make a sacrifice for national identity, and wasting the pets is the price we have to pay for the practice of having a pet: "It shows we are sincere." At one point, as he explains monumentality, the visual track shows an old movie scene of a human sacrifice where the shamanistic priest rips out a young woman's heart. We still make human sacrifices and recognize those in memorials to soldiers killed in war. A reluctance to make sacrifices could either mean a contradiction in our values (sympathy and love for available pets versus the need to avoid having animals overrun cities and towns) or it might mean we do not know ourselves as a nation. "We don't realize that our existence depends on an enormous amount of waste." Loss is complicated as part of a circuit of waste to sacrifice to mourning to identity formation, and that loss cycle depends on the sincere effort to carry on a legacy. Reluctance to accept any legacy—to give birth to yourself as an original thinker—ignores, but does not eliminate, that sinking feeling: progress pushes the angel backward into a future without past, without mourning, without pause.

In the Introduction to *Sound Tracks: A Musical ABC (Volumes 1–3),* Michael Jarrett discusses a method of using personal analogies, of a self-revelation used for narrative, expository, and poetic effects. He quotes Ray: "An author producing a text always finds himself, like someone playing a video game, provided with three knobs, labeled narrative, expository, poetic. At any point during the text's creation, he can adjust the balance (as one would adjust a television's colors), thereby increasing (or reducing) the level of any of the three"(5; quoting Ray, 1995, 200). The legacy of the Florida School has to with this mode of the essay that telescopes the personal anecdote through narrative, exposition, and poetic shifts. Jarrett's Florida School approach, like Ray's in the essay Jarrett cites, constructs innovative essays that both describe and use music and popular musical culture. You can see this musical essay approach in many of the Florida School works; the other approach involves the joke: jokes and music demonstrate how entertainment becomes the popularizing institutional setting for pedagogy.

Many have argued that those, like Plato and Aristotle, who inherit a legacy and follow, often get it wrong, distorted, reversed, or, for example, convert radically defiant pedagogy into the arms and legs of complacent power. Aristotle, Alexander's tutor and mentor, became a parody of Socrates who taught in the streets and died for corrupting young minds. The birth of children is the death of parents in a Hegelian formation. Likewise, the Florida School's legacy continues only in its disciples' (mis)recognitions (to borrow the psychoanalytic term) and projective understandings. While you cannot take your legacy with you, others will read what is left behind as best they can from where they stand—mispronunciations, puns, misunderstandings, and all. The personal analogies function in a web of comparisons and *differances.* As Barbara Stafford explains in her brilliant *Visual Analogies,* explicitly building on Ulmer's *heuretic* strategies, analogistic reasoning functions as a method of scholarship, a process, something that calls one to think and does not limit thinking with an end product. *Allegoresis,* rather than allegory, to borrow a comparison from Maureen Quilligan, does not ornament for a popular consumption an algorithmic solution, nor does it find a singular ground of meaning, but uses analogies, including those drawn from personal, popular, and expert discourses as method rather than mere expression. Making was always an end to the process, but Ulmer's epistemology of doing situates making, theory as hobby, as a pedagogical relay in which students learn a method of scholarship—the method of the humanities—by trying it on and running with it. It is not the study of creative geniuses, but an artificial or prosthetic version of the processes involved. Once the issue shifts from using analogies to consider literature, film, or culture in general to ana-logistic thinking, then the question concerning infrastructure emerges. The *sociopoetic* work of networked art suggests that one might organize a productive system that uses the consideration of the infrastructural, School formation, for example, as a poetic analogy. The changes to scholarship, in turn, function as analogies for new ways of thinking. If this is the legacy of the Florida School, from media studies and poststructuralism to *sociopoetic infrastructuralism,* then the problem of legacy returns to find its resolutions in analogy: not in the abstract view but in the absolutely particular. What follows, then, is a reading of this legacy using the mystory. One could then re-read the explanatory essay above as emerging from the ana-logic experiment that follows here.

Recently, my old and ailing father, part of Leslie Fiedler's generation, told me that he was worried about his death, not scared of dying, but worried that no one would carry on his legacy; that his life would be for naught, insignificant. He showed me a group of boxes filled with papers, notes, outlines, and photocopies. He told me that he wanted me to write that book (on Jewish jokes in the context of a psychological theory of humor and healing). He asked me to finish what he had only started. "All you need to do," he pleaded, "is write the book" using the notes and outlines. I hemmed and hawed, and remained uncommitted to making any promises. This was a kind of pun on the traditional Freudian Oedipal conflicts (the tradition describes the allegory of damaging the child's foot to keep them at bay and to not interfere with the father's desire; only creating resentment of the constraints as the child becomes conscious of the family drama). To use these stories differently, as an allegoresis instead of traditional psychoanalysis, scholars use personal stories as the tropes for new theories. This sometimes twists the stories and imbues them with the air of parody as they become grist for the mill rather than significant in and of themselves.

The boxes are still in his house. My wife gently protested that I was not solicitous enough, and should have humored his wishes; the promise to carry on the legacy would be enough. Anyone given that task, the task of an apprentice learning the family trade—and in our job specific world, it is a task too few experience—anxiously worries not just about the umbilical ties of influence, as in Harold Bloom's Romantic conception, but more intensely about not living up to the demand. For, legacy always has the stench of parody floating around even the most conscientious inheritors. If history repeats itself: the first time as tragedy, the second as farce, then legacy never seems to find its intended destination. My father later gave my son a group of videotapes and books on the same topic, and instructed me to put all of them in a bookshelf across from his bed, "So that every morning, he would wake up and see those books and videos." Of course, the Jewish joke usually contains guilt, food, therapy, and wordplay, and sometimes the fool's quest. Read through Fiedler and mystory, the Florida School's legacy looks more and more like a Jewish joke—not just any joke, but a surreal mix of Talmudic word play and somewhat forced Borscht-belt type of joke. Just as some might complain that Ulmer's experiments often conclude with a clever, cute, pun filled, and merely joking mystories, my stories and word-play may fall on deaf ears mistaking the artificiality of the unfunny joke on personal tragedies about family legacies as merely a literal story. Certainly, this is the only volume that would even consider, perhaps begrudgingly, to accept this type of *mystoriological* experimentation, and to allow (as Ulmer's works do) for the reader to connect the *scenes of discovery,* below, to the arguments and justifications, above, in this essay.

My father-in-law, whose avocation is growing heirloom apple trees and studying the history of apple growing and cider making (he also has an unfinished manuscript), also talks of his historical scholarship and actual orchard as his legacy to my children (skipping a generation). Through his efforts (collecting specimens all over the country, grafting, cultivating, and protecting the trees until they bear fruit), he has compiled the most complete group of Pennsylvania apple trees (hundreds of types). He is particularly proud of one accomplishment. He recently donated a group of pear trees he grafted from the only remaining stock of John Bartram's pear trees (he found the specimen in Maryland) to Bartram Gardens (a park celebrating Bartram's naturalist journeys). Of course, Bartram was the naturalist who traveled from his gardens adjacent to Philadelphia (where I lived and where generations of my in-law's family lived) to Florida (where I now live) and stood at the very spot where Ulmer made his video about reading on TV. Ulmer explains that Coleridge had based his notion of Edenic paradise, Xanadu, on Bartram's descriptions of north central Florida (coincidentally, I gave my son the middle name Eden to honor his birth on a farm near Bartram Gardens). Hamlet, Prince Hal, Lear, Macbeth, and many others find themselves caught in the problem of legacy; they want to escape their legacies, or to pass it on to children, so that they may idle away their hours in an Edenic (childlike) paradise. But, to their dismay, and the delight of the audience, they find themselves haunted to death by the problem expressed in the old saying, the apple always falls close to the tree. These are the mundane personal analogies and entertaining mythic versions, played out everyday in countless family and scholarly dramas, that also illuminate the profound legacies that mark not just School formations, like psychoanalysis following after Freud, but whole epochs of thought, from Aristotle building on Plato, who before had built on (a fictionalized) Socrates.

The thinking about how to handle legacy reminded me of an earlier scene in my life: my primal scene of legacy. When I was a bit younger than my son is now and a bit older than my daughter is now, my grandfather died. His name was Selig pronounced like the later famous character from Woody Allen's film *Zelig* (1983). I don't remember him ever talking; he would sit outside his apartment and watch life go by. Sometimes I sat with him. We went to his home, a two-room first floor apartment, in a run-down neighborhood of Brooklyn, New York. An uncle and his family lived upstairs, and when my father was a child, he lived there too (or in a similarly dilapidated apartment in Brooklyn) with at least some of his many siblings (some of the older ones had probably moved out already). He was born in Williamsburg and lived in East New York (Brooklyn) through high school. In this apartment, the first room was the kitchen. The second room was the bedroom with one bed.

After the funeral, the entire family was in the apartment sitting *Shiva* (Yiddish for a type of mourning ritual in which the participants sit on unevenly balanced three legged low stools so that they cannot sit comfortably). All the mirrors are covered; although I don't remember any mirrors in the apartment. Mourners sit for seven days, and visitors come by to sit with them all the while talking about the deceased and praying and mourning. Earlier, at the funeral, all the men had their ties cut in half as part of the mourning ritual, and they still had their half ties on to remind them of their loss. Everyone was sitting in the cramped and dark apartment; my grandmother (although I remember calling her Gran(d)ma; she was to all of my many cousins, I imagine, *Bubbie*—Yiddish for grandmother) was cooking a big pot of something (although I may be conflating other memories since cooking, food, and guilt played a large role in my extended family). My immediate family was "modern," educated, secular, more Philip Roth than Sholem Aleichem. We lived upstate; some of my uncles had never left the boroughs. The rest of the extended clan always worried that my family did not feed me, and would demand that I "eat, eat" whenever I appeared. One uncle owned a delicatessen, and I remember eating some delicious stuffed cabbages with a *mish mash* (Yiddish for combination, mess, hodgepodge, collage) of ingredients inside during another visit a few years later at my grandmother's funeral. I wandered around the apartment like the boy in a Mordecai Richler story, "The Street," who confronts the guilt and contradictions of mourning. The boy gets his room back after his grandmother dies, and he comes to appreciate the guilt that haunts the living as he wanders around the apartment while the family sits *Shiva*.

While my relatives were mourning and talking, I looked in a small closet and found something that disturbed me. The adjective to describe what I felt was *fahrblunget* (Yiddish for mixed up, bemused, confused) that later became a kind of mana-word for my earliest research with the Florida School on Moses Maimonides's *The Guide Of The Perplexed* (yes, "of the perplexed," not "for the perplexed"). I came back into the bedroom where everyone was sitting Shiva and talking. I tugged on my dad's sleeve and told him "Grandpa left something behind." Everyone stopped talking and looked over at me. Someone said, *oy vey* (Yiddish expression for dismay, pain, grief, but also, with *vey* pronounced by Sephardic Jews as *way,* poetically connected to *wah,* the interjection on joyous occasions, leading to much wordplay in the Talmud to suggest the porous connection between woe and joyous tears). So *oy vey* marks those domestic troubles like "*Oy vey,* my kid only eats candy," or "*Oy vey,* you'll have your hands full with that one," those certain types of parental and familial torments that we learn to prefer over the alternatives. My father asked me what grandpa had left behind. "Grandpa left his leg behind," I announced, and I wondered to everyone's stunned silence, how we would get it back to him. Someone gently told me that it was my grandfather's *false* leg and since he was dead, he did not need it anymore, and we should leave it in the closet. I did not know he had a false leg until that moment, and worried, in spite of the reassurances, that we should have done more to get him his leg back. It was a residue from the Devil's Millhopper kicked back out as a legacy just in time to pull out the stopper. Or, in Joycean terms Wah, wah, water, "riverrun, past Eve and Adam's, from swerve of shore to bend of bay, brings us by a commodius vicus of recirculation"(Joyce 1). It is, in other words, best described poetically by, for example, William Carlos Williams (uncatalogued page fragment, c. 1930–1931; cf. Dworkin 83 n. 14):

> Come O orthopedic Muse,
> Analyze the funny feet
> That all the modern poets use.
> Put my senses all to rout
> And make my brain a muddy mess
> So I may trace and write about
> The gutter of my conscience.

This fragment has guided my analysis here on the Florida School's legacy, and suggests a new model of inspiration, a new Muse, and a new scholarship of footnotes.

Works Cited

Benjamin, Walter. *Illuminations: Essays and Reflections*. New York: Harcourt Brace Jovanovich, Inc, 1968.

Barthes, Roland. *Camera Lucida*. New York: Hill & Wang, 1980.

Dworkin, Craig. " 'Seeing Words Machinewise': Technology and Visual Prosody," in *Sagetrieb: Poetry and Poetics After Modernism,* 18.1 (Spring 1999).

Fiedler, Leslie. "Montana: P.S.," in *The Collected Essays of Leslie Fiedler,* vol. II. New York: Stein and Day, 1971, 331–36.

—. "Montana: P.S.S.," in *The Collected Essays of Leslie Fiedler,* Volume II. New York: Stein and Day, 1971, 337–42.

—. "Montana; or The End of Jean-Jacques Rousseau," in *The Collected Essays of Leslie Fiedler,* vol. I. New York: Stein and Day, 1971, 131–41.

—. "On Remembering Freshman Comp," in *The Collected Essays of Leslie Fiedler,* Volume II. New York: Stein and Day, 1971, 355–60.

—. "The Death of Avant-Garde Literature," in *The Collected Essays of Leslie Fiedler,* Volume II. New York: Stein and Day, 1971, 454–60.

Jarrett, Michael. *Sound Tracks: A Musical ABC (Volumes 1–3).* Philadelphia: Temple UP, 1998.

Ray, Robert B. *The Avant-Garde finds Andy Hardy.* Cambridge, MA: Harvard UP, 1995.

Ray, Robert. *How A Film Theory Got Lost and Other Mysteries of Cultural Studies.* Bloomington: Indiana UP, 2001.

Richler, Mordecai. *The Street.* Washington: The New Republic Book Co., 1975, c1969.

Saper, Craig. "A Nervous Theory: The Troubling Gaze of Psychoanalysis in Media Studies" *diacritics* (Summer 1992): 33–52.

—. *Artificial Mythologies: A Guide to Cultural Invention* U of Minnesota P, 1997.

—. "Electronic Media Studies," *SubStance* (December 1992): 114-134.

—. "Fluxacademy: From Intermedia to Interactive Education," *Visible Language,* 26.1/2 (Winter/Spring 1992): 79–96.

—. "Instant Theory: Making Thinking Popular," *Visible Language* 22.4 (Spring 1989): 371–98.

—. "Learning From Being Lost," *Journal of Urban and Cultural Studies* 1.2: no. (Fall 1990): 67–86.

—. *Networked Art.* U of Minnesota P, 2001.

Stafford, Barbara Maria. *Visual Analogy: Consciousness as the Art of Connecting.* Cambridge, MA: MIT Press, 1999.

Tanenhaus, Sam. "Fear and Loathing: How Leslie Fiedler Turned American Criticism on Its Head." *Slate* (Tuesday, Feb. 4, 2003, at 2:26 PM PT/ http://slate.msn.com/id/2078106).

Ulmer, Gregory. *Greg Ulmer Reads Reading on Television.* (video) Paper Tiger TV.

—. *Mr. Mentality.* (video)

—. *Internet Invention: From Literacy to Electracy.* New York: Longman, 2003.

—. "The Making of "Derrida at the Little Bighorn" (An Interview), in *Strategies for Theory: From Marx to Madonna.* Ed., Rutsky, R.L. & MacDonald, Bradley J. Albany: SUNY Press, 2003, 145–68.

—. *Heuretics: The Logic of Invention.* Johns Hopkins UP, 1994.

Part 2

Theory: Inventing New Modes of Scholarly Discourse

4 Hypericonomy, Negatively Defined

Marcel O'Gorman

Indeed, if after the death of God (Nietzsche), the end of grand Narratives of Enlightenment (Lyotard), and the arrival of the Web (Tim Berners-Lee), the world appears to us as an endless and unstructured collection of images, texts, and other data records, it is only appropriate that we would want to develop a poetics, aesthetics, and ethics of this database.

—Lev Manovich, *The Language of New Media*

Those who can, think up feminism or structuralism; those who can't, apply such insights to Moby-Dick or The Cat in the Hat.

—Terry Eagleton, *After Theory*

Hypericonomy Is Not Collage

I have been taking an inventory of the tools necessary for the invention of a new mode of academic discourse, one that is suitable to a culture in which identity formation takes place in an environment of image bombardment and digital communications. Recently, I added yet one more tool to this kit in order to round things off. It is a tool that I happened upon most recently in my own garage, and it appears at a nodal point through which scholarly discourse, avant-garde art, popular culture, and my own autobiography all pass. The tool in question is the vise: "a holding device attached to a workbench; has two jaws to hold workpiece firmly in place" (hyperdictionary.com). With the vise—a solid, tangible object—my inventory of theoretical tools takes a very literal and materialistic, though perhaps nonsensical, turn. But I require the vise temporarily to hold all the pieces of a makeshift appliance in place while the new form of discourse takes shape. I have dubbed this theoretical appliance *hypericonomy,*[1] a methodical device that combines the interdisciplinary, networked thinking of Michel Foucault with the picture theory of W. J. T. Mitchell, including his concept of the "hypericon," an image that that "encapsulates an entire episteme, a theory of knowledge" (49). The result is an approach to scholarly praxis, and ultimately an approach to (academic) institutional reform, centered on the management, distribution and arrangement of hypericons over space and time. I'm just not sure what this method "looks like," or how it works, exactly.

With this in mind, it's more productive, I would suggest—or rather, more generative—to discuss what hypericonomy "isn't," rather than discussing exactly what "it is." I will proceed then, in the manner of a tinkerer, a *bricoleur,* cobbling (theoretical) objects together, keeping some of the parts and discarding the rest, based on an informed intuition of the mode of discourse I am trying to invent.

Hypericonomy, like most inventions, originates anecdotally, in this case with a scene from a film that cut into me affectively, psychically, cognitively. The film in question is Martin Scorsese's *Casino.* I viewed it for the first time in 1996, the same year that the Art Gallery of Windsor (my home town in Ontario) leased out its entire building to make room for a Vegas-style casino. The art, everyone supposed, would get more attention in the local shopping mall, and indeed it did. In any case, the hypericonic media scene from *Casino* that I have in mind is the one involving a vise and the head of a gangster named Tony Dogs.[2]

INT. SLOT-MACHINE SHOP, LAS VEGAS—NIGHT

MARINO and BLUE are dragging TONY DOGS, who is beaten to a pulp, across the floor towards a workshop table. NICKY follows them.

NICKY: (Voiceover) To be truthful with you, I had to admire this fuckin' guy. He was one of the toughest Irishmen I ever met. . . . In the end, I had to put his fuckin' head in a vise.

NICKY: Dogs. Dogs, can your hear me, Dogs?

(DOGS gasps and mumbles.) Listen to me, Anthony. I got your head in a fuckin' vise. I'm gonna squash your fuckin' head like a grapefruit if you don't give me a name. Don't make me have to do this, please. Come on. Don't make me be a bad guy. Come on.

TONY DOGS: (With what strength he has left) Fuck you!

NICKY: (To MARINO and BLUE) This motherfucker, do you believe this? Two fuckin' days and nights!

(To DOGS.) Fuck me?

(NICKY begins to tighten the vise.) Fuck me, you motherfucker? (Turning the vise.) Fuck my mother? That's what you fuckin' tell me?

(NICKY angrily keeps spinning the vise handle until suddenly one of DOGS's eyes bulges out of the socket.) Huh? You motherfucker, you, huh?

(MARINO and BLUE are horrified by the sight. Everybody freezes.) Oh, God! Give me the fuckin' name!

TONY DOGS: Ch-Charlie M!

NICKY: Charlie M?

TONY DOGS: (Blood streaming out of his mouth) Charlie M.

NICKY: (Screaming) Charlie M? You make me pop your fuckin' eye out of your head to protect that piece of shit? Charlie M? You dumb motherfucker!

TONY DOGS: (Pleading) Kill me, you fuck, kill me.

NICKY: Kill you, (unwinds the crank) you motherfucker you!

(To MARINO.) Frankie, do him a fuckin' favor.

ACE: (Voice-over) The word got around that finally . . .

(MARINO places a knife against DOGS's neck.) . . . there was a real gangster in town. Nicky was the new boss of Las Vegas.[3]

Tony Dogs, the tough Irishman who, according to Micky, was "just beggin' to be made an example of," might be looked upon as the iconic apotheosis of daily life in our late-capital culture of information overload. Unlike the casualties in typical information-age films (*Videodrome, Strange Days, Vanilla Sky, Feardotcom,* etc.), Dogs does not meet his demise at the hands of an electrical apparatus; he is the victim of an ideological apparatus, a primitively-armed war machine that draws its power from the withholding, extraction, and dissemination of information.[4] Seen this way, the vise scene might also represent a certain tendency of print culture toward closure, specificity, specialization, even rigor, the horrific epitome of the human mind and body placed under the pressure of a remorseless informational/disciplinary apparatus.

But Dogs is only a fictional character; it is the viewer of this film who is the real victim here. The viewer's mental and emotional capacities are being impressed upon by real machine: the movie camera and the screen. It is the viewer who is being zoomed in on, the viewer whose eyes pop out; that is, if she can stand to watch. This mirror scene of a squirming viewer witnessing a torture session is iconic as well, representing a different sort of confrontation between the human head and an informational apparatus. This second scene might be looked upon as the apotheosis and archetype of a digital culture, a culture of hypervisualization.

Of course, scenes of crushed, imploding or exploding heads are not rare in American popular culture, as may be witnessed in any number of essays which fall under the rubric of cultural studies and are dedicated to uncovering the mass-media symptoms of postmodernity or post-humanity. We see cyborgic, hypervisual heads everywhere, from video games to magazine ads, and their profusion is such that one could, from a single issue of *WIRED Magazine,* easily assemble and elaborate collage of such images suitable for deconstruction in the name of cultural criticism. This might be, I suppose, an appropriate strategy for a cultural critic living in an age of image-bombardment. I myself have created a series of collages, drawing on this precise strategy. The image of the Saturn Girl, which was used to launch Sega's ill-fated Saturn video game console, was the initial impetus for this activity of bricolage.

Is this sort of collage-work the type of image-rich, critical discourse that I am talking about when I use the term hypericonomy? Collecting digital heads and pasting them into a collage may result in a certain, easily digestible theory about what has come to be called "cyberculture"; but this activity of fragmentation and pictorialization may be

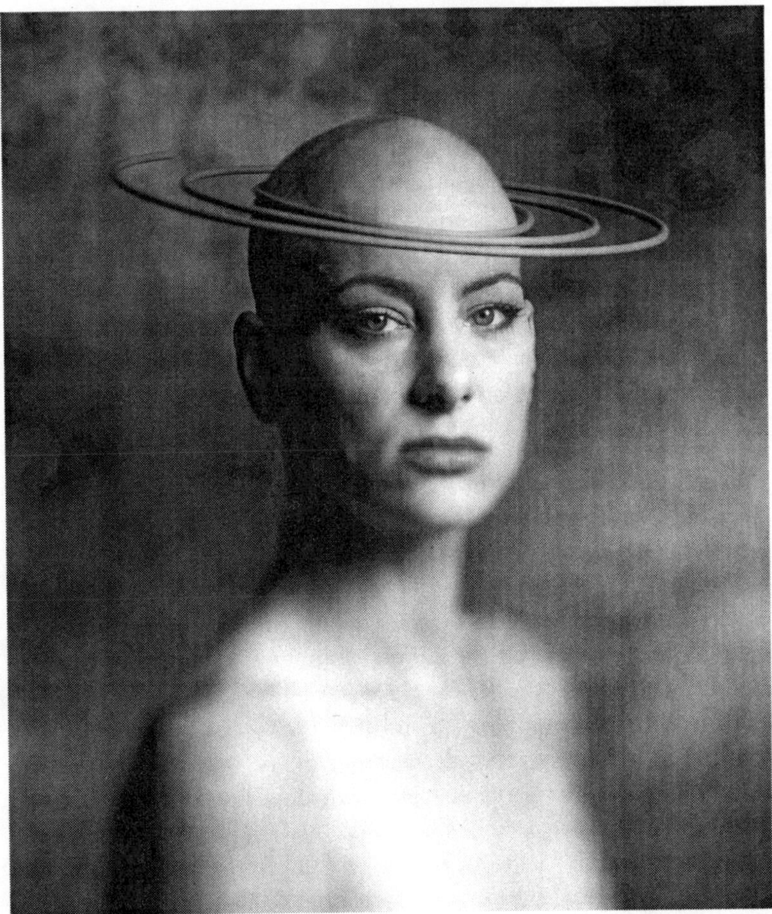

"Saturn Girl," courtesy of Eric Tucker.

viewed as symptomatic of the very consumer oriented ideology that produced the original images.[5] Furthermore, commenting on these images as symptoms of a posthuman, visual culture is merely an act of cataloguing, a simple process of archiving and hermeneutic interpretation, which has been typical of scholarly work ever since cultural theorists stopped inventing new methods of research, and started mechanically applying pre-packaged theories to texts of all shapes and sizes.

In *The Avant Garde Finds Andy Hardy,* Robert Ray describes how film studies has "constructed an enormously powerful theoretical machine for exposing the ideological abuse hidden by the apparently natural stories and images of popular culture. That machine, however, now runs on automatic pilot, producing predictable essays and books on individual cases" (7). This is the very situation that, more recently, prompted Terry Eagleton to proclaim an end to the age of "high theory." In Eagleton's terms,

> the older generation [of critical theorists] proved a hard act to follow. No doubt the new century will in time give birth to its own clutch of gurus. For the moment, however, we are still trading on the past—and this is a world which has changed dramatically since Foucault and Lacan first settled to their typewriters What kind of fresh thinking does the new era demand? (2)

In response to this, and following Greg Ulmer, I would suggest that "the new era" demands not the reductive, hermeneutical, vise-like thinking that characterizes the majority of today's critical work, but rather the *conductive thinking* (a concept I will outline in greater detail below) which is more appropriate to an age of digital media. As Lev Manovich suggests in *The Language of New Media,* "the cultural technologies of an industrial society—cinema and fashion—asked us to identify with someone else's bodily image. Interactive media ask us to identify with someone else's mental structure. . . . The computer user is asked to follow the mental trajectory of the new media designer" (61). What I would suggest then is that the inventors of a new scholarly poetics should learn to more consciously materialize their own mental trajectories, and this requires a more profound engagement with interdisciplinarity, visual culture, and even cognitive science.

While Marshall McLuhan and Katherine Hayles worked with designers in completing, respectively, *The Medium is the Massage* and *Writing Machines,* hypericonomy asks scholars to think and work as designers themselves (albeit 'amateur' designers), and to work with still images and video in both the initial generation and final material instantiation of a research project. Simple collage work, such as that mentioned above, can therefore NOT be defined as a hypericonomy for the following reasons:

1. First of all, the images in my *WIRED Magazine* collages were not consciously chosen as echoes of events in the researcher's (my) own life. In order for an image to function as part of the new discourse, it must be subjectively motivated.[6] The scene from *Casino,* for example, is very much a replay of my own personal history, echoing an incident (fortunately less tragic)

in which my brother, in the course of an argument, attempted to place my head in a vise. The images from the magazine, however, hold no such claim over my personal cosmology. We could argue that I have chosen them out of some unconscious drive of which I am not aware. But what's important is that none of the pictures used in my collages provoked me to engage with them immediately on a conscious, affective level, as did the image of Tony Dogs with his head in the vise.

2. Images pasted together from a single issue of a magazine represent a *synchronic* view of a given cultural phenomenon. In fact, they couldn't be much more synchronic. Hypericonomy, on the other hand, strives for diachrony. The point of the new discourse is to trace the presence of a discursive circuit as it appears at various nodal points over time.

3. Although the pictures in my collages all repeat a single theme—the confrontation of the head with an informational apparatus—they are not iconologically consistent. Certainly, they represent a series of heads undergoing transformation by a variety of technological implements (e.g.: VR glasses, microchip implants, fluorescent eyes), but there is no specific visual leitmotif beyond the technologization of the head. Hypericonomy requires the consistent treatment of a very specific scene or pictorial element that is discernible in various contexts. The simpler the element, the more effective the hypericon. For example, in *E-Crit,* I draw on the vise as a visual link to connect the following nodal points in the history of print: the *Casino* scene above; Peter Ramus' binarizing, logical brackets; the printing press; the upright hands of a nurse compressing the head of a child in a William Blake poem; Stephen Gibb's painting titled "No Parole," which appears at the end of this essay.[7] .

The three elements listed above might be classified under the following categories: subjectivation, diachrony, and (iconic) repetition. These are the constituent elements of a hypericonomy, which should not be confused with the traditional study of visual culture. Unlike typical cultural studies research, hypericonomy is a subjectively motivated composition process for crossing disciplinary and discursive boundaries. A hypericonomist might, for example, focus on the pouting face of the adolescent, saturnine girl [8] pictured above. The Saturn

Girl, cut and pasted from an advertisement for a now defunct video game system, might take the central role in a (imaginary) research project. This investigation would attempt to trace the various discursive lines of flight that travel through the node of the Saturn Girl, from Burton's *Anatomy of Melancholy* to current research in adolescent depression, drawing perhaps on images from the history of visual culture that correlate baldness, melancholia, and femininity (images from the holocaust, ads from the American Cancer Society, etc.).

The goal of such a project would not be to engage in a semiotic deconstruction of the Saturn ad campaign, but perhaps to remotivate the image in the invention of a new, post-Saturnine mode of academic discourse, one that is inspired more by humor than by academic melancholia. This would not result in a truly effective hypericonomy, however, unless the Saturn Girl was initially chosen out of the personal, affective motivation of the hypericonomist. Perhaps, for example, the researcher might recognize in the Saturn Girl a trace of himself, the melancholy scholar.

Of course, all of this is conjecture, a "thought experiment" (to borrow the words of John Guillory, whose work I will discuss below) in the service of re-imagining academic practices and disciplinary structures. Rather than provide a comprehensive set of instructions for how to practice this method, I will proceed by offering some theoretical directives, the utility of which will vary according to each individual reader, as he or she works toward the invention of a new mode of academic discourse. After all, my goal is not to prescribe a specific, perfectly replicable methodology, but to provide the reader with the equivalent of a software package with a number of menu items with which readers must tinker in order to achieve a satisfactory level of proficiency, though not necessarily expertise. There are no experts in hypericonomy, only (hopefully) what Terry Eagleton would call "well-informed dilettantes," an expression he uses to describe intellectuals, from Voltaire and Rousseau to Sartre, Sontag and Foucault, who paid no heed to a culture that fosters narrow specialization (81).

At a recent conference of the International Digital Media and Arts Association, several educators in new media expressed their frustration at the impossibility of teaching software applications to students. To put it simply, as soon as the course is over, a new version of the software comes out or hardware configurations change in ways that render the software obsolete. The only way of dealing with this, I proposed, is to teach students how to be digital dilettantes. That is, rather than instructing them in the full range of menu items in a software interface, show them some basics and let them discover the rest as they work toward the completion of a project. Their ability to independently learn 'enough to get by' in a given situation will in many ways determine their success as designers in an environment where they will always be contending with "new media"; that is, media that are constantly changing, always "new." Consider the following section then, a series of theoretical exemplars, as a selection of menu items from a complex software tool that may be put to use in the invention of a digital/pictorial mode of scholarly discourse.

Hypericonomy Is Not Picture Theory

The term *hypericon* was defined by W.J.T. Mitchell as "a piece of moveable cultural apparatus, one which may serve a marginal role as illustrative device or a central role as a kind of summary image . . . that encapsulates an entire episteme, a theory of knowledge" (*Picture Theory,* 49). The most concrete example of a hypericon offered by Mitchell is René Magritte's *La trahison des images,* as hypericonized by Michel Foucault in "Ceci n'est pas une pipe." Instances of the hypericon seem to abound in the history of philosophy: "Plato's cave, Aristotle's wax tablet, Locke's dark room, Wittgenstein's hieroglyphic are all examples of the 'hypericon'that, along with the popular trope of the 'mirror of nature,' provide our models for thinking about all sorts of images—mental, verbal, pictorial, and perceptual" (*Iconology* 6). It is important to note that these examples, including Magritte's painting, which Foucault transforms into a hypericon of "the crucial faultline in 'scopic regimes'"(12), are not only hypericons, but each one is a *metapicture* as well—a picture "that is used to show what a picture is" (35). In fact, I would argue that *all* hypericons are metapictures, in the sense that each one encapsulates a theory of seeing, a way of picturing things.[9] Mitchell himself reminds us that "as the words 'reflection,' 'speculation,' and 'theory,' indicate, there is more than a casual relation between visual representation and the practice called theorizing (*theoria* comes from the Greek word 'to see')" (82). To be a hypericonomist, one must also be a creator of metapictures, a creature of pictures about picturing, viewing the metapicture not as a "subgenre within the fine arts but a fundamental potentiality inherent in pictorial representation as such" (82).

This inevitably raises the following question: how does someone who has little or no training in the fine arts invent or discover a metapicture, let alone a hypericon? My answer would be that *anyone* engaged in critical or philosophical praxis can create a metapicture or hypericon. All Wittgenstein had to do was sketch the simple outline of an optical illusion known as "duck-rabbit" in his notebook, and he had created a hypericon that encapsulates his theories on the instability of signification (*Picture Theory* 50). The duck-rabbit is not a sophisticated image such as *Las Meninas,* which Foucault hypericonizes in *The Order of Things,* nor is it as complex as the Allegory of the Cave, yet it serves to enframe an entire episteme. Hypericons, then, can be found almost anywhere, even as "occasions of middle-brow leisure and amusement," in magazines, comics, and children's books. Mitchell himself transforms a cover of *Mad*—a magazine that targets adolescent boys—into a site "where power, desire, and knowledge converge in strategies of representation" (82). Of course, the duck-rabbit and the image from *Mad* were not hypericons or even metapictures until Wittgenstein and Mitchell, respectively, made them so. Anyone, then, can create metapictures or hypericons, as long as s/he is willing "to give theory a body and visible shape that it often wants to deny, to reveal theory as representation" (*Picture Theory* 418).

If a picture is to exist as a hypericon, then, it must be accompanied by a verbal discourse, a theory that is, at last, *given a body.* When this encounter of the visual and verbal is materialized in the same space, we have what Mitchell has dubbed quite simply as an *imagetext.* It appears then, that the metapicture, hypericon, and imagetext, are interdependent, each one playing a role in Mitchell's picture theory. And when all three are rolled together, this hybrid mode of discourse can be used to demonstrate "the inescapable heterogeneity of representation, to show that the body we give to theory is an assemblage of prostheses and artificial supplements, not a natural or organic form" (418). Hypericonomy simultaneously constructs and undermines a theoretical edifice. It is not shy about admitting its rootedness in subjectivity and identity formation. With this in mind, hypericonomy is a mode of picture theory, a form of meta-discourse that produces knowledge while calling into question the techniques of that production.

I should note, however, that Mitchell's "picture theory" is not hypericonomy. Although Mitchell's hypericon is the most essential cog in the methodical machine I am constructing here, I still require the elements of subjectivation, diachrony, and repetition to transform the theory of the hypericon into a method. If I were to ask 'How does the *Mad* image position the subject, W.J.T. Mitchell?,' or 'How and where is this *Mad* image, or the shapes that constitute it, repeated throughout the history of visual culture?,' or again, 'How does this picture define a given discursive circuit?,' then I would be thinking as a hypericonomist. In order for a hypericonomy to function, the "notoriously migratory" metapicture must be examined as a node in a network of discourses (*Picture Theory* 57).

Hypericonomy Is Not Iconology

Hypericonomy is not picture theory then; nor is it iconology, although it draws on the archaeological methods of this science. No essay that concerns the icon can escape the shadow of the master iconologist, Erwin Panofsky. Mitchell suggests that Panofsky's "magisterial range, his ability to move with authority from ancient to modern art, to borrow provocative and telling insights from philosophy, optics, theology, psychology, and philology, make him an inevitable model and starting point for any general account of what is now called 'visual culture'" (*Picture Theory,* 16). Indeed, Panofsky is an impressive and imposing figure in the history of cultural criticism. His complex interdisciplinary strategy may certainly be considered as a model for how to conduct research in our picture-saturated culture. Unfortunately, Panofsky's model of interdisciplinarity leaves no room for multivocality, or even for the individual subject for that matter. Panofsky's method of pursuing an image (e.g., Father Time, Blind Cupid) across time and space, bringing diverse fields of information into a single hermeneutical decipherment of that image is, in effect, the inverse of hypericonomy. Whereas Panofsky views the icon as the subject of inquiry, and the various specialized discourses of inquiry as the *tools* of his trade, a hypericonomist views the icon as the methodological tool, and the discourses as the subjects of inquiry—what's important in hypericonomy is not the history of the icon, but the way in which it gathers discourses at a nodal point, displaying their interrelatedness.

Panofsky fulfils the requirements of *diachrony* and *repetition* required in hypericonomy, but his method, as diversely informed as it is, is conducted as if it were an objective science, or in his terms, "an organic and indivisible process," (*Iconology* 17). Panofsky's iconology is, above all, a method of containment, a totalizing strategy that advances by refusing to accept the body of theory as "an assemblage of prostheses and artificial supplements." Hypericonomy, on the other hand, advances "not by totalizing but by relaying, connecting, converging and prolonging" (Deleuze, *Foucault* 30). Hypericonomy is a method of dispersion, and has no pretensions of being indivisible or universal.[10]

It is useful to note that the model of cultural studies as practised by Panofsky is nearly impossible to emulate. Panofsky is, without a doubt, a Renaissance man versed in a variety of specialized languages. But in spite of this specialization, Panofsky's work is also individual, unique, even as he claims for it a certain universality, a certain organicity. To put it bluntly, there are leaks in Panofsky's supposedly scientific method. Panofsky's notion of "synthetic intuition" for example, an essential tool in his "equipment for interpretation," demonstrates that iconology is not as much of an exact science as he would like it to be. Described as "familiarity with the *essential tendencies of the human mind* . . . conditioned by personal psychology and *'Weltanschauung,'*" synthetic intuition inserts the subject into the *objective* science of iconology (*Iconology* 15, my emphasis). Tip-toeing on the shadowy edge of rigorous method, Panofsky is willing to admit that *synthetic intuition* is a faculty that "may be better developed in a talented layman than in an erudite scholar" (15). But rather than admitting to, or even embracing, the presence of contingency, subjectivity, and dilettantism in his work, Panofsky warns that *synthetic intuition* can be "dangerous," and must therefore be "controlled by an insight into the manner in which, under varying historical conditions, the *general and essential tendencies of the human mind* were expressed by specific *themes* and *concepts*" (16, my emphasis). This, in turn, implies a knowledge of what Panofsky calls the "history of style." Synthetic intuition, then, is grudgingly admitted into the critical process, but only to be tempered by an objectifying conception of history.

This is where hypericonomy must depart altogether from Panofsky's version of iconology, for iconology refuses to allow the subject—even when faced by its inevitable presence—into the method, while hypericonomy relies entirely on the admission of the subject in(to) the research methodology. And if this means that hypericonomy threatens to behave "not like ethnology as opposed to ethnography, but like astrology as opposed to astrogrography," then so be it (Panofsky, *Meaning* 32). Perhaps astrology, a mode of knowledge-acquisition that relies heavily on chance encounters and blind intuition, is a much better analogy for the mode of discourse I am seeking. In a sense, then, the forms of research and pedagogy I am seeking ask scholars to be more like Panofsky, an intellectual who took chances in breaching the boundaries of disciplinary specialization. Unlike Panofsky, however, the hypericonomist should harbor no pretense about "being rigorous" or engaging in "hard science." Hypericonomy rebuffs the taboo of dilettantism, embraces desire and subjectivity, and self-consciously remobilizes these as a research strategy.

Hypericonomy Is Not Archetypology

The exemplar in Panofsky should be supplemented with Carl Jung, another expert dabbler in iconology, one who understood and subsequently ignored the danger of dilettantism. In Jung's terms, society expects that "only the cobbler who is not a poet can supply workmanlike shoes" (*Essays* par. 305). But this did not stop Jung from rooting his psychoanalytic theory in the *archetype,* a concept that is more akin to art history or anthropology than psychology. Drawing on Freud's notion of "archaic remnants," Jung describes the archetype as a mental form "whose presence cannot be explained by anything in the individual's own life and which seem to be aboriginal, innate, inherited shapes of the human mind" (*Symbols* 67). Jung's theory of the archetype seems to cover the ground that Panofsky fears to tread: the ground of the individual subject. Not only does Jung harbor a belief in the diachronic repetition of symbolic images, but he also connects these images to the pervasiveness of subjective motivation, and to identity formation. To counter Panofsky's positivistic iconology, we have Jung's ultra-subjective physio/cognitive theory that "every experience contains an indefinite number of unknown factors, not to speak of the fact that every concrete object is always unknown in certain respects, because we cannot know the ultimate nature of matter itself" (23).

Unfortunately, the inscrutability of the "ultimate nature of matter" did not deter Jung from issuing a more or less "totalizing" psychiatric apparatus. The role of the archetype is to provide evidence of a certain homogeneity that makes human experience more explicable. This ultimately results in the production of sameness, a flattening of subjective experience that works primarily to the advantage of the analyst. Jung's theory of the collective unconscious, "'collective representations,' emanating from primeval dreams and creative fantasies" (55) is, in essence, a method of containment; so much so, in fact, that it was easily adopted by literary scholars as a prefab critical methodology.[11] Hypericonomy, on the other hand, does not work according to a logic of assimilation, but according to one of difference and dispersion. Jung's notions of "symbol" and "archetype," especially as they were systematized by literary critics in the 1960s, are too restrictive to serve as models in a hypericonomy. Hypericonomists invent their own symbols and archetypes. Whereas Jung claims that "No genius has ever sat down with a pen or a brush in his hand and said: 'Now I am going to invent a symbol,'" the hypericonomist claims that anyone can invent a symbol (a hypericon) that "hints at something not yet known" (*Symbols* 55), and use it as a tool for the acquisition, storage, and dissemination of knowledge.

The preceding constellation of theoretical summaries, terse reflections on complex concepts, will certainly fail to please the specialist—art critic, psychologist, anthropologist, etc.—in any of the fields considered above. But it is in the nature of hypericonomy to be terse, epigrammatic, even ideogrammatic, and thus to plow across many fields, causing offshoots to grow from the plants that others have sown. Consider the previous collection of theories, then, not as a formal taxonomy, but as a set of tools or implements with many purposes, some of which are useful to the hypericonomist. As they appear in this essay, these theories are more or less a digression, a bricoleur's hodge-podge,[12] a Barthesian list of "likes and dislikes."

Hypericonomy Is Conduction

In a move which places this essay directly in the path of an oncoming accusation—i.e., 'This is too clever, too cute, too ludic, too *pomo*'—allow me to hijack the "con" of conduction as an example of how conductive logic works in hypericonomy. The reason for this contraband is to demonstrate how I might trace myself in(to) this essay while simultaneously demonstrating the logic of conduction. In this case, everything revolves around the "o" at the center of "con." The o is the (w)hole that draws me in. How do I, personally, enter into a theoretical discussion of visual culture, identity formation and scholarly discourse? I must, above all, employ my knowledge of travelling by train in Canada; not by VIA Rail (a passenger system), but by CN (Canadian National Railways), a cargo system. A passenger train (VIA) would do me no good in this situation, even though it may be equipped with a conductor. What I need is a passing freight train (CN) to latch onto as it flies by. Only by placing the o, or rather, the O (i.e., O'Gorman) in the CN can I think conductively. I must situate myself not at the front (where the engineer plies his trade), nor at the end, (where the caboose should be), but at the center of the discourse, with the cargo, that which allows itself to be conducted across the networks of tracks. This is how the *con* game of conduction (in Italian, a game of *with,* in French, a game of *stupidity*[13]) works in hypericonomy.

As nonsensical as this conductive language may seem, it demonstrates in text the signatorial,[14] ideographic, pun-centred type of discourse suitable to an age of electronic media, an age where identity may be formed entirely by the internalization of media images. This mode of discourse may indeed belong to what Greg Ulmer has called *electracy.* Central to the emergent phenomenon of electracy (and present signaturally in the name Ulmer gives it: elec-**trace**-*y*) is Derrida's notion of the *trace.* The trace, according to Gayatri Spivak "is the mark of the absence of a presence, an always already absent present, of the lack at the origin that is the condition of thought and experience" (xvi). Conductive logic gives us a way of writing this nothing that is everything, this w/hole (O, 0) that we call the *trace.* The purveyors of electracy understand that "the authority of the text is provisional, the origin is a trace" (Spivak, xviii), and hence we must learn to devise our own organizational systems, our own origins for the text, even while understanding that such an origin is contingent upon our own subjectivation (in the example above, the "O" in "CON" marks the spot of this subjectivation, traces my signature into the discourse). In electracy, "we must learn to use and erase our language at the same time" (Spivak xviii).

As an organizational mechanism, conduction gathers disparate types of information into a single location or node. Evidently, there are analogies that must be drawn here, first of all, between conduction and the Freudian concept of condensation in dreamwork. This is more than an analogy, however, since conduction does indeed rely upon the logic of the unconscious, i.e., an individual's psychic capacity to gather associations at a single ideational node.[15] More appropriately, perhaps, the concept of conductive thinking is analogous to emergent technologies of representation that have appropriated the term "node" to designate a single document within a hypertextual network. In a demonstration of how the language of conduction can be at once heuretic and heuristic, inventive and instructive for an electronic age, Ulmer asks:

> How should we conduct ourselves in the age of television? Electronically. How might we keep cur-

> rent in education? Electronically. Conduction, that is, carries the simple form of the pun into a learned extrapolation in theory. When we pose the ancient question of the ground of reason in the context of teletheory we think first of all of the pun that gives us an electronic ground. *Ground:* a conducting connection between an electric circuit or equipment and the earth or some other conducting body. Reasoning by conduction involves, then, the flow of energy through a circuit. . . . [This] gives us a new definition of truth as "a relationship of conduction between disparate fields of information," as illustrated here in the conduction between the vocabulary of electricity and that of logic. (*Teletheory,* 63)

The pun, that annoying device that may very well have been the demise of Marshall McLuhan's academic legitimacy, is essential in conduction. In hypericonomy, the pun is pictorial, and not verbal, although the two may merge in the alphabetic ideograph. By employing the logic of conduction in hypericonomy, a researcher assimilates disparate surges of information into ideational, pictorial nodes as a strategy for managing information and acquiring knowledge in an age of digital media and visual overload, an age of electracy.

For the Sake of Institutional Reform

In *Writing Machines,* a book that takes very seriously the materiality of scholarly work, Katherine Hayles makes a similar suggestion about integrating subject positioning into academic discourse: "Maybe now is a good time for a double-braided text where the generalities of theory and the particularities of personal experience can both speak, though necessarily in different voices. A text where both voices can be heard, at first very different but then gradually coming closer until finally they are indistinguishable." (106)

What Hayles is asking for in critical theory is essentially a form of resistance to the demand for objective distance and "rigor" placed upon academic discourse by what John Guillory has identified as the technobureaucratic, professional-managerial class. This may seem like a strange turn for theory to take, given that, as Guillory suggests, it is the "scientific" aura of critical theory that permitted its canonization in the humanities (via literary studies) in the first place. In Guillory's words, theory permitted the humanities to achieve a "rapprochement with the technobureaucratic constraints upon intellectual labor, symptomatically registered as a fetishization of 'rigor'" (xii). To return to the vise hypericon, mentioned briefly above, the current academic apparatus is rooted in specialization, a model of productivity recognizable in the logic of the assembly line and in the compartmentalization of knowledge achieved through a vise-like containment of academic departments. This model has infected theory as well, turning the wide-ranging intellectual work of Derrida, Barthes, Foucault, etc. into punch presses, hydraulic powered vises if you will, that spit out predictable readings of texts and culture.

Hypericonomy asks scholars to engage in a form of resistance toward the technobureaucratic constraints that are in place in the current academic apparatus, and that account for the lack of cultural capital in the humanities. Not only does the method require a more concerted focus on identity formation, but its visual style, its very materiality, rooted in the imagetext, asks for a degree of interdisciplinarity that likely cannot be accommodated by any traditional academic department. As W.J.T. Mitchell suggests, "the corporate, departmental structure of universities reinforces the sense that verbal and visual media are to be seen as distinct, separate, and parallel spheres that convene only at some higher level of abstraction" (*Picture Theory* 85). Hypericonomy challenges this distinction, and calls for a new, integrative model of education that interconnects and synthesizes specialized discourses, and unabashedly fosters generalization as opposed to specialization, even at the risk of being accused of dilettantism. Hypericonomy, then, as I have imagined it in this essay, is only a microcosm of the sort of integrative, wide-scope thinking that is lacking in academic administration today.

In a *Chronicle of Higher Education* article titled "Colleges Must Reconstruct the Unity of Knowledge," Vartan Gregorian brings his point home by referencing T.S. Eliot:

> "Where is the wisdom we have lost in knowledge?" T.S. Eliot once asked. "Where is the knowledge we have lost in information?" Colleges and universities must, once more, play a critical role in rediscovering that knowledge and that wisdom. Otherwise they will resemble what Eliot described in a commentary on

> Dante's *Inferno,* when he wrote to the effect that hell is a place where nothing connects with nothing. (B 14)

Hypericonomists must specialize in the interconnectedness of information. In short, they must prove that it is possible—and valuable—to be both a cobbler and a poet.

Stephen Gibb, *No Parole*, Oil on plywood, 1990. Courtesy of the artist.]

Notes

1. This method was originally conceived of as "hypericonology," but this denotes more of a science or discipline directed toward the study of hypericons, and not a praxis or economy of the hypericon. Hypericonology is the science that W .J. T. Mitchell adheres to in *Picture Theory,* and that incites him to confess that his "aim has not been to produce a 'picture theory' (much less a theory of pictures), but to *picture theory* as a practical activity in the formation of representations" (6). Hypericonomy is indeed a 'picture theory,' and the term can be used to denote either a method or a particular text, print or electronic, in which that method has been employed. Hence, we can say "this or that hypericonomy" is generated by a method called hypericonomy.

2. Although some readers may object to the inclusion of such a violent scene, or to its relevance here, it is an essential part of this study, and hopefully, an effective mnemonic device. Mnemotechnics, which are most effective when they draw on shocking or grotesque images, are a supplementary, yet necessary element of hypericonomy.

3. The screenplay for *Casino,* cited here, was written by Nicholas Pileggi.

4. There is an inevitable resonance here with Deleuze and Guattari's notion of the face as an "abstract machine" which facilitates the operation of certain *assemblages of power* through its cipherability (*Plateaus,* 175). Based on this concept of faciality, one could easily envisage an essay which depicts the vise scene in *Casino* as a Deleuze/Guattarian one-act play.

5. The "ideology" to which I am referring here can be vaguely described as "posthuman marketing," a strategy of consumer engagement built on anxieties and desires surrounding the morphing of human and machine, the fragmentation of identity. My former colleague Nick Rombes, while reading this manuscript, questioned whether hypericonomy is yet another symptom of our culture's hypervisual drive toward simulacrum and noise. My response is that the method is geared toward a critical consumption and careful redistribution of images. In this sense, the hypericonomist is more of a film director and writer than a film viewer or reader.

6. The notion of the discourse being "subjectively motivated" falls in line with Barthes's concepts of "studium" and "punctum" as outlined in *Camera Lucida.* Whereas the studium is that which draws us into positioning ourselves subjectively within or vis-à-vis the photograph, the punctum is an element of the photograph that provokes a greater level of emotion ("love," as opposed to "like"). In Barthes's words, A photograph's *punctum* is that accident which pricks me (but also bruises me, is poignant to me)" (26). Hypericonomy, then, begins with the punctum, and proceeds by means of the pun.

7. I draw this example from Chapter 3 of my book, *E-Crit: Digital Media, Critical Theory, and the Humanities* (U of Toronto P, 2006).

8. This example is taken from a paper entitled "Born Under Saturn: Anatomy of the Digital melancholic" which I presented at the 1996 Conference of the Society of Literature and Science.

9. My goal here is not to confuse the concepts of *metapicture* and *hypericon* as defined by Mitchell, but to *fuse* them. Any metapicture—a picture which self-reflexively conveys a theory of visualization—can be seen as a hypericon, since a theory of visualization necessarily implies an episteme, a theory of knowledge, a way of looking at things. The point of this apparent syllogism is to foster an awareness of the interplay between content and materiality in theoretical praxis. Theories of visualization are theories of knowledge; representation is theory; and yes, the medium can be the message.

10. In *The Archaeology of Knowledge,* Foucault asserts that "a total description draws all phenomena around a single centre—a principle, a meaning, a spirit, a world-view, an overall shape; a general history, on the contrary, would deploy the space of a dispersion" (10). In this sense, Hypericonomy—a method that resists the notion of a universal principle, meaning or world-view—might be used to devise a "general history," a method of dispersion, and not a totalizing methodology.

11. The most famous example, perhaps, of the application of the archetype to critical theory is Northrop Frye's classic *The Anatomy of Criticism.* For an extended critique of myth-criticism, see Norman Holland, *The Dynamics of Literary Response* (New York: Oxford, 1968), esp. pp. 243–61.

12. This approach to knowledge has distinct affiliations with the *bricoleur,* that tinkering figure first identified by Claude-Levi Strauss, and further elaborated upon by Deleuze and Guattari: "When Claude Levi Strauss defines *bricolage,* he does so in terms of a set of closely related characteristics: the possession of a stock of materials or of rules of thumb that are fairly extensive, though more or less a hodgepodge—multiple and at the same time limited; the ability to rearrange fragments continually in new and different patterns or configurations" (*Anti-Oedipus*7).

13. The meaning of stupidity (connerie) that I am grasping for here is best expressed by Rosalind Kraus, who, in reference to the impossibility of the viewing subject to achieve objective distance from the object of his gaze, draws on an expression from Jean-Francois Lyotard:

> There is no way to concentrate on the threshold of vision, to capture something *en tournant la tête,* without siting vision in the body and positioning that body, in turn, within the grip of desire. Vision is then caught up within the meshes of projection and identification, within the specularity of substitution that is also a search for an origin lost. *Con,* as they say, *celui qui voit.* (140)

14. Here, I am invoking Derrida's notion of the signature as a form of pun. The signature can function at the abyssal level of the hypericon, in order to mark the trace of the author whose authority is erased in the very act of writing. To deliver one's name to the signatory mode is to "monumentalize, institute, and erect it into a thing or a stony object. But in doing so, you also lose the identity, the title of ownership over the text" (Derrida 56). Ulmer considers the signature as a central tool in the invention of a new method of electronic writing. "In hyperrhetoric," Ulmer suggests, "the pattern formed by the signature *en abyme* functions as the electronic alternative to concept formation for gathering heterogeneous materials in a set" ("Miranda,"184). The signature is a short-cut, a short-circuit, a tool for conductive thinkers.

15. See Freud's *Interpretation of Dreams,* Penguin, 1976, pp. 383ff.

Works Cited

Barthes, Roland. *Camera Lucida.* Translated by Richard Howard. New York: Hill and Wang, 1981.

Casino. Directed by Martin Scorsese. With Robert DeNiro, Joe Pesce, Sharon Stone, and Alan King. Universal Pictures, 1995.

Deleuze, Gilles. *Foucault.* Minneapolis: U of Minnesota P, 1986.

—. Anti-Oedipus: Schizophrenia and Capitalism. Minneapolis: U of Minnesota P, 1983.

—, and Felix Guattari. *A Thousand Plateaus: Capitalism and Schizophrenia.* Minneapolis: U of Minnesota P, 1987.

Derrida, Jacques. *Of Grammatology.* Baltimore and London: Johns Hopkins U P, 1984.

Eagleton, Terry. *After Theory.* New York: Basic Books, 2003.

Foucault, Michel. *This Is Not a Pipe.* Translated by James Harkness. Berkeley: U of California P, 1982.

Foucault, Michel. *The Archaeology of Knowledge and the Discourse on Language.* Trans. A.M. Sheridan Smith. New York: Pantheon, 1971.

Freud, Sigmund. New York: *Interpretation of Dreams,* Penguin, 1976.

Gregorian, Vartan. "Colleges Must Reconstruct the Unity of Knowledge." *The Chronicle of Higher Education* (June 4, 2004).

Guillory, John. *Cultural Capital: The Problem of Literary Canon formation.* Chicago: U of Chicago P, 1993.

Hayles, Katherine. *Writing Machines.* Cambridge: MIT Press, 2002.

Holland, Norman. *The Dynamics of Literary Response* . New York: Oxford UP, 1968.

Jung, Carl G. *Two Essays on Analytical Psychology.* Princeton: Princeton UP, 1972.

—. *Man and His Symbols.* New York: Doubleday, 1964.

Krauss, Rosalind E. *The Optical Unconscious.* Cambridge: MIT Press, 1994.

Manovich, Lev. *The Language of New Media.* Cambridge: MIT Press, 2000.

Mitchell, W. J. T. *Picture Theory.* Chicago: U of Chicago P, 1994.

—. *Iconology: Image, Text, Ideology.* Chicago: U of Chicago P, 1986.

O'Gorman, Marcel. *E-Crit: Digital Media, Critical Theory and the Humanities.* Toronto: U of Toronto P, 2006.

Panofsky, Erwin. *Studies in Iconology.* New York: Harper & Row, 1962.

—. *Meaning in the Visual Arts.* Chicago: U of Chicago P, 1955.

Ray, Robert. *The Avant-Garde Finds Andy Hardy.* Cambridge: Harvard U P, 1995.

Spivak, Gayatri. "Translator's Preface." Jacques Derrida. *Of Grammatology.* Baltimore: Johns Hopkins U P, 1976.

Ulmer, Gregory. *Heuretics: The Logic of Invention.* Baltimore: Johns Hopkins UP, 1994.

—. "The Miranda Warnings." *Hypertext Theory.* Ed. George P. Landow. Baltimore: Johns Hopkins U P, 1994.

—. *Teletheory: Grammatology in the Age of Video.* New York: Routledge, 1989.

Wittgenstein, Ludwig. *Philosophical Investigations* . Cambridge, MA: Blackwell Publishers, 1958.

5 Ease and Electracy

Bradley Dilger

Introduction

Technology's presence in everyday life has increased steadily over the past two centuries. This evolution has been documented in academic and popular writing, with almost as many perspectives on technological change as there are texts. Many writers explicitly suggest, or otherwise indicate, that ease, or "making it easy," can successfully help us understand technology, learn to use technological systems, and confront the development of electronic technology—even the changing nature of technology itself.[1] Contemporary American culture provides numerous examples of ease functioning in this role. It figures prominently in the marketing of products and services as different as DVD players, car insurance, hair dye, and appliances. Ease has incredibly profound effects on the development of electronic communication, especially computing and the Internet.

In the familiar context of personal computing and consumer electronics—what many people might name when asked for examples of "technology"—ease is defined by rapid learning, comfort in use, and high usability. Ease often means refusing to see the code: preferring a simple, pragmatic approach which doesn't involve the complication of complete understanding. But ease has a very complex definition which has evolved over hundreds of years, and its connection to technology is by no means limited to computers and electronics. Demands for ease support a powerful system of representation which defines and shapes our experiences with, and understanding of, technology and technological systems. In ongoing research into the history of ease, I have observed a complexity of definition, a deeply paradoxical nature, and a history of gradually broadening power and influence which began hundreds of years ago and continues to this day. Ease supports disturbing patterns in the cultural role of technology discussed by Langdon Winner, Cynthia Selfe, and other scholars. However, perhaps most importantly, I have also learned that as early as the eighteenth century, ease was motivated to teach children the technology of writing—as today it teaches the technology of networked computing. Ease and writing are very closely connected, and any history of one needs to recognize the important role of the other.[2]

All kinds of writing, in and beyond the discipline of rhetoric and composition, involve learning new technologies and questioning one's relationship with technology. If, as I believe, ease shapes the way we understand the concept of technology, then composition instructors—who have always been "teaching with technology"—should understand ease. Whether or not one is considering "new media," computing and ease influence writing at all levels, profoundly shaping its study and production.

In this essay, I focus on the role ease plays in composition pedagogy which involves the production of new media.[3] After outlining the history of ease, and its connection to rhetoric and composition, I will discuss the implications of ease for new media. My essay concludes with the outline of four concepts thatcan be explored as the apparatus of electracy takes shape—either as pedagogical alternatives to ease or redefinitions more adapted to the technology of new media.

A Brief History of Ease

The history of ease can be considered as two interrelated strands—the connection of ease and writing, and the role of ease in the consumer economy—both building on a common original meaning.

In its oldest sense, ease was primarily economic, meaning the "opportunity, means or ability to do something" ("Ease" 31). Though ease still connotes financial well-being (as in the phrase "easy street"), the second historical sense, "comfort [or] absence of pain or trouble" (32), is the most common meaning, from the earliest definitions until today. With *comfort,* the first widespread concept of ease relied on two other qualities: *effortlessness,* the reduction or elimination of physical labor and intensive activity; and perhaps the most important, *transparency,* or freedom from concern with complications or unnecessary attention to details and procedures.[4]

Early definitions of ease were often quite ambivalent. It could indicate detachment, an aloofness or sublime state of mind made possible by disconnection from the rigors of daily life—sometimes possible because of privileged economic status, sometimes the result of behavior seen as idleness and sloth. As the economic and technological changes of industrialization reduced the amount of manual labor necessary for sustenance, ease was less often seen negatively, and even became a desirable goal. However, ambivalence still often surrounds ease, whether in the economic sense (for example, in concepts like Thorstein Veblen's "conspicuous consumption") or perpetuation of the belief that reliance on ease indicates laziness or unwillingness to learn something comprehensible with a little hard work.

Ease and Writing

The connection of ease and writing forms the first historical strand I consider here. As ease was motivated to understand the technology of writing, its definition became more complex, and a complicated relationship between the two developed. Two new meanings of ease emerged as writing and composition pedagogies were developed in the early eighteenth century: *simplicity,* the apparent absence of complexity or difficulty; and *pragmatism,* disengagement from general understanding which fails to produce immediate reward.

The *OED* shows that in 1711, writing "showing no trace of effort; smooth, flowing" was considered easy. To be sure, an easy style of communication was venerated long before that time, as in I Corinthians 14:9, "So likewise ye, except ye utter by the tongue words easy to be understood, how shall it be known what is spoken? For ye shall speak into the air." Joseph M. Williams, discussing the development of modern English prose (6–7), points to Thomas Sprat, who called for "a close, naked, natural way of speaking; positive expressions; clear senses; a native easiness: bringing all things as near the Mathematical plainness" as possible (Sprat 111). Sprat saw complex prose as a willfully bloated form of language, which was naturally pure and clear, and attacked writers whose prose was "swollen" or "extravagant." Other British writers such as Joseph Addison and Richard Steele are often credited with creating modern techniques of essay writing, such as "equitone prose" (McLuhan, *Gutenberg Galaxy* 273). However, as Francis-Noël Thomas and Mark Turner observe, style is not a mere matter of surface-level features (26–28), and the shift to easy style in

English reflected the larger epistemological changes which occurred in the early Enlightenment.

Around the turn of the seventeenth century, more philosophers and rhetoricians believed language could transparently and accurately represent an individual's knowledge or observations of the environment. Clarity, distinction, and ease—named as such and appearing in other forms—played an increasingly important role in Enlightenment philosophy. Sharon Crowley shows that as modern epistemology developed, knowledge production was increasingly seen as an individual phenomenon, and was no longer "enshrined in authoritative books and commentaries or in God's law made manifest in the nature of things" (5). Arguments could be without reference to divine texts or law: "an orderly completed text, which reproduced the history of the thinker's investigation, was assumed to constitute sufficient testimony to the authenticity of its findings" (8). Writers who chose an orderly, transparent, and enjoyable style—an easy style—created authoritativeness through their easy manner of presentation.

These ideas were quickly applied to teaching writing. As Crowley and other scholars have demonstrated, the English schoolmasters Isaac Watts and John Holmes adapted Enlightenment philosophy to pedagogical use by using ease to teach reading and writing—or, to cast the work of Watts and Holmes in technological terms, for consumption and production of the technology of writing. Watts, while better known today for his Christian hymns, was instrumental in making Cartesian method workable for composition pedagogy (Crowley 40–2, 177). An avid follower of John Locke, Watts championed Locke's ideas, and attempted to enact his vision of gentler educational practices which "shared a concern for tailoring education to coincide with the child's developmental level" (Schultz 63). Like Watts, Holmes embraced educational change, presenting an increasingly pragmatic curriculum and new techniques for improving the efficacy of writing instruction (Howell 125).

In his 1725 *Logick,* Watts transformed the four basic rules of Cartesian method—accept no unclear judgments, divide difficulties into parts, think in order from simple to complex, and be complete, leaving nothing from consideration—into learning strategies. His work combined Cartesian method and Locke's proposals for atomization (dividing a complex or difficult subject into smaller chunks so that it could be taught) and gradation (using atomization to slow the presentation of difficulty over time), key strategies still used in writing pedagogy to this day. Watts's second rule of method stands out: "Let your *Method* be *plain and easy,* so that your Hearers or Readers, as well as your self, may run thro' it without Embarrassment, and may take a clear and comprehensive View of the whole Scheme" (351). He argued that both teachers and students should move "by regular and easy steps" from simple matters to more difficult ideas, keeping sentence structure simple, and arguments as brief as possible (352, 356).

Like Watts, in the preface to *The Art of Rhetoric Made Easy,* Holmes argued that his new approach was well-suited to the character of contemporary students. Transferring the ambivalence of ease to the classroom, Holmes built a pedagogy of ease, but simultaneously regretted the need to do so. Stating the relevance of his book, he remarked:

> [I]n this Day,[. . .] School-boys are expected to be led, sooth'd, and entic'd to their studies by the Easiness and Pleasure of the Practice, rather than by Force or harsh Discipline drove, as in days of Yore. For while some of them are *too Copious* in Things not so immediately the Concern of Boys at School, most are *too Brief* in Things really necessary for Youth to be inform'd of, and none at all so happy or methodical as *to distinguish* between One and T'Other. (xiii)[5]

This slightly pejorative cast was well-represented in contemporary senses of ease as an immaturity or naïvete, "moved without difficulty to action or belief" ("Easy" 33). Holmes engages the language of method here and in numerous other places, calling for students to be "methodical" and to "distinguish" between unities—an ability critical in Cartesian schema. Following Watts, Holmes makes writing easy through content and in presentation: he prints critical sections in larger type, annotating them with large capital letters, and ensures that chief tropes and figures are shortly stated, "for the more easy attaining and the longer retaining them in Memory" (xvi). American proto-compositionists such as John Frost and John Walker selectively embraced and extended the work of Watts and Holmes. Later writers like Barrett Wendell would be even more pragmatic, simplifying composition by completely jettisoning the classical rhetoric at the core of this early work (Connors 273–75).

As American composition matured, the reductive approach to writing often called "current-traditional rhetoric" developed.[6] Important histories such as Alfred Kitzhaber's pioneering study *Rhetoric in American Colleges: 1850–1900,* Crowley's *The Methodical Memory,* and Robert Connors's *Composition-Rhetoric* all provide evidence for considering ease as the fundamental quality which organizes current-traditional rhetoric and pedagogy. My comparison of the work of Kitzhaber, Crowley, Connors, and others shows that four trends involving ease characterize this approach to writing:

1. Pedagogy: students should find writing easy.

2. Teacher education: teachers should find teaching writing easy.

3. Rhetoric: students should produce prose which is easy to read.

4. Societal function: writing is the gatekeeper to the life of ease.

Ease was even applied *recursively,* guiding the subdivision of composition into separate entities, and legitimizing application of single concepts at multiple levels—such as the use of the "unity-mass-coherence" triad to guide the structure of sentences, paragraphs, and entire compositions. This universal application of ease is the ultimate realization of the "microcosmic to macrocosmic" structure Crowley calls "a nest of Chinese boxes" (132).[7]

But making composition easy for teachers didn't necessarily make it easy for students. The assumption of close correspondence of thought and language allowed open questioning of the intelligence and work ethic of those who wrote poorly. As was true for Sprat years earlier, producing "good writing" was seen as a matter of refusing complication and ornament, and allowing the natural clarity, brevity, and simplicity of expression to assert itself. The push for mechanical correctness—well-documented by Connors (112–70)—simplified grading, but raised the bar of "good writing" far above the ability of most writers. Since teaching writing was (allegedly) easy, it was impossible for students to question the quality of their instruction based on a lack of teacher preparation. And few acknowledged the paradoxical nature of ease, such as the difficulty of writing brief, clear, easy prose—well-summarized by Thoreau, who quipped, "Not that the story need be long, but it will take a long while to make it short" (320).

Ease was embraced ambivalently, seen as a necessary evil, a technique composition teachers were forced to use because of the illiteracy of their students. And though critics of current-traditional methods have offered successful alternatives to many of its questionable practices—acknowledging the complexity and difficulty of writing, and raising questions about the institution of English—ease still enjoys tremendous goodwill in composition and writing. Ease sells handbooks, with titles such as *Easy Writer* (Lunsford) and *Easy Access* (Keene and Adams), and marketing slogans like "the easiest textbook for students to use." Numerous popular forms correlate good writing and easy reading, from Strunk & White's *The Elements of Style* to Jakob Nielsen's prescriptions for writing for websites ("How Users Read"), with little or no mention of the effort often required to write clear, brief, simple prose. Finally, despite years of research which points elsewhere, there is tremendous pressure to model writing, and also composition programs, on the transactional models of the marketplace and the consumer economy—which, notably, are driven by ease.

Ease and the Development of Consumer Culture

Since the turn of the twentieth century, ease has been widely employed to understand many technologies, especially those involved with consumer goods and services. The definition of ease became even more complex as ease became more attainable and as the penetration of technology in everyday life deepened. These changes would alter ease in three ways: highlighting the correspondence of ease with *femininity;* a demand for *expediency,* which supplemented pragmatism's filter of relevance with a demand for speed; and finally *pictorialism,* a mutation of transparency which recognized the rising importance of the visual.

At the turn of the twentieth century, the advertising techniques, branding, centralized distribution, mass production, and widespread consumption which characterizes today's economy were being developed (Strasser 17). But Americans used to making their own bread, soap, and other sundries had to be convinced store-bought goods were worth the expense. Much of the argument was made using ease. As the consultant and author Christine Frederick repeatedly argued in *Household Engineering,* store-bought products were easier to use—why not buy the ready-to-use name brands, and save the trouble of making one's own? Marketing for labor-saving devices such as washing machines followed suit, highlighting the comfort and increased leisure time they made possible. Interestingly, these products were not easy to use by today's standards. For example, washing clothes required manual operation of multiple valves and switches. There were no automatically controlled wash, rinse, and spin cycles. Additionally, poorly insulated electrical components and unshielded moving parts made these machines extremely dangerous (Maxwell). Regardless, washing via electricity was much easier than by hand—and manufacturers made sure Americans repeatedly saw household technology and consumer goods portrayed as a means for making life easy.

Before World War II, consumer deployment of ease was largely divided among gender lines: it was suitable for family matters, for women and children, at home and school. Men at work had little need for ease (except, perhaps, if they wrote). The identification of ease with femininity continues today, often in a demeaning fashion: women allegedly need ease because they can't handle difficulty.[8] However, as rapid mechanization, electrification, and electronification transformed America in the 1930s and 1940s, demands for ease began to ignore gender lines. Since there were numerous new technologies to learn and use, speed and simplicity became critical. The war effort hammered this point home, as scientists realized weapons and other war machines which were easy to operate were often more lethal—for example, an easily controlled mortar could be fired more quickly. Military-sponsored "knob and dial studies" led to the growth of new disciplines. Lessons learned with munitions and communications technology were soon applied to automobiles and other consumer goods, as demonstrated by the appearance of the journals *Human Factors* and *Ergonomics* soon after the war. Ease of use quickly became a requirement for technology, on the battlefield and at home as well. The washing machine model—hard-to-use, but acceptable for its labor saving properties—began to disappear, and was replaced with the automatic, drive-in, just-add-water model—technology not only created a sense of ease (comfort, effortlessness, etc.) but was easy to use as well.

But ease was not applied consistently—computers and other very "high-tech" systems remained arcane, hard to use, the realm of expertise. Apple famously attacked this assertion head on after introducing its Macintosh in 1984, presenting it as "the computer for the rest of us" (Turkle 41). And if the computer, which represented the pinnacle of technological advancement and development, could be made easy, couldn't anything be made easy? Donald Norman's *The Psychology of Everyday Things* embodies this attitude, calling for ease in the design of nearly all technological systems. However, though the function and scope of applicability of ease had changed considerably since its first application to the technology of writing more than 250 years before, it remained paradoxical and ambivalent. Macintosh critics argued it was a toy, a pretty little curiosity, not a serious computer for real work. Some derided the Mac OS along gender lines; John C. Dvorak called its rival, the IBM PC, a "man's computer designed by men for men" (Levy 197).[9] Similarly, America Online (AOL) users were often attacked for "cluelessness" and stupidity. While the popular "For Dummies" series of self-help books has undercut the negativity associated with preferring technologies considered easy, regardless, it is often considered pejoratively.

Unfortunately, the paradoxical character of ease is still inconsistently acknowledged. "Overwhelmed by Tech," a January 2001 cover story from *U. S. News & World Report,* admits that "It takes enormous computer power and programming know-how to make something complicated look simple," but envisions the movement toward ease as a mere matter of time: "Continuing leaps in processing power and computer storage promise more horsepower to make complex products easier to use . . . as effortless as breathing" (Lardner *et al.* 33, 34). The Western view of technology seldom admits the challenge "making it easy" poses—one of the central reasons I am carefully investigating the role of ease in learning and understanding technology.

Ease and New Media

For teachers and theorists of hypertext, digital cinema, weblogs, and other new media, I believe ease creates two related clusters of difficulty: the first associated with the conceptualization of technology encouraged by ease; the second related to the differences between the print-oriented heritage of ease and the electronic apparatus of new media.

The Easy View of Technology

Generally speaking, ease encourages a paradoxical technological determinism which, while venerating technology, downplays human involvement in its creation and control, and encourages adopting a lackadaisical, even cynical attitude towards it. In the easy view, technology is a natural force, like weather, which we embrace if pleasant, but grudgingly tolerate otherwise. Ease supports five assumptions about technology (all present in the influential application of ease to writing):

a) Technology is not innately difficult; it can be made easy. Only extremely complicated technology must be complex or difficult.

b) Simple, transparent, easy technology is good and normal; anything different is a failure or aberration.

c) Technology works best when it emulates natural objects, systems, and practices.

d) Technology development and economic growth correlate (personally and nationally).

e) Technological progress is constant, consistent, natural, and inevitable.[10]

New media are produced and displayed using computers and other electronics. Compared to writing—which has been made easy and thus appears natural and transparent—new media appear highly technological, disassociated from the tradition of the humanities, an intrusive and misguided attempt to replace poets and artists with programmers and algorithms. Overzealous hypertext advocates like Mark Bernstein perpetuate this belief by portraying established textual forms as inadequate relics, providing fodder for classifying new media an "extremely complicated" or "bad/failure" technology in the five-part schema above. Hypertext proponents who sneer at literate forms help perpetuate the belief that emergent technologies (and media) replace and destroy their predecessors—the oversimplified "supersession" model which remains powerful though frequently debunked by Marshall McLuhan, Paul Duguid, and others. Combined with the easy view of technology, this perspective reinforces the belief that the best response to new media is no response at all—better to wait for the next emergent technology, or for new media made easy.

The high profile of transparency in this view of technology can create additional repercussions. Marcel O'Gorman illustrates that valorizing transparency dissolves most conscious confrontation with the workings of technology, following the assumption that the best communication and technology appears without mediation. But unlike most writing, new media often calls attention to its mediation, through components such as scroll bars and download progress indicators. Interface control elements are sometimes even presented as part of the "content" itself, as is the case with many video games, which display the inventory, health, or game completion conspicuously (Manovich 210). Some games allow quick shifts between topographic and cinematic points of view—a direct manipulation of the cinematic language which mediates game play (Manovich 83–4). This heavily interactive relationship flies in the face of "easy" norms.

O'Gorman and others have also argued that consistent demands for transparent, easy technology can lead to dependency on ease which discourages learning generalized approaches to tasks, or understanding the conceptual model behind a certain form of technology. Practical knowledge, if developed, is highly contextualized; for example, instead of learning how hypertext links function, one learns how to make links with a certain program. Robert R. Johnson has shown that for users of such systems, the lack of generalized practical knowledge can can cause serious difficulty if trouble arises:

> [User-friendly interfaces] can mask the complexities of the system to such an extent that if there is a system breakdown, such as when you receive a cryptic error message that explains the problem in virtually encrypted language . . . you are left helpless, unable to solve the problem, and continue with your work because you are dependent on external expertise not available to you in any useful form. (28)

This has certainly been the case with new media. Consider the web-based course support software Blackboard, widely used because it makes website production easy—with it, creating a sophisticated course website requires minimal technical knowledge of hypertext. To the instructor using it, the complex hypertext file structure is transparent. However, in Fall 2001, when Blackboard began charging some users for courseware server access which had previously been free, composition instructors had to download their course materials, lose their work, or pay for continued use. At the time, to move content from Blackboard elsewhere, hundreds of files of different types had to be transferred individually (Harris). The sudden suspension of transparency turned "a course web site" into "a collection of hierarchically organized files," pushing many into the helplessness Johnson notes above.[11]

Novice/Expert Separation

Johnson's advocacy of a user-centered model of technology includes a critique of the forced novice/expert separation created by system-centered technology. Ease supports this distinction in the process of simplification, in which experts render complexity and difficulty palatable for novices (for example, in composition, classical rhetorical theory and the essay were simplified into static abstractions and the five-paragraph theme). For most users of technology, expertise remains reserved for the system and its creators:

> the system is powerfully hegemonic: the system is the source and ultimately the determiner of all. System-centered technology . . . locates the technological system or artifact in a primary position. There is no need for the user to be involved with system or artifact development, this perspective suggests, because the system is too complex and therefore should be designed and developed by experts who know what is most appropriate in the system design. (26)

Ease even encourages novices to *cultivate* their "inability" to comprehend the complex and instead defer to expertise (both human and computer agency—for example, by considering that programming is impossible without a sophisticated "helper" application). Perhaps acknowledging the self-deprecating, yet very popular, "For Dummies" book series, Johnson calls acceptance of the disenfranchising system-centered model "technological idiocy":

> Users reside on the weak side of the idiot/genius binary. We have embedded the notion of technological idiocy so strongly in our culture that we actually begin to think of ourselves as idiots when we encounter technological breakdowns. Experts are the ones who "know," so we let them have the power, which of course means we accept whatever is given to us. (45)

Due to the emergent character of new media, expertise should be less powerful, since to some extent, everyone using new media is a novice. However, the novice/expert binary is well-established. Software for producing digital films, hypertext, and other new media is separated into "consumer" and "professional" markets (such as Apple's film editing applications iMovie, Final Cut Express, and Final Cut Pro). The resistance to seeing code typical of ease backs reduced support or exclusion of scripting or programming languages from consumer-level applications, since programming is presumably for experts only. Generally speaking, the assumption that new media are too complex for most folks to fully understand, let alone produce, allows the spread of the novice/expert system to new media. While students might be asked to build hypertexts or make simple new media objects, classroom use more often encourages consumption through web-based research or viewing and analysis, further enforcing the novice/expert division.

Discouraging Experimentation

The pragmatic and expedient character of ease, and its associated portrayal of technological systems as foreign and potentially hazardous, discourages novelty and experimentation. Physical and systemic constraints often present in easy technologies enforce this restriction. The "information appliance" model Norman advocates in *The Invisible Computer* replaces general-purpose technology (like the personal computer) with highly specialized systems. Instead of a PC, one would have a document making computer, a music computer, a cooking computer, etc. Certainly, there are advantages to this framework (consider electronic organizers like the PDA), but these machines make experimentation less possible by restricting their function. Similarly, in the *U. S. News* article mentioned earlier, human-computer interaction expert Ben Shneiderman suggested making computers work like automobiles: put the working parts under the hood, out of the reach and concern of most. However, the hood is often welded shut, literally or metaphorically, excluding both would-be experimenters and those looking to repair technology on their own.[12] In writing and in new media, the use of "easy" forms discourages divergence from the norm. For example, using the templates or "wizards" in PowerPoint encourages creation of a series of slides which each have three or four bullet points, colorful charts and graphs, and an "inspirational" conclusion (Parker 76–77). Creating unconventional presentations is not supported by the software "wizards"—those in the application, in Redmond, or in Cupertino.

Given that new media *are* new, it's reasonable to expect some freedom to experiment with form, and a little less pressure to be conventional. But at least with web-based hypertext, constraints and demands for standardization have appeared rapidly. Influential writers like Jakob Nielsen have actively discouraged experimentation and deviation from the norm, even if conventional principles are questionable from a designer's perspective: "If 80% or more of the big sites do things in a single way, then this is the de-facto standard and you *have* to comply. . . . I recommend following the conventions even in those cases where a different design would be better if seen in isolation ("When Bad Design"). In this model, templates and wizards become the logical method for production of new media. Given the problems Parker has observed with templates in PowerPoint, this seems extremely problematic—would a template- or wizard-created argumentative essay be acceptable in a first-year composition course? Perhaps more importantly, discouragement of experimentation also reinforces the pragmatic, vocational, even transactional character of education. Nielsen actively discourages use of the web that doesn't fit the "e-commerce" model: "While I acknowledge that there is a need for art, fun, and a general good time on the web, I believe that the main goal of most web projects should be to make it easy for customers to perform useful tasks" (*Designing Web Usability* 11).[13]

New Media, Literacy, and Electracy

What happens when we try to make the technology of computing easy?

When pedagogical strategies developed using ease entered widespread use in the eighteenth century, there was strong correspondence between the epistemological foundation that backed ease (the modern world-view of the Enlightenment) and its dominant technology of expression (writing). As shown above, the bond of ease and literacy strengthened dramatically in the nineteenth century. Ease and literacy grew up together, affecting each other in a complex relationship with huge ramifications for technology and culture as a whole. For this reason, I see three possibilities: (1) ease will change to adapt to embrace the epistemology, subjectivity, and technology of electracy; (2) the application of ease to electronic communication technology will result in the reproduction of literate-oriented forms which use electronic means of delivery; (3) ease is simply irrelevant, and attempts to make new media easy will be ineffective. Since some evidence exists for each of these conclusions, I will consider each of them in turn.

I have already outlined changes in the definition of ease, many responses to the increased ubiquity and changing nature of technological systems. It is reasonable to expect more changes in ease, both the introduction of new meanings and changes in the relative importance of specific denotations. Recently, ease has embraced pictorialism, an awareness of the visual which reflects the ongoing shift in thinking W. J. T. Mitchell calls "the pictorial turn." As Mitchell defines it, this change is a recognition of the rising importance of the visual in many forms—icons, images, film, video, and more (3, 8–12). Like Mitchell's pictorial turn itself, the alliance of ease and the pictorial is deeply ambivalent; as shown above, the usefulness of images in graphical user interfaces is recognized, but simultaneously derided as "pretty pictures."

However, this development could be a manifestation of the second possibility: does the pictorialism of ease domesticate the visual, making it comprehensible with the tools of literacy? Patterns of making pictures easy often imply a specific approach, such as Edward Tufte's "chartjunk" and "data ink" (91–133)—visualization concepts which have much in common with the brevity, clarity and simplicity triumvirate often motivated to make writing easy. The use of literate forms to organize new media is not surprising; after all, at least at first, "the content of any medium is always another medium" (McLuhan, *Understanding Media* 8). Walter Ong has also shown that electronic communication produces a "secondary orality," a self-conscious return to qualities of speech in electronic form (11). However, is the current situation hybridization, or just wrapping literacy in an electric shell? Development of World Wide Web Consortium (W3C) standards for web encoding, which first addressed expanding functionality and capability, has shifted to the establishment of technologies which promise to achieve the separation of form and content—that is, the transparency of perfect communication (Brooke). Web-based hypertext has developed features much more closely allied to traditional printing and publishing than the patterns of "trailblazing" proposed by Vannevar Bush, or the complex interconnections of the Xanadu hypertext system envisioned by Ted Nelson.

To be sure, the presence of literate features in hypertext, such a top-to-bottom, left-to-right organization, doesn't mean that its development will remain tied to print literacy. It would be difficult, if not impossible, to create print versions of specialized forms like concurrent versioning system (CVS) browsers, which allow collaborative development and distribution of computer program code, and weblogs, which do move the web's hypertext structure in the direction of Bush and Nelson. These and other forms represent significant departures from literate patterns of organizing and displaying information. But it's difficult to understand what limits will be placed on the creation of expression with computers if we expect web technology "to function like the technology of printed words" (Wysocki and Johnson-Eilola 349). Is the dominance of the web by literate forms the result of attempts to make computing easy—from the original conception of the graphical user interface as a metaphorical paper filing system, to usability standards which rely on literate-oriented methodologies like alphabetization, gradation, and simplification? Are demands for literate models like ease keeping the web and computing tied to print oriented epistemology?

The promise of fantastic 3D interfaces notwithstanding, serious questions about computer technology still remain, and articles similar to "Overwhelmed by Tech" regularly complain that technology has not yet been made easy enough, and manufacturers need to redouble efforts to make it easy. This brings me to the third possibility presented above: what if ease is ineffective outside of the context of literacy? In *Heuretics,* Gregory Ulmer, building on Crowley's argument about the epistemological shift behind the methodical memory, argues that the problems faced by those creating communication using computer technology are radically different than those confronting writers in the nineteenth century. Given the movement toward postmodern epistemology, subjectivity, and electronic technology, we should question the use of atomizing and simplifying technologies designed for Cartesian method and the technology of writing.

Gradation and simplification assume that breaking things down into steps presented over time leads to understanding. But that assumes a linear, sequential approach is the best method. I believe many people prefer experimental "learning by doing" to linear tutorials and manuals because graphical user interfaces organize information using a variety of patterns, with many paths to the same goal (such as keyboard shortcuts, application menus, and mouse interactions). Sometimes it's better to consider the "difficult" whole, not the "simple" parts. Applying literate values and methods to computing may be as ludicrous as insisting that computer program code be written using rhymed iambic pentameter so that it will be easy to memorize.

If the strategies which defined classroom use ease are irrelevant, might ease be irrelevant too? In *The Language of New Media,* Lev Manovich repeatedly notes that computers make some processes considered difficult for writing quite easy. For example, the question of invention, deeply affected by the shift to a modern epistemology (Crowley *passim*), is once again radically altered. For new media, creating material from scratch is unneeded thanks to the ready-mades available in "media databases" of various kinds. Invention involves "modification of an already existing signal . . . one does not have to add any original writing; it is enough to select from what already exists" (126, 127):

> The practice of putting together a media object from already existing commercially distributed media elements existed with old media, but new media technology further standardized it and made it much easier to perform. What before involved scissors and glue now involves simply clicking on "cut" and "paste." . . . Pulling elements from databases and libraries becomes the default; creating the from scratch becomes the exception. (Manovich 130)

As Ulmer points out, and Manovich recognizes, it's not that new media are the first to engage this "logic of selection"; obviously, academic citation and quotation practices, the tradition of commonplaces in rhetoric, and the study of intertextuality all engage this logic in various forms. Making writing easy called for disposal of the canon of invention and the logic of selection, since both were considered too difficult, and too much borrowing was disgraceful. But this is no longer the case. Making writing easy was a monumental breakthrough. Making new media easy? It's no big deal, at least when the question of invention is considered.

What's Next?

If we assume the nature of the orality and literacy relationship applies to literacy and electracy, of the three possibilities for ease in electracy, the second and third possibilities discussed here will be critical; we'll need to consider the establishment of new techniques which redefine "ease." In the early eighteenth century, economic meanings of ease dominated; in the twentieth century, the most powerful meanings shifted to transparency. Though predicting the character of "ease" for the twenty-first century is difficult, if not impossible, I believe we can examine alternatives to the narrow noetic field of ease. I have four ideas in mind.

Models of Technology: Hybridity and the Complex

The technological model associated with ease ignores the hybridity often associated with technology, bifurcating its character into inferior and superior, new and old, natural and technological, as well as novice and expert. Though this logic of binary oppositions has been thoroughly discredited, it remains powerful. For computer technology, escaping these oversimplifications is necessary for a variety of reasons, the first related to the hybrid character of technological change. The "user-centered rhetorical complex of technology" envisioned by Johnson (34–40) offers a viable alternative to this model with added benefit of design tailored to reducing negative effects of ease discussed above.

Wysocki and Johnson-Eilola argue that Western culture's current obsession with literacy is restrictive. I've already noted that overcorrection—rejection of the nature of literacy out hand—is just as regrettable. Instead, we need to understand that literacy has developed, and electracy will be developed, not only through the production of new concepts, but by finding new ways to use old concepts, and by finding value in concepts which once seemed irrelevant. The ideas bracketed by Ramus, Descartes, and their contemporaries might be quite useful in the apparatus of electracy. Ulmer's attempt to develop a poetics for electracy in his textbook *Internet Invention* follows this model. Considering the usefulness of Roland Barthes' concept of the obtuse meaning for working with images, he writes:

> It is important to remember that the obtuse or "third" meaning has been at work all along, but that the literate apparatus was not suited to exploit it fully. We are speaking of an imaging technology, and the arts never left off making images throughout the epoch of literacy, even if images were rarely granted cognitive, let alone scientific, status. (*Internet Invention* 45)

In some ways, all of Ulmer's research focuses on reassessment of practices made transparent by the conventions of the academic essay and the application of ease to the technology of writing. This explains his interdisciplinary approach—valuable ideas may appear outside of "English" structures, and will be missed unless we keep an open mind. It's not surprising, then, that the exercises in Ulmer's textbook involve decidedly non-literate, non-composition activities—which may seem as strange to our literate-minded students as the pragmatic exercises of Watts and Holmes appeared to eighteenth century students used to the declamations and recitations of classical rhetoric.

Embracing the Image

The highly visual nature of new media, and Mitchell's concepts of "pictorial turn" and "imagetext," suggest the concept of "image" will be at issue in electracy in numerous ways. In *Internet Invention,* Ulmer shows that "image" is not only a matter of the pictorial and visual, but a component of numerous artistic forms, alternately expressed as atmosphere, voice, or mood, with established methodologies in literacy (many associated with the development of poetic or figurative language). His assignments confront the development of image-oriented forms, based on the assertion that the strong visual component of electronic media will reinvigorate "image reason"—a conductive method of inference which complements the deduction and induction of literacy (9–10). Manovich provides strong technological support for this assertion, pointing that computers represent new media objects which seem heterogeneous—a research paper, the score of a symphony, a clip from a film, an algorithm for reducing the red-eye in amateur photography—using the same representational code:

> All new media objects, whether created from scratch on computers or converted from analog media sources, are composed of digital code; they are numerical representations. . . . For although from one point of view new media is another type of media, from another it is simply a particular type of computer data, something stored in files and databases, retrieved and sorted, run through algorithms and written to the output device. That the data represent pixels and that

> this device happens to be an output screen is beside the point. (27, 46–47)

Therefore, hybridizing "text" and "image" (or, really, any two forms of computer expression) is not only quite easy, but normal. Systems for creating and editing such mixtures appear in new media software—compositing, morphing, blending, layering—making media programmable, manipulable by human- and machine-operated processes. Manovich points out that computer science has developed concepts like "transcoding" to describe the ability of computers to perform these operations, and broadens its definition to include exchange between forms which exist on computers—bits, bytes, packets, and pixels—but between human-oriented forms as well—both the words, sentences, and paragraphs of literacy, and the visual components excluded from it (46). If Ulmer and Mitchell are right, developments in ease will have to address images *and* text, and the connection of ease and the pictorial will have to be more sophisticated than the common-sense notion that visualizing words makes them easy. Mitchell's insistence that the pictorial turn indicates a problem, not merely the "rise of images," is one step towards recognizing the need for new thinking in this arena.

Translucence, not Transparency

New media pedagogy needs to develop concepts which will enable learners to confront the representational code of new media and in fact the very nature of encoding and mediation made invisible by ease-oriented models of communication, such as George Orwell's characterization of good writing as a windowpane. I believe that pedagogical use of translucence, rather than transparency, would motivate some of the framework of ease, but with critical differences which acknowledge the technological nature of new media and the conductive logic native to electracy. Of course, the new media notions of "filters" aren't strictly a visual construction, nor is translucence, and we should imagine it in many possible ways. As we work with new media and translucence more often, it should be possible to consider both without assuming a visual character.

Manovich points out that the relationship between the different parts of new media objects is fundamentally different than that of writing. New media objects are *modular:* they can be stored independently of each other, as well as combined into other objects, while retaining both independent and coexistent properties. A new media object "consists of independent parts, each of which consists of independent parts, and so on, down to the level of the smallest 'atoms'—pixels, 3-D points, or text characters" (31). This modular character affects the structure of metaforms of new media, like the Web, as well as the logic and practice of computer programming and new media creation: "the modular structure of new media makes such deletion and substitution of parts particularly easy" (31). In turn, this gives rise to a second critical property, *variability:*

> Old media involved a human creator who manually assembled textual, visual, and/or audio elements into a particular composition or sequence. This sequence was stored in some material, its order determined once and for all. . . . New media, in contrast, is characterized by variability. . . . Instead of identical copies, a new media object typically gives rise to many different versions. (36)

From a pedagogical perspective, these fundamental differences have several important consequences, all of which call into question concealing the code of new media, or erasing the borders of the objects of which it is composed. Generally speaking, making the modular structure or variable character of new media transparent would cripple our ability to deal with it. Better to make it translucent, that is, to hide the code only partially. First, if the relationship between the parts of a new media object can be easily altered, it might be less difficult to determine the desired arrangement through trial and error (or other creative processes). In writing, arrangement of compositions was made easy by the imposition of a recursive hierarchical structure of word, sentence, paragraph, and essay. This allowed readers to avoid the difficulty of developing a mental representation of a complicated linear argument, and the trouble caused by rearranging or rewriting prose. Such strict forms are unnecessary for new media. Because it's possible to alter arrangement quickly—and to use computer-controlled processes to do so—there's no need to restrict arrangement to hierarchical, linear forms, or to invent strategies for their domestication.

Second, new media won't necessarily involve the production of a single end product, with a simple author, which is duplicated and shared by all readers or viewers, but variations on a theme customized according to individual preferences—some controlled by the producer, some by the consumer (Manovich 36–37, 125). Therefore, new media producers would need to understand the relationships between the various parts of new media compositions under construction, as well as the ways those parts might be articulated into wholes. It might also be desirable for producers and consumers to more regularly communicate about new media objects they share, as opposed to current practices, where authors often write for an unseen "General Reader." Indeed, Manovich points out that strict separation of producer and consumer is a view of communication typical of high literacy not supported by contemporary literary theory (119).[14]

Third, the form-content relationship is fundamentally altered if form is mutable and if it's possible to quickly alter the content associated with a form, or vice-versa. As Manovich puts it, "A number of different interfaces can be created from the same data" (37). Producers of new media will need to understand ways that "media databases" harness modularity and variability to create different sorts of texts, images, and other creative forms which haven't yet been invented. The pattern encouraged to make composition easy—selection of an established form optimized for the desired message—is not likely to be workable.

The concept of translucence could help answer these pedagogical needs by allowing the appearance of codes and the boundaries of objects—which I believe will be necessary in order to teach the production of new media. The largest difference, however, would be degree; unlike the dichotomies of literacy and ease, which enforce the belief that "it's transparent or it's not," translucence would allow variations in the foregrounded technological character of an object, system, or practice. From a pedagogical standpoint, this makes much more sense than all-or-nothing transparency. While students are learning the function of a new media object or creation tool, its borders and algorithms would be only as translucent as necessary. As learning proceeded, translucence could be increased, if so desired, or the visibility of encoding retained. In some ways, this strategy would be an update to the literate idea of "gradation;" a new media object or practice would be presented in its entirety, with the visibility of its encoding presented in whole or part for pedagogical purposes. Translucence is also better suited to acknowledgment of hybridity, which, as noted above, didn't fit well with the highly dichotomized perspective of literacy. The choice between transparent and opaque forbids the interaction of multiple objects or practices, whereas translucence would permit much more complex relationships—the programmability of new media Manovich proposes.

Confronting Expediency and Pragmatism: Iteration

The final practice I wish to propose confronts the pragmatism and expediency which often characterizes ease. Complementing translucence, which I see as a property to be cultivated in new media objects and technological systems under production, iteration is an approach to creating new media (the analogue to "writing process"). If, as Manovich argues, the fundamental difference between new and old media is that the former are "programmable," those who wish to produce new media might employ methods of programming, which is heavily reliant on loops of various kinds. In fact, many of the computer systems we imagine as the most sophisticated (IBM's chess-playing Deep Blue, weather simulators, and encryption-breaking tools) operate by repetitively performing the same tasks on slightly different sets of relevant data.

Manovich considers the loop extensively, in both programming and as a narrative device important in literature, in new media, and the moving pictures which preceded cinema (314–22). Repetition—simply performing a task over and over—and iteration—repeating the same task with slight differences each time—both harness the modularity and variability principles of new media, in conjunction with another property, automation, which shifts tasks from human control to computer-regulated processes. Iteration is more relevant for new media, since its production with variation more closely follows the post-industrial logic of customization than repetition's industrial logic of exact duplication.

Internet Invention suggests students use an iterative loop to construct the central project of a new media course. Students perform the same function (documentation) on a set of variables (the four areas of Ulmer's "Popcycle": Career, Family, Entertainment, and Community) in order to produce data (the central project, the "widesite") intended to support the production of the "image of wide scope" which is the ultimate goal.[15] I believe the method Ulmer has selected is not particular to the production of the wide image, but a reasonable method of invention suitable for any new media project. A pedagogy that actively sought to teach students how to displace repetitive tasks to computers which could perform them more quickly and effectively, and to use iteration as an process for both invention and analysis, would take the place of similar movements in ease (atomization, alliteration, and alphabetization, which shifted some decisions to Cartesian method or the form of the essay).

I don't mean to turn students into programmers, but rather, as Johnson argued, to disrupt two assumptions: (1) some people are programmers, and some people are not; (2) programming is an advanced form of computer usage exclusive to experts. The parallel to writing is obvious: some are writers, some aren't; literature is the advanced, elite form. I hope that as computers develop, what's considered "programming" will change. To continue thinking analogically, this has already occurred in document production. Everyday word processors allow writers to make decisions about page numbers, font selection, and other book encodings previously restricted to expert designers or printers. Similarly, as the programmable nature of new media becomes less esoteric, and more tools for programming are invented, methodologies which support programming should affect the formation of new practices of writing.

Writing process pedagogy offers a relay for bringing iteration into the classroom. However, the practice of iteration I envision differs from the step-by-step mode of research, prewriting, drafting, and revising essays because it does not necessarily shape the final artifact, but produces material and methodologies which support it. Whereas from the "drafting" stage forward, writers work on their final utterance in some form, iterative development often focuses developing procedures for computer-generated final products based on human-designed scripting, or systems for processing data and displaying incremental results. The programming language Perl began this way, and grew from a tool for processing text in certain situations to a widely used general-purpose language (Wall *et al.* 645–47). Iterative thinking and creating offer ways to leverage the processing power of computing and the characteristics of new media to construct the "different interfaces for the same data" Manovich envisions; in addition to "writing processes," the creators of new media can "process writing."

Iteration would also provoke student interest in the creation of technologies by offering direct contact with creative processes, and showing direct connections between technologies and human agents.

In this way, the simplistic view of technology typical of ease would be disrupted; it would be difficult for students to claim technologies they shaped were natural forces completely beyond their control. Once again, the change would follow process pedagogy's attempts to suggest students have control over their own writing and language.

I offer iteration and the other ideas for teaching presented here knowing that a lot more study is necessary to develop my work into a comprehensive pedagogy. Though my research is incomplete, I believe it shows the merit of considering the role of ease in composition and new media pedagogy. On the one hand, ease helped make widespread literacy possible. But on the other hand, ease shapes the understanding of technology in a manner which needs to be carefully considered by composition instructors teaching the production of new media.

Notes

1. In the preface to *User-Centered Technology,* Robert R. Johnson notes that review of the study of technology could continue for a very long time (xiii). Like Johnson, I believe that definition of "technology" varies widely, and I favor a user-centered perspective which highlights its constructed nature, ubiquity, and connection to human agency.

2. I realize the provocative nature of some of these claims. I am currently continuing my research with the long-term goal of creating a comprehensive history of ease which methodically demonstrates its importance. My dissertation *Ease in Composition Studies* includes extensive documentation of the connection between ease and writing, as well as a more detailed history of ease. For my latest work on ease, please visit my web site, <http://faculty.wiu.edu/CB-Dilger/>.

3. Like "technology," the term "new media" is somewhat problematic, as Paul Leonardi and others have noted: at one point, all media were new. I rely heavily on Lev Manovich's definition from *The Language of New Media,* recognizing the important cinematic heritage of new media, and evaluating the form based on his five "principles of new media" (27–48).

4. The concept of transparency has been discussed extensively, often in very conflicting ways. Sherry Turkle outlines some of the debate when comparing the Mac OS and MS-DOS interfaces (32–42), labeling the former "opaque" and "postmodernist" (23). Conversely, Manovich sees the Mac OS as transparent and modernist (63). In Turkle's framework, technology is hidden by opaque masks that conceal inner workings. I follow Marcel O'Gorman's definition, discussed in detail later in this essay, which sees transparency as concealing technology by making it invisible.

5. Holmes's frontmatter is unnumbered; I cite *The Art of Rhetoric Made Easy* as if its title page was numbered "i," the next page "ii," and so on.

6. Robert Connors suggests that what is meant by "current-traditional rhetoric" became undefined as it became the "whipping boy" of composition studies (4–7). While I hope to avoid a thoughtless attack here, I am not persuaded by Connors's attempt to rehabilitate the rhetoric and pedagogy which, as clearly demonstrated by primary and secondary sources, had sad consequences for nineteenth-century students.

7. For more on the extensive connections between ease and current-traditional rhetoric, from Watts and Holmes to the end of nineteenth century, see the fourth chapter of *Ease in Composition Studies*.

8.See *Ease in Composition Studies* 34–5 and 65–7.

9. Dvorak's attacks on the Macintosh are numerous; his gender-based criticism of the iBook in 1999 is especially heinous.

10. This framework relies on Winner's argument about the role of technology in Western culture, and is similar to the conclusions he makes in "Luddism as Epistemology" (325–9).

11. Norman considers helplessness extensively, considering both "learned" and "taught" varieties (*Psychology of Everyday Things* 41–3).

12. See Evan Watkins's discussion of repairing automobiles in *Throwaways*, 89–92).

13. Nielsen has recently softened this stance somewhat. However, generally speaking, his advice about Web design is much more prescriptive than his pioneering work on usability testing (e. g. *Usability Engineering*).

14. "Producer" and "consumer" are another terminological challenge, with "consumer" in particular having undesirable connotations of the mass-produced convenience products associated with ease.

15. This could be expressed in Perl pseudocode as: @Popcycle = qw(career family entertainment community); foreach (@Popcycle) { $Widesite .= &Document_area($_); }

Works Cited

Brooke, Collin G. "The Substance of <Style>: HTML Degree Zero." Unpublished ms. 2003.

Bush, Vannevar. "As We May Think." *The Atlantic Monthly* 176.1 (July 1945), 101–8.

Connors, Robert J. *Composition-Rhetoric: Backgrounds, Theory, and Pedagogy*. Pittsburgh Series in Composition, Literacy, and Culture. Pittsburgh: U of Pittsburgh P, 1997.

Coogan, Michael D., Marc Z. Brettler, Carol A. Newsom, and Pheme Perkins, eds. *The New Oxford Annotated NRSV Bible with the Apocryphal: Indexed*. London: Oxford UP, 2001.

Crowley, Sharon. *The Methodical Memory: Invention in Current-Traditional Rhetoric.* Carbondale: Southern Illinois UP, 1990.

Dilger, Bradley. *Ease in Composition Studies.* Diss. U of Florida, 2003 <http://faculty.wiu.edu/CB-Dilger/texts/ease-comp-studies.pdf>.

Duguid, Paul. "Material Matters: Aspects of the Past and Futurology of the Book." *The Future of the Book.* Geoffrey Nunberg, ed. Berkeley: U of California P, 1996: 63–102.

Dvorak, John C. "The iBook Disaster." *PC Magazine* July 26, 1999: 34+.

"Ease." *The Oxford English Dictionary.* 2nd ed, 1989.

"Easy." *The Oxford English Dictionary.* 2nd ed, 1989.

Frederick, Christine M. *Household Engineering: Scientific Management in the Home.* Chicago: American School of Home Economics, 1919. History of Women 7381. Woodbridge: Research Publications, 1976.

Harris, Trish. "Re: [techrhet] Blackboard or WebCT conversion to pay services?" Email to the author. September 15, 2002.

Holmes, John. *The Art of Rhetoric Made Easy: Or, the Elements of Oratory Briefly Stated, and Fitted for the Practice of the Studious Youth of Great-Britain and Ireland: in Two Books.* 2nd ed. London: Hitch & Hawes, 1755. *The Eighteenth Century,* reel 547, no. 25. Woodbridge: Research Publications, 1983.

Howell, Wilbur Samuel. *Eighteenth-Century British Logic and Rhetoric.* Princeton: Princeton UP, 1971.

Johnson, Robert R. *User-Centered Technology: a Rhetorical Theory for Computers and Other Mundane Artifacts.* Studies in Scientific and Technical Communication Series. Albany: SUNY P, 1998.

Keene, Michael L., and Katherine H. Adams. *Easy Access: The Reference Handbook for Writers.* 3rd ed. New York: McGraw-Hill, 2002.

Kitzhaber, Albert R. *Rhetoric in American Colleges, 1850–1900.* Dallas: Southern Methodist UP, 1990.

Lardner, James, David LaGesse, and Janet Rae-Dupree. "Overwhelmed by Tech." *U. S. News and World Report.* January 15, 2001: 34+.

Leonardi, Paul. "Problematizing 'New Media': Culturally Based Perceptions of Cell Phones, Computers, and the Internet among United States Latinos." *Critical Studies in Media Communication,* 20(2), 160–179.

Levy, Steven. *Insanely Great: the Life and Times of the Macintosh, the Computer that Changed Everything.* Penguin Books, 1994.

Locke, John. *Some Thoughts Concerning Education.* Harvard Classics 37. New York: P.F. Collier & Son, 1910.

Lunsford, Andrea. *Easy Writer: A Pocket Guide.* 2nd ed. Boston: Bedford/St. Martin's, 2002.

Manovich, Lev. *The Language of New Media.* Cambridge: MIT P, 2001.

Maxwell, Lee. Email to the author. August 21, 2002.

McLuhan, Marshall. *The Gutenberg Galaxy.* Toronto: U of Toronto P, 1967.

—. *Understanding Media: The Extensions of Man.* Cambridge; MIT Press, 1994.

Mitchell, W. J. T. *Picture Theory: Essays on Verbal and Visual Representation.* Chicago: U of Chicago P, 1994.

Nelson, Theodor H. "Xanalogical Structure, Needed Now More than Ever: Parallel Documents, Deep Links to Content, Deep Versioning, and Deep Re-Use ." *ACM Computing Surveys* 31.4es (December 1999), No. 33.

"Newest Electronics Short on Simplicity." *CNN.com.* January 30, 2004. March 1, 2004. <http://www.cnn.com/2004/TECH/ptech/01/30/unfriendlier.electronics.ap/>

Nielsen, Jakob. *Designing Web Usability: The Practice of Simplicity.* Indianapolis: New Riders, 2001.

—. "How Users Read on the Web: Alertbox, October 1, 1997." March 1, 2004. <http://www.useit.com/alertbox/9710a.html>.

—. "When Bad Design Elements Become the Standard: Alertbox, November 14, 1999." March 1, 2004. <http://www.useit.com/alertbox/991114.html>.

Norman, Donald. *The Invisible Computer: Why Good Products Can Fail, the Personal Computer is so Complex, and Information Appliances are the Solution.* Cambridge: MIT P, 1998.

—. *The Psychology of Everyday Things.* New York: Basic Books, 1986.

O'Gorman, Marcel. "You Can't Always Get What You Want." *Ctheory,* December 6, 2000. March 1, 2004. <http://www.ctheory.net/text_file.asp?pick=227>.

Ong, Walter. *Orality and Literacy: The Technologizing of the Word.* London: Routledge, 1982.

Parker, Ian. "Absolute PowerPoint: Can a Software Package Edit Our Thoughts?" *New Yorker,* May 28, 2001, 76+.

Schultz, Lucille M. *The Young Composers: Composition's Beginnings in Nineteenth-Century Schools. Studies in Writing and Rhetoric.* Carbondale: Southern Illinois UP, 1999.

Selfe, Cynthia. *Technology and Literacy in the Twenty-First Century: The Importance of Paying Attention.* Studies in Writing and Rhetoric. Carbondale: Southern Illinois UP, 1999.

Sprat, Thomas. *History of the Royal Society.* Washington University Studies Series 3, no. 7. St. Louis: Washington UP, 1958.

Strasser, Susan. *Waste and Want: A Social History of Trash.* New York: Owl Books, 1999.

Strunk, William Jr., and E. B. White. *The Elements of Style.* 3rd ed. New York: MacMillan Publishing, 1979.

Thomas, Francis-Noël, and Mark Turner. *Clear and Simple as the Truth: Writing Classic Prose.* Princeton: Princeton UP, 1996.

Thoreau, Henry D. Letter to Harrison Blake, Nov 16, 1857. *The Writings of Henry David Thoreau.* Ed. F. B. Sanborn. Vol. 6. Boston: Houghton Mifflin & Company, 1906. 320.

Tufte, Edward. *The Visual Display of Quantitative Information.* 2nd ed. Cheshire: Graphics Press, 2001.

Turkle, Sherry. *Life on the Screen: Identity in the Age of the Internet.* New York: Simon & Schuster, 1995.

Ulmer, Gregory L. *Heuretics: The Logic of Invention.* New York: Longman, 2003.

—. *Internet Invention: From Literacy to Electracy.* New York: Longman, 2003.

Veblen, Thorstein. *The Theory of the Leisure Class: An Economic Study of Institutions.* New York: Macmillan, 1902.

Wall, Larry, Tom Christiansen, and Jon Orwant. *Programming Perl.* 3rd ed. Sebastopol: O'Reilly & Associates, 2000.

Watkins, Evan. *Throwaways: Work Culture and Consumer Education.* Stanford: Stanford UP, 1993.

Watts, Isaac. *Logick: or, the Use of Right Reason in the Inquiry after Truth.* 2nd ed. London: Clarke, Hett, Mathews, & Ford, 1726. The Eighteenth Century, reel 2107, no. 4. Woodbridge: Research Publications, Inc, 1986.

Williams, Joseph. *Style: Ten Lessons in Clarity and Grace.* 7th ed. New York: Longman, 2003.

Winner, Langdon. *Autonomous Technology: Technics-out-of-Control as a Theme in Political Thought.* Cambridge: MIT P, 1977.

Wysocki, Anne Frances, and Johndan Johnson-Eilola. "Blinded by the Letter: " *Passions,*

Pedagogies, and Twenty-First Century Technologies. Ed. Gail E. Hawisher and Cynthia L. Selfe. Logan: Utah State UP, 1999.

Part 3

Research: Media Performance in Media Studies

6 Elvis (The Florida School Remix)

Michael Jarrett

Since Manny, my real barber, died of a heart attack, I have gotten my hair cut at Barberama. A year ago, after marking a stack of papers, I drove to the shop to get a trim. No appointment necessary: Walk in, have a seat, wait for an open slot, and take your chances with any one of nine "stylists." But who am I kidding? There's no chance taken. No risk involved. Given the "material conditions" that govern my middle-age scalp, anyone competent on a weed whacker could cut my hair. This story's complicating action has nothing to do with barbering.

I was sitting in her chair, my haircut halfway finished, when my barber-for-the-day called attention to the easy-listening radio station that provides Barberama with an innocuous soundtrack. "Listen to that," she said to no one in particular. "Can you believe it? 'Stairway to Heaven.'"

"Pretty funny," I said, though I wondered whether this was the first time my barber had noticed a rock song strung up and hanged—as wallpaper.

Before I could draw a breath and comment further, the keeper of music and owner of the shop sneered, "What's that?" He walked two booths over to where my barber was working. "What do you mean, 'Stairway to Heaven'?"

"It's Led Zeppelin," said my barber. "You know, 'Stairway to Heaven'?"

"Nope. I don't know what you're talking about."

His response galled me. The guy was, max, twelve years older than me. My barber, on the other hand, wasn't a day over twenty-five. "Come on," I said to the shop owner, whose ignorance I found disingenuous—utterly feigned and fabricated. "Did you spend the last thirty-five years under a rock? I guess you've never heard of Elvis Presley, either."

"Of course I've heard of Elvis. I saw him on *Ed Sullivan.* But I'll tell you something most people don't realize. Elvis wasn't any good. I mean, as a singer, he was nothing special. And he admitted it! He said that Roy Orbison was better."

"Well, let me tell you something," I said in haste, fumbling toward some route that led out of an argument I imagined flaring up and dying down in that exact spot since 1956. "I'll bet you didn't build up this business by insulting your customers or their religions. So please, sir"—and I have to admit that, maybe, I didn't actually say "sir"—"I'd appreciate it if you don't say anything more about Elvis." I managed a weak laugh.

The shop owner shook his head and walked back to his booth. As for my barber, she didn't say anything I can remember, and the next time I stopped in to get a haircut, she was gone. I haven't seen her since. Barberama has a pretty fast turnover, especially among its younger employees.

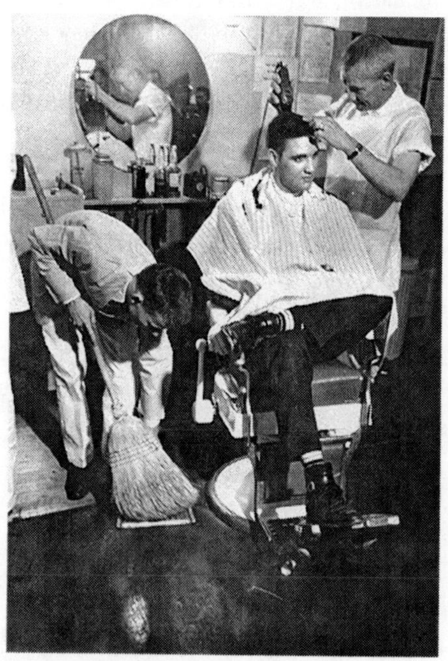

Elvis gets clipped. *This is Elvis*, Warner Bros, © 1981

I

In my teaching I try to take advantage of the free association method in order to set aside critique.

—Gregory L. Ulmer, *Seulemonde Conversation*

[I]n a world in which we are entertained from cradle to grave whether we like it or not, the ability to rework image and dialogue, light and sound, may be the key to psychic and political health.

—Colin MacCabe
Godard: A Portrait of the Artist at Seventy

But I can guarantee you one thing: we will never again agree on anything as we agreed on Elvis.

—Lester Bangs
"Where Were You When Elvis Died?"

I am tempted to justify the telling of my haircut anecdote by pressing it into service as an allegory about education in new media. Barberama is the classroom. I play the role of teacher—the protector of truth and tradition. The shop owner plays a student. My initial reading goes something like this: Confronted by a student so ill-acquainted with academic culture that he mistakes judgment for analysis, audacity for authority, and yesterday's battleground for today's *avant-garde,* the teacher is flummoxed. He falls back on received truths and squelches dissent. "Some matters—pillars of faith—are not to be questioned." But that is overstated. The teacher is not doctrinaire. He is no self-appointed protector of canonical precepts. He is jaded or flummoxed. All significant battles have been fought and won; there is little gained by staging reenactments. The teacher expresses his weariness with irony and a chuckle. Or at least that is one reading of the scene. There are lots more plausible interpretations. For example, I could occupy the position of student. Let the shop owner play teacher. But what about my barber? I am troubled that she is relegated to the sidelines. What is her role? Her presence at the margins of the story genders the conflict that excludes her. That is certainly a lesson worth pursuing.

For my purposes, however, I have to ask, why interpret? Why render the text as allegory? As much as possible in the pages that follow, I intend to deemphasize hermeneutics, the path of interpretation—but not because my anecdote collapses under careful scrutiny. Its quality may not rival the shorter works of Shakespeare, Proust, or Dave Barry, but the anecdote is sufficiently "literary" to bear any type of interpretive operation. And it is "literary" because it is built of ordinary language. All texts work this way. No, I am deemphasizing allegories of reading for other reasons. I wrote the anecdote not to set up an exercise in interpretation, but to set in motion an experiment with invention. Confronted with a text, we have two basic options: read or write. Barthes made this point in *S/Z* when he pushed reading (consumption) so far and so hard that it became writing (production). Textual production informed by theory is my goal—not the creation of better consumers (though better readers might be a happy effect of educating better writers). Robert Scholes calls this emphasis on invention over interpretation "textual power." Students capable of exercising it not only understand literature (as traditionally construed) and texts of all sorts—oral, print, and electronic. They are able to emulate texts, to reproduce their motions (133). To equip students to attain "textual power," Scholes recommends a methodology "organized around a canon of concepts, precepts, and practices rather than a canon of texts" (120). The particular methods that I and others have labeled Florida School theory—because they were developed by the University of Florida's Gregory Ulmer (*Teletheory* and *Heuretics*), Robert Ray (*The Avant-Garde Finds Andy Hardy*), and contributors to this book—represent an especially viable and transferable application of textuality (Jarrett 188). At its most ambitious, Florida School theory seeks to push textual experimentation until it yields new ways of thinking and writing, ways especially suited to electronic culture.

Heuretics instead of hermeneutics, Ulmer would say. So let me briefly explain. "Heuretics" developed as a theological term in the Middle Ages. It was the inverse operation of "hermeneutics." One could interpret scripture: strain it through a hermeneutic grid; subject it to literal, allegorical, moral, and anagogical readings. The result was truth encoded as doctrine or lessons. One could also use scripture as a means of invention: employ it heuretically (Ulmer 15). Interpretive communities might respond in a couple of ways. They could embrace the invention (Eureka! we've been illuminated), or they could reject it (accuse the inventor of heresy). Sometimes approve and, then, reject (think Joan of Arc). Hermeneutics produced "readings" that seemed to emanate from scripture, readings that seemed discovered. They were verifications of truth. The interpreter found what had been placed in the text by its (ultimate) author. He did not impose meaning, bring it to the text. Meaning arose. It was resurrected. Or at least these were effects of hermeneutics. Heuretics, on the other hand, was failed hermeneutics, interpretation become opaque, its operations visible. Heuretics employed scripture generatively, to manufacture meaning. Or rather, it produced readings that seemed more created or fashioned than recovered. It used scripture as a means to invention. Whenever interpretation was received as invention, hermeneutics had become heuretics.

I started this essay with an anecdote, then, to announce Florida School leanings: an interest in new methods that foster heuretics over hermeneutics. First, as an alternative to interpretation and critique (to *writing about*), my anecdote stands as a reminder: One can always work obliquely, respond to a text by making another text. As John Cage famously demonstrated in *Silence,* anecdotes can effectively stage a deconstruction of critical and creative writing. Instead of verifying what is already known, they function as myths that evoke alternative explanations or theories. Second, my anecdote stages the scene—the diegesis—in which new methods must now function. Any useful textual practice must come to terms with—it must, ultimately, *write with*—new media: photography, radio, audio recording, film, television, and digital composition. Textuality is no longer thinkable within a "purely literary" context. Or better, keep in mind what we must know by now. Elvis is a text; he is new media. (Can we know him otherwise?) He is constituted by a convergence of discourses. Third, my anecdote signals a desire for new types of writing motivated by interest or "amateur" knowledge. I want to spend my time learning and writing about topics that arrest me. I cringe to recall advice I have given students: "Have you thought that, maybe, you might like this movie too much to write effectively about it?" Or worse, "I'll bet you could write more analytically if you chose a book you liked less." Better I should assign students a much more difficult task: invent a new kind of theoretical writing that emerges from your love for an "object of study" (an "object" that addresses, authors, or interpellates you as the "subject" of knowledge).

If Florida School theory is valid, presenting new methods for new media, shouldn't it be able to prove itself by engaging the figure Elvis Presley? Which is to say, shouldn't it engage those discourses that converge to construct the sonic and visual image—the electronic figure—we call Elvis? My answer is, of course, "Yes." But my reason might not be obvious. Elvis is not essential to study because he looms large in a rapidly forming canon of texts: something like, "Elvis is an ideal test case for what Ulmer calls 'electracy.' Media-studies scholars ought to understand him just as psychoanalysts understood Oedipus and New critics understood Keats." Certainly, new methods organized around canons of texts expanded to include electronic media—methods favored by more and more English departments as they transform into cultural studies departments—must now attend to Elvis. Elvis matters. Methods built for the literary canon, as a rule, continue to compel the study of major figures and works (and so-called "minority literatures" excluded by major figures and works). But Florida School theory does not engage Elvis because of his iconic place in an emerging canon, or because the validity of its methods depends on comprehending a major figure of electronic culture. Instead of an ever-expanding and an increasingly unmanageable canon of texts, Florida School theory works toward the creation an emerging canon of method. It has to—it simply must—address Elvis. Why? Any new method should want to make something of Elvis. He has much to teach us about invention, about writing within electronic culture.

Back at the time of that haircut, probably because of that haircut, I got the notion to use Elvis heuretically. More daringly, I wanted to make something of Elvis movies, to let them teach lessons in film studies. I was working with a small group of students in a second-semester film course (none was a communication major). I was confident that they possessed a basic understanding of Hollywood's formal and thematic paradigms. And I was weary, sick to death, of reading their papers. Moreover, I knew exactly what the problem was: a gap between ideas and discourse. Students had plenty of insights into film, as they routinely demonstrated during class conversations. But a lack of fluency in analytical languages led to student writing that was frequently clumsy and inarticulate. There was a wide gap between thought and expression. However clever my assignments might have been, they inevitably required students to explain films. In effect they put students in the role of teacher; me in the role of student. ("What can you folks show me?") But what might students learn, I wondered, if they got a new teacher? What if they allowed Elvis—his movies—to be their teacher? What if I called upon students to invent instead of verifying what was already known? That is when Florida School Elvis entered my classroom at Penn State University.

2

Fame is a form of incomprehension, perhaps the worst.

—Jorge Luis Borges,
"Pierre Menard, Author of the *Quixote*"

On record, Elvis Presley was audacious; on stage, magnetic; and on television, charismatic. He was a risk, however, for only a few months (and risky for a little while longer). After that, he was bankable—bankable beyond the wildest imaginings of most sane people and, perhaps, bankable forever. As the surest of sure bets ever placed by Hollywood, Presley prompted a fiscally conservative industry to adopt the most risk-aversive approach to filmmaking ever undertaken. With Elvis movies one rule obtained; it was overseen and enforced by Colonel Tom Parker: Don't fool around and lose what you already have. For example, there was no need to find an audience for Elvis pictures. Presley had already summoned one, and he delivered it to Hollywood's doorstep. And acting was not necessary, either. It was totally optional. Presley needed only to be seen on screen as "Elvis." That was mandated. Seeing "Elvis acting" was gravy. Presley's roles—and, especially, the really bad ones—had the effect of assuring moviegoers that the real Elvis, a "presence" (in Derrida's sense of the word), resided behind the roles, and that they had been granted privileged access to him. He hadn't yet left the building. Lester Bangs wrote: "Elvis never even had to move a muscle, not even in his face—he always, from day one up till almost the very end, had that *glow*" (326).

Elvis works the studio. *Jailhouse Rock*, Warner Bros./Turner Entertainment, 1957.

The moviemaker's challenge was how not to lose what casting Presley in a role thoroughly guaranteed. Production meant minimizing risk.

> The basic problem with Presley's films was clear from the start: with their semi-serious, linearly developed plots, highly choreographed dance numbers, and stylized backgrounds, they represented updated versions of the old-fashioned Hollywood musical whose form had evolved around exactly that kind of Tin Pan Alley song against which Presley's rock and roll was in revolt. (Ray 1885:164)

Thus, Hollywood reversed the route Presley had taken to fame, the route summarized in a precept fit for the bathroom wall at Sun Studios or as an "oblique strategy" or a rock anthem: "When you've got nothin,' you've got nothin' to lose."

The "old-fashioned Hollywood musical" that Presley updated thirty-one times represents a vaudeville-derived pattern that Paramount perfected for the screen in the 1930s and 1940s. Gerald Mast describes it as "a cross between the wacky nonsense of silent comedy, the verbal jokes of sound comedy, and the singing of musical comedy" (224). "Paramount comedy-musicals were as cheap, trashy, and silly as movies could get" (225). Fault Hollywood for path dependency in charting Presley's career, but also consider two significant points. First, there are fewer years between the advent of sound cinema and Presley's first movie than between his final movie and the present. Second, as Mast observes, "Paramount musicals were the swingiest of the Swing Era," made "not for the genteel adult market but for the snappy youth market," and "Bing Crosby was the sun of Paramount's musical solar system" (225, 223). It is hardly surprising that Paramount saw Elvis—whose musical success began in Sun Studios—as a possible successor to Crosby. "[I]n Paramount musicals," writes Mast, "the music itself was parenthetical to what were personality pictures with music." "Film stars," notes Ray, "have always been less actors than personalities" (2001:104).

Hollywood has generally "saved its biggest rewards for men and women who, by theatrical standards, didn't much act at all" (Ray 2001:103). During the studio era, this phenomenon meant that the job of casting actors in roles, indeed the entire task of producing movies, often resembled the surrealist game Exquisite Corpse (Ray 1995:53). (Want an Elvis version of this game? After reading the second draft of *Spinout,* Colonel Parker said, "This is great. Just one thing. Put a dog in it" [Simpson 305].) Or as Mast describes moviemaking with Crosby, "Casting a musical meant playing Bingo. Paramount spun the talent bin and the first four names to fall out went on the Bingle card. Crosby made sense with anything and everything Paramount put around him" (223). "If Goldwyn recycled Eddie Cantor as Danny Kaye, Paramount recycled Crosby as Elvis Presley. Elvis, like Bing, was a singer who slid (or writhed, wriggled, and rocked) through life" (225). *Blue Hawaii, Harum Scarum, Girl Happy, Clambake* and *Double Trouble* bear more than a passing resemblance to Crosby vehicles such as *Road to Singapore, Rhythm on the Range, Sing You Sinners* and *Waikiki Wedding* (in which Crosby croons "Blue Hawaii"). "Who is that fast-talking hillbilly son of a bitch that nobody can understand?" Presley cynically joked, in syntax that scans like a parody of "Shaft"'s opening line ("Who's the black private dick that's a sex machine to all the chicks"). "One day he's singing to a dog, then to a car, then to a cow. They are all the same damn movie with that Southerner just singing to something different" (Simpson 307). In this movie, a master narrative if there ever was one,

> Presley had to have a manly occupation (he was a racing driver three times, a boxer, a rodeo rider, a soldier and an ex-frogman) or be a professional singer. His inevitable buddy could either be as dodgy as Elvis was basically good, or straight if Presley was a lovable wild boy. Where possible, cute children should

> be on display; but to balance things, Elvis should get into a fight, in which he was invariably the innocent party. Thanks probably to Parker, carnivals, shows and fairgrounds were never far away. And, for reasons that remain unclear, Elvis should go to jail, be put on trial, or at least be harried by a tax inspector, before finally managing to get his car, or perhaps his speedboat, ready to win the race. It would be nice if he could also find the time to sing on the back of a truck. (305–306)

No wonder film studies—oriented toward interpretation and critique—has not figured out what to do with Presley's cinematic *oeuvre:* multiple remakes of remakes.

What sort of film might have accommodated Presley's sizable, but utterly misdirected, gifts? In his essay, "The Riddle of Elvis-the-Actor," Robert Ray answers: "[Elvis] would have perfectly suited Godard's approach to filmmaking." Presley was certainly no method actor, though he is too frequently cast as a failed one. That approach to acting may have been all the rage when Presley went to Hollywood in the mid-50s. And Presley may have been exceptionally forthright about his admiration for James Dean and other students of Lee Strasberg's Actor's Studio, where the Method was taught. But it is extremely important to note that Presley studied actors—not approaches to acting. If we are looking for an equivalent to Elvis-as-actor, we should turn to Godard's *Breathless* and "the moment . . . when Michel Poiccard, confronting Bogart's face on a movie poster, does his own version of Bogart's gestures. As a character, Michel results from his imitation of Bogart, his desire for a life like those in American film noirs." Instead of deriving performance from "some preexisting inner self" (as recommended by the Method), Godard has his actor, Jean-Paul Belmondo, treat Michel's self as an effect of performance (107).

Reflecting on his and the French New Wave's place in history, Godard writes: "A young author writing today knows that Molière and Shakespeare exist. We were the first directors to know that Griffith exists" (1986:172). At the "exact moment," the middle of the century, the moment of the French New Wave, cinema was old enough to have a history, and it was young enough to have a history "that could still be recounted." You inherited "a history that was already rich and complicated, and turbulent," says Godard in *Histoire(s) du Cinéma.* And you had "taken enough time to see enough films as a cinephile and then as a critic to have acquired a personal view of what was important or less important in that history" (29). Of course, Elvis's film-going experience could not match Godard's. Memphis boasted no theater comparable to the *Cinémathèque Française.* But Elvis loved movies. However unschooled (formally), he was both cinephile and critic. His approach to acting bears an uncanny resemblance to Godard's. It was decidedly less reliant on affective memory than on cinematic recollection. Elvis, like Godard in the middle of the century, understood (intuited, perhaps) that cinema had a history, and that performance could be derived from it. In place of the autonomous self posited by the Method, cinephilia positioned another corpus: cinema. It offered a databank or thesaurus of artificial memories from which one could recollect. It was from this trove that Elvis derived his performances. Instead of a naturalistic approach to acting, he advanced an alternative. Elvis displayed codes that signified "role playing." Was he conscious of, or analytical about, this approach? That is unlikely and irrelevant. He employed it.

Matthau studies Presley's acting style (*King Creole,* Paramount, 1958.)

"He was very intelligent," said Walter Matthau, who worked with Elvis on *King Creole.* "Also, he was intelligent enough to understand what a character was and how to play the character simply by being himself through the means of the story" (Guarlnick 451). Matthau does not emphasize, however, that Elvis never enjoyed the luxury of *being himself.* With Elvis that phrase—it's so Hegelian—becomes meaningless. Why? It is thinkable only within a paradigm (logocentrism) that excludes the conditions of Elvis's own success: conditions we might call grammatological because they depend on conceptualizing cinema as an apparatus for composing selves, not for self-expression. Elvis created characters not by "being himself," but by drawing upon cinema. Moreover, Elvis's first task as an actor—and it was the same with every role—was to recollect Elvis. ("How could the Method help him prepare for that role?" asked my friend David Russell.) He had to play Elvis before going on to play any subsequent part. And playing Elvis (or, rather, Elvis playing Elvis playing, say, a cowboy or a carnival hand) created a self named Elvis. In other words, within the paradigm of grammatology selves emerge as a consequence of performance. You can't be yourself. You play yourself. It's complicated. But it is why Elvis was brought to Hollywood. Bass player Norbert Putnam recalls:

> "It was kind of camp in a way but he was just being this creature that he created called Elvis Presley. He could turn that on and off in an instant. I remember once, he and I were having a sandwich, one of the few times I was one-on-one with him, and he said to me, 'Put, what time is it?' I told him it was about 1am and he tapped me and said, 'Put, it's time for me to go and be Elvis Presley.' And then he walked across the studio, picked up the mike and his voice changed and he became Elvis Presley." (qtd. in Simpson 90–91)

"[T]hink of a lost Godard film," writes Ray, "a sequel perhaps to *Masculine-Feminine,* with Elvis in—what else?—the hero's role" (2001:107).

3

> *Writing was already a way of making films, for the difference between writing and directing is quantitative not qualitative.*
>
> —Jean-Luc Godard, *Godard on Godard*

> *One day the experiment goes very nicely, and another day it doesn't.*
>
> —Jean-Luc Godard,
> *Les Lettres Françaises* (qtd. in MacCabe)

Elvis, I have discovered, is a big, knotty problem. He is a particularly productive means of thinking and writing about new media. In fact, Elvis is one name for new media. How could I enable college students to learn him? To engage and answer that question, I transformed Robert Ray's provocation into an assignment. I issued the following charge to a group of students: Think of Elvis Presley in a lost Godard movie. Create a scene—a script and a detailed list of shots—from this hybrid movie. Your scene should combine Hollywood conventions with *auteurist* tactics.

The brief I wrote for students fleshed out this charge, gave it some context, and evoked a few models: Revolutionary Russian filmmakers often used found footage in cobbling together new movies. And Francis Ford Coppola—to use a term favored by Jamaican DJs—has "versioned" *The Godfather* several times. *Blade Runner* received similar treatment from Ridley Scott. Arguably, there isn't an "original film" subsequently remixed—but only versions of *Blade Runner.* Walter Murch reedited *Touch of Evil* to yield a film more in keeping with Orson Welles' stated intentions. Downloading and desk-top digital editing enabled amateurs to reedit *Star Wars: Episode 1—The Phantom Menace,* reportedly making it watchable. Imagine, then, what one could accomplish with all the raw material available that features Presley? What if every film—thirty-one versions of what amounts to "the same damn movie"—and every TV show starring Presley were available, right now, on the hard drive of your computer, just begging to be remixed? Out of this ash can of memory, picture a phoenix rising: "a sequel perhaps to *Masculine-Feminine,* with Elvis in—what else?—the hero's role." Instead of writing an interpretation or a critique of a Presley movie—i.e., following a predictable path that would lead to the verification of what we already know about Presley, ideology, and film theory—describe the movie that Godard would have made if he had only taken the chance. A brief synopsis is all that is needed. Tell what happens in each act. Then, in detail describe one scene from this movie: provide script and storyboard. Your vocabulary, therefore, is a given. It is set. Nothing is to be shot. You should use found footage—video and audio—that features Elvis, but you may also appropriate material from other films, any movie you want. Invention, therefore, equals arrangement. Making the scene will prompt learning.

Although my class watched several New Wave films (*Breathless* and *A Hard Day's Night;* parts of *Masculine-Feminine, A Woman Is a*

Woman, and *Shoot the Piano Player*) and only one Elvis movie (*Viva Las Vegas*), students constructed scenes that invariably replicated Paramount's vaudeville-derived template for musicals. Nothing hinted at a lost Godard film starring Elvis Presley. Students submitted reiterations of the Elvis formula instead of remixed scenes from an alternative type of film. Of *Breathless,* Godard had declared, "What I wanted was to take a conventional story and remake, but differently, everything the cinema had done. I also wanted to give the feeling that the techniques of film-making had just been discovered or experienced for the first time" (1986:173). Students remade conventional stories—but not differently. What had gone wrong with my assignment? What was the problem? I kept getting flashes, intimations, of two terrific movies. One involved a plot that implicated Elvis in accusations of forgery. How it would resolve I was not sure, but the movie resonated with incidents and themes from Presley's life: Vernon Presley's jail time for check forgery, Ira Louvin calling Elvis a "fuckin' white nigger" (a rock-and-roll version of Philip Roth's *The Human Stain?*), and mob-associated goons conning Elvis out of $950,000 (Simpson 83, 64). My working title? *Passing Checks.* My second movie would advance without much of a plot: very *nouvelle vague.* In it a parade of actresses talks to Elvis on the telephone. Mostly, we see the actresses, and we hear Elvis talking. Every one in awhile, there is a reverse shot. Elvis says, "Baby, I gotta go on stage" or "Hold on while I take care of business" or something to that effect (audio, I figured, that must be readily available). Then, there is a cutaway shot to an appropriated performance. The movie is a musical, even more rambling and minimalist than Godard's *A Woman Is a Woman,* but with much better tunes. And the telephone call, the spark that ignites so many plots, would take us almost nowhere.

Run Lola Run, Sony Pictures Classics, © 1999.

Jailhouse Rock, Warner Bros./Turner Entertainment, © 1957.

Day for Night, Warner Bros./Les Films du Carrosse S.A., © 1973/2001.

Jailhouse Rock, Warner Bros./Turner Entertainment, © 1957.

Touch of Evil, Universal, © 1958/2000.

In the end, I realized that the two films I had imagined might qualify as possible sequels to *Masculine-Feminine*—but only in my mind. Rendered on paper, scenes from these films looked suspiciously like the work my students had submitted. Call it rationalization, but I concluded that nothing had gone wrong with my assignment, so long as I recognized and accepted that the scene I had called for simply could not be made. It was impossible—at least with footage taken from Elvis movies. There was, however, no doubt that scenes could be imagined. My students and I demonstrated that. Further, the charge to imagine and assemble the scene called upon students to exercise—to employ in a hands-on way—a range of basic knowledge about film that conventional testing methods routinely assess but can hardly teach. Still, a little foresight on my part would have been nice. I should have required students to explain why the scenes they created fell so far short of what the models pictured. Why did these scenes—mine and theirs—resist translation into the language of the New Wave? Answering that question would have elicited rudimentary film theory. It would have demanded that students report what invention had taught them. For example, the phone-tag sequence looks pretty good on paper, but the rapid-fire dialogue and the shot-reverse figures that structure the movies from which these images were captured provide almost no raw material for building anything new. Found footage—and certainly found footage from Elvis movies—provides no wiggle room for working differently. Any New Wave Elvis picture, any might-have-been movie, was long ago cut out and left lying on an editing-room floor (to be swept up like clipped hairs under a barbershop chair). The movies my students and I imagined exist, all right, but only as traces in the cracks of the Elvis films we have seen. Look very closely at *King Creole,* and you might see the ghost of another picture, "a sequel perhaps to *Masculine-Feminine,* with Elvis in—what else?—the hero's role." The problem is how to access this elusive movie.

4

The worst films I've ever seen, the ones that send me to sleep, contain ten or fifteen marvelous minutes. The best films I've ever seen only contain ten or fifteen valid minutes.

—Man Ray, qtd. in Robert Ray, "Invention Finds a Method: Surrealist Research and Games"

I made G.I. Blues, lemme see, what else did I do, Blue Hawaii, Viva Las Vegas, and, uh, Girls, Girls, Girls, and a little eight-millimeter black-and-white underground film that hasn't come out yet.

—Elvis Presley, qtd. in Greil Marcus, "Elvis Again,"

And then, as fate would have it, I was nearly knocked off my feet by an astounding discovery. Into my hands fell undeniable evidence—barely sketchy, hardly tenuous, and, therefore, wholly convincing—that the film I was trying to imagine actually existed—albeit unfinished. What was once a whisper materialized into something more than tangible. Jean-Luc Godard had authored a sequel to *Masculine-Feminine,* with Elvis in—what else?—the hero's role. In his much lauded two-volume biography of Presley, *Last Train to Memphis* and *Careless Love,* Peter Guralnick never once mentions Godard. For his part, Colin MacCabe, in *Godard,* mentions Presley in passing but only as a historical referent. No relationship between French film director and rock and roller is documented. Such a lack of evidence could not be more telling.

I want to turn now to this subterranean work for it is, perhaps, the most significant of Godard and Elvis—if not of our time. The film in question consists of portions of two scenes, several discrete shots, and an odd frame here and there (autonomous images, really, what the *Cahiers* crew called "the *mise-en-scène*")—all from *King Creole.* Admittedly, in terms of quantity it is not much. Moreover, I am well aware that my claim may seem patently absurd: Godard, through great effort, made fragments of an already made movie. To justify this "absurdity," however, is the primordial object of this note. Indeed, it has become the chief aim of my career.

It appears that soon after releasing *Masculine-Feminine* in 1966, but definitely before he filmed *One Plus One (Sympathy for the Devil)* with the Rolling Stones (released in 1968), Godard turned his attention almost obsessively to *King Creole.* Elvis's fourth movie, *King Creole* had been originally directed by a 69-year-old veteran filmmaker, Michael Curtiz, for Paramount. It was released in 1958. That year is, of course, a milestone in cinema. It falls on the eve of the New Wave's *annus mirabilis* and Godard's directorial debut, *Breathless.* And so we are immediately confronted by an enigma, a research problem of monumental proportions. Why might Godard—in 1966, the very emblem of *la politique des auteurs*—direct his gaze to *King Creole,* late work of a director that, perhaps, best epitomizes the Hollywood Studio System at its most typical? Was it because Curtiz had directed *Casablanca* in 1942 and also *Mildred Pierce* and *Young Man with a Horn?* No, says the evidence—what little there is of it. Godard's choice of director and movie appears, at first blush, counterintuitive. It is, in fact, highly logical. Curtiz and *King Creole* had been absolutely unnecessary to Godard's development (Godard was very open about his influences). Thus, the filmmaker could premeditate making the film without "falling into a tautology." Even more puzzling, why did Godard not want to direct another *King Creole*—that is, remake the original as a New Wave film—but, rather, to make *King Creole* itself? Needless to say, Godard sought not to copy the film; he intended to shoot a movie perfectly congruent—that coincided frame for frame—with *King Creole.* Distinctions between original and copy would vanish. Godard's *King Creole* would reconstruct literally Curtiz's *King Creole.* Bizarre and audacious, this project stands as a full realization of Godard's goal "to do research in the form of a spectacle" (1986:181). Perhaps it was merely the next step in a story that began with petty theft (jail time in 1952) and moved on to brazen appropriations and remakes. Reportedly, while on the set, Godard said: "My intent is no more than astonishing" (Borges 39).

Not surprisingly, the first strategy that Godard conceived, as he set about making *King Creole,* was to cast himself as—to become—the express image of a Hollywood director. With ordinary directors such a transformation might prove exceedingly challenging; it might even call for a version of method acting. Godard discarded this strategy as entirely too easy. More like impossible, skeptics will say. Granted, the project was always impossible, but of all the ways to stage the impossible, Godard found this one the least interesting. Instead, he purposed to go on being Jean-Luc Godard and reach *King Creole* through his own experience as a filmmaker.

Forgetfulness and indifference had reduced Godard's recollection of *King Creole* to a nebulous pool of images, to the status of a film not yet produced. Back in 1958, had Godard actually viewed the film in part or whole? It did not matter. Under no circumstances would he view it in the mid-'60s. And thus, his task was far more daunting than Curtiz's had ever been. It was governed by "two polar laws": the first licensed a wide variety of formal and thematic experimentation; the second limited experimentation to absolute fealty to the "original" film. From this dialectic had to emerge a practice that unfailingly yielded a film—if only in bits and pieces—already made.

The rest is, as they say, history. Godard's fragmentary *King Creole* turns out to be substantially more nuanced than Curtiz's completed film. And it is a revelation to compare Godard's Elvis with Curtiz's. It is hard to believe they are one and the same actor. Curtiz, for example, offers the following shot:

Curtiz shoots Elvis. *King Creole*, Paramount © 1958.

Three or four minutes into *King Creole,* Curtiz delivers an establishing shot that plants Elvis's feet firmly in the French Quarter of New Orleans. But ultimately, it is nothing more than a tease. The shot constructs a *mise-en-scène* so alluring that it almost stalls the movie, bringing the barely begun story to a halt. Curtiz will use the remainder of the film to dispel its magic. Indeed, we are given this tantalizing glimpse of a possible filmic world so that it can be replaced by a Hollywood youth-rebellion noir musical (that gets "real gone for a change"). Godard, on the other hand, provides the following:

Godard shoots Elvis] (***King Creole,*** Paramount© 1958.

Exactly the same image as above? *Au contraire.* While it is unmistakably the work of Godard, we cannot claim that it was "authored" by him in any conventional sense of that term. Therein lies the brilliance of the shot, visible here even in its representation as a frame. The shot manifests a vision adamantly—laboriously—not unique. Remarkably, it critiques *la politique des auteurs.* It is vintage Godard, documenting the truth of cinema. And it documents Elvis, convincingly playing a younger Elvis. It announces Presley's comeback (in particular, prefiguring the bordello sequence cut from the 1968 television special), and by laying bare a cinematic means of production, it models a revolutionary gesture (foreshadowing events of May 1968). With an image that recalls photographs by Henri Cartier-Bresson (snapshots that capture "decisive moments"), Godard—the director as a "visionary, well-educated, sensitive elect"—reveals himself as an effect, a creation of cinema (Ray 2001a:70). The bride is stripped bare by an image that offers a most radical self-critique. *Mise-en-scène,* as the shot clearly shows, is sufficient to create the director as *auteur.* It is the machine that generates him, the apparatus that calls him forth (much like the perception of an "orderly world," Darwin maintained, elicits a creator). *Cahier*-style film theory had resurrected the director as the divine source or superintending consciousness, thus designating an effect as the cause (59). Godard, *auteurism's* most ardent proponent, exposes this mechanism as a type of forgery. (The wrought iron in the shot puns on this idea and visually links Godard and Elvis: partners in aesthetics.) The director's name—his signature—authenticates the movie as a thing authored or forged by a guiding consciousness, instead of something generated by a machine (that retroactively elicits an author). While Curtiz offers a rather empty virtuosity, Godard, to adopt a phrase coined by Christian Keathley, is "modest enough to employ the camera's fundamental automatism as a means for discovery" (129). His critique is astonishing. (We might say Godard practices heuretics.) And so the contrast in style between Godard's shot and Curtiz's is vivid and obvious. Godard's is self-reflexive. Its lack of ease with conventional cinema manifests a hint of willed gawkiness and more than a hint of anti-Americanism (the bitter irony of "French Quarter" underscores the tendency of meaning to double). It suffers from a very slight but certain affectation. As a compliment, Gilles Deleuze called Godard a stammerer, gifted with the ability to remain a foreigner in his own language (MacCabe 258). To detractors, the street scene will look clichéd; the deep focus too much like homage to André Bazin. Not so Curtiz. He handles the language of Hollywood as easily as Cervantes handled the Spanish of his time.

5

> *I would say that all important research in the humanities is simply teaching by other means than the lecture or the seminar.*
>
> —Robert Scholes, *The Rise and Fall of English*

I am hopeful that, quite some time ago, readers spotted this business of Godard remixing *King Creole* as fabulation pure, if not so simple. It is an invention—a forgery in the best sense of the word. Keathley labels experiments with attribution *signateurism.* Like Ray, he expands upon Derrida's theories in *Signsponge* and redirects them toward film studies. They generate knowledge by exploring information that can be extrapolated from names associated with particular films. While Ray and Keathley's approach differs from mine, all three of us read in order to write heuretically. Instead of retrieving meaning from films, we project meaning onto them: locate motivations that were formerly unobserved, repressed, weak, or absent. But here's the rub. The *signateurist* method, as I have employed it, is "both initiated by and limited to the meanings and associations available in the name of the [assigned] author": that is, in the name as a synonym for a "distinguishable personality" (Andrew Sarris's concept of *auteur*) or an "inimitable idiom" or "style" (Derrida's concept of *signateur*). It is not a "freely projected" reading "in the manner of reader-response criticism (Keathley 216–17).

The next time I try an Elvis experiment in a film course, I am going to require my students to extend this *signateurist* exercise into a full-blown experiment. Their job will be to find other scenes, shots, and frames in *King Creole* that Godard could have made and to provide DVD commentary on them. Or I might have them explore other possibilities. Didn't Fellini attempt *Viva Las Vegas,* or was it *Jailhouse Rock?* No . . . wait. That was Visconti, and the movie was *Roustabout.* The Coen brothers shot parts of *Clambake* or *Tickle Me.* Preston Sturges or Lubitsch worked on something or other. Was it *Frankie and Johnny?* The hand of John Ford is, of course, visible throughout *Flaming Star.* It is not clear which Elvis movie Douglas Sirk directed under a pseudonym. And why didn't Allen Smithee direct Elvis? My students constantly want to write about films they find difficult, while I had rather they imbue the most ordinary material with magic. An elaborate experiment with attribution satisfies both of our desires. And students get to learn about (and learn from) new media.

The model for my experiment—and I followed it closely—was Jorge Luis Borges's short story, "Pierre Menard, Author of the Quixote." I have shamelessly cribbed from it (and in cribbing, learned much about its inner workings). Call my remix sustained allusion or homage to Borges, if you like. His story amounts to a primer for working heuretically, a set of instructions for pushing interpretation until it becomes invention. Borges identifies his version of *signateurism* as "the deliberate anachronism and the erroneous attribution." Taking it seriously and applying it to film might be a typically Florida School thing to do. I have tried to suggest—and, even more, to demonstrate—that Borges's method could be generalized very easily into a genre capable of generating knowledge. Practicing "deliberate anachronism and erroneous attribution" is worthwhile, not because it is postmodern or fashionable (or a fulfillment of Socrates' fears and misgivings about writing). Rather, it is an enormously powerful method for approaching media, new and old. It has the potential, claims Borges, to fill "the most placid works with adventure" (44). I can think of no better motivation for writing than that.

Works Cited

Bangs, Lester. *Psychotic Reactions and Carburetor Dung.* Ed., Greil Marcus. New York: Alfred A. Knopf, 1988.

Borges, Jorge Luis. "Pierre Menard, Author of the *Quixote.*" In *Labyrinths: Selected Stories & Other Writings.* Ed., Donald A. Yates and James E. Irby. Trans. James E. Irby. New York: New Directions, 1964.

Godard, Jean-Luc. *Godard on Godard.* Trans. Tom Milne. New York: Da Capo, 1986.

—. "Chapitre deux (a) seul le cinema." *Histoire(s) du Cinéma.* New York: ECM New Series, 1999.

Guralnick, Peter. *Last Train to Memphis: The Rise of Elvis Presley.* New York: Little, Brown, 1994.

Jarrett, Michael. *Drifting on a Read: Jazz as a Model for Writing.* Albany: SUNY P, 1999.

Keathley, Christian. "*Signateurism* and the Case of Allen Smithee." In *Directed by Allen Smithee.* Ed. Jeremy Braddock and Stephen Hock. Minneapolis: U of Minnesota P, 2001.

Mast, Gerald. *Can't Help Singin': The American Musical on Stage and Screen.* Woodstock, New York: Overlook Press, 1987.

MacCabe, Colin. *Godard: A Portrait of the Artist at Seventy.* New York: Farrar, Straus and Giroux, 2003.

Ray, Robert B. *A Certain Tendency of the Hollywood Cinema, 1930–1980.* Princeton: Princeton UP, 1985.

—. *The Avant-Garde Finds Andy Hardy.* Cambridge: Harvard UP, 1995.

—. *How a Film Theory Got Lost and Other Mysteries in Cultural Studies.* Bloomington: Indiana UP, 2001.

—. "The Automatic Auteur; or, a Certain Tendency in Film Criticism." In *Directed by Allen Smithee.* Ed. Jeremy Braddock and Stephen Hock. Minneapolis: U of Minnesota P, 2001a.

Scholes, Robert. *The Rise and Fall of English: Reconstructing English As a Discipline.* New Haven, CT: Yale UP, 1998.
Simpson, Paul. *The Rough Guide to Elvis.* London: Rough Guide, 2002.
Ulmer, Gregory L. *Teletheory: Grammatology in the Age of Video.* New York: Routledge, 1989.

7 Speculating a Hollywood, Finding Picture City

Denise K. Cummings

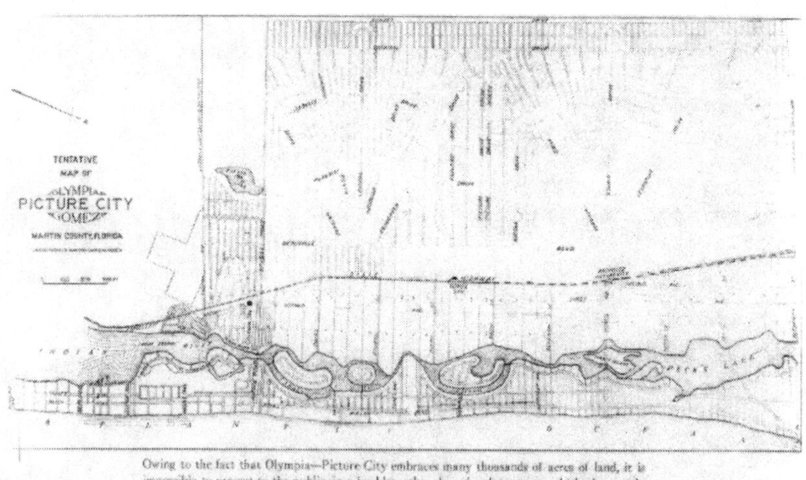

Tentative Map of Olympia—Picture City, c 1925. Original Caption: "Owing to the fact that Olympia—Picture City embraces many thousands of acres of land, it is impossible to present to the public, in a booklet, other than the above map—which shows only in very small detail, the size and magnitude of the property."

Robert Ray goes back to the early days of film criticism in order to explore paths that are no longer taken. In doing so, he claims to examine what constitutes knowledge in film studies. If the cinema, he argues, is a new way of seeing, then approaches to it must reconsider this perceptual organization. If you begin with a particular case, Ray reasons, you may not be able to predict where it will lead, and with that unpredictability comes the possibility for knowledge. He puts forward one such novel approach in his review of *Reinventing Film Studies* (Gledhill and Williams 2000), Take a walking tour of a single movie, Ray suggests, and from the moments, the images, and the details that are striking, "compose a set of histories or stories that provide us with new ways of understanding those flickering images made so long ago" ("Mystery Trains"), an idea in the spirit of Sergei Eisenstein's c1937 effort to link architectural ensemble to film ("Montage and Architecture").

While I have often focused on the traditional essay format for the writing of film history, I confess I am struck by the potential in proposing a similar tactic as Ray's; that is, starting cultural and film historical research from a detail. In my case here, the detail is part of the landscape in Martin County, Florida. By practicing Ray's geographical approach, with its emphasis on fragmentation, I take a tour of an actual place while simultaneously following a trail of seemingly disparate discursively produced details—maps, various kinds of deeds and documents, films, newspaper articles and advertisements, billboards, anecdotes, oral and written histories, accounts of natural disasters—to see where they will lead. My encounters result in a form of writing, a weaving together of travel journal entries, historical narratives, and provocative theoretical strands.

In addition to making a case for alternative ways of writing about cinema history, this project seeks to participate in that process by offering certain spatializing operations. The travel journal entries largely comprise my tour of Martin County (the successive events that took place in the course of my journey); the tour conditions the map, a surveyor's sketch. In the interlacing of the two, the tour and the map, an action permits one to see something. Stories of journeys and actions are marked out by citation of the places that result from them or authorize them. Although foregoing the element of mapping that presupposes a certain itinerary, the map is not alone on the stage. The tour describer materializes; in this way, practices that inform the writing of history are thus exposed.

speculate

1 a : To meditate on or ponder a subject: REFLECT b : to review something idly or casually and often inconclusively 2 : to assume a

business risk in hope of gain, *esp* : to buy or sell in expectation of profiting from market fluctuations.[1]

My opening title refers at once to land speculation and to the acts of looking and theorizing. As per its Latin root, *speculatus* (past participle of *speculari*), "to speculate" implies an action: to spy out, examine. I spy out places and locate cinema's cultural history alongside geography, economic development, and wild dreams in order to give us something for film studies to think about.

January 2003. Winter Break. Palm Beach County, Fla.

When traveling just outside of the Palm Beaches, I noticed huge bright orange billboards beside the north- and south-bound lanes of the Florida Turnpike. They hype the "new golden age" of living, a planned housing community dubbed "Olympia."

March 1996. Spring Break. Hobe Sound, Fla.

Today, while driving south along Highway A-1-A—also known as old Dixie Highway—in the town of Hobe Sound in Martin County, Florida, I noticed many slender obelisks fashioned from stone and cement. Their lichen and mold-covered surfaces look pockmarked and weathered. For a half mile or so these modernistic posts, towering about eleven feet above crumbling sidewalks, appear primarily in pairs along the right side of the road and collectively create a curious aberration on the landscape. They demand a traveler's attention.

The posts materialize on a section of A-1-A that whips neatly through a sprawling flatland of scrub pine and saw palmetto dotted with occasional subdivisions, a small neighborhood market, a few billboards and business signs, a Texaco gas station (Diamond's Filling Station, c1942), and a yellow blinker that hangs over the highway at the turnoff for old Hobe Sound's modest business district.[2] U.S. Highway No.1 and Jonathan Dickinson State Park[3] lie to the west; the Intracoastal Waterway and the Atlantic to the east. Parallel to Highway A-1-A are railroad tracks, vestige of Henry Flagler's Florida East Coast Railway (F.E.C.)—an ambitious project that helped build South Florida a century earlier.

For a few seconds, I wondered: what are these posts? What is their purpose? When were they erected? At the turnoff for the business district, I instead took a left on Bridge Road and traveled towards Jupiter Island's Hobe Sound Beach, forgetting about the posts.

The signs bequeathed by history, the memories of cities, are engraved in visible traces, architecture, monuments, ruins of any kind, and onomastics—street or square names, all kinds of acronyms. This heritage tells us about the past; it makes up an urban memory, historical records for the one trying to decipher the various signs displayed before her—either she is a stroller, tourist, historian, artist, writer, or filmmaker taking the city as the setting or the main character of her work. This heritage also tells us about the present and the future, for like in the fictional world of film, the simultaneity of past, present, and future marks our landscapes.

> *The filmic path is the modern version of the architectural itinerary and the geographic exploration. Film follows a historical course. It ventures to draw on the multiple viewpoints of the "picturesque" route, reinventing this practice in modern ways. It does so by leaving it to a spectatorial body to take unexpected paths of exploration.*
>
> —Guiliana Bruno
> "Site-Seeing: Architecture and the Moving Image"

October 26, 2000. Gainesville, Fla.

An intriguing Palm Beach Post newspaper article arrived in my mail today. Sent by my father in Hobe Sound, he also attached a letter and wrote, "Thought you might enjoy reading. . . ." Indeed, the first few lines captured my attention . . .

The Palm Beach Post. October 2, 2000 "The Lost City of Olympia," by Paul Reid.

"There is always the road not taken. And sometimes there is the road not finished—hardtop, shell and sand by ways in Hobe Sound that never went beyond the drawing board during Florida's land boom of the 1920s" (1E). Reid goes on to briefly describe a metropolis that was to rise out of the mangroves along the Intracoastal, where Hobe Sound stands today. Olympia, also known as Picture City, was going to be bigger than Hollywood, CA, bigger than Palm Beach, bigger than Miami.[4] "Picture City as in moving pictures, movies, silent movies. Hollywood producers were interested" (4E). Although a few infrastructures were established, Reid concludes that the only place to find Olympia—Picture City today is on "a map. Nowhere but a map. An old map. . . . It was the city that died before it drew a breath or a resident" (4E).

. . . I remembered what I had once seen on old Dixie Highway. According to Reid's account, the posts and deteriorating walkways must be the old light standards and remaining sidewalks of a lost city. A movie capital, no less! I want to learn more. . . .

To take the light standards seriously, I believe, is to re-find Olympia—Picture City as the artistic representation of a city at the crossroads of geography, economic development, and history—indeed, as a kind of chronotope turning it into a high place of historical memory.

When I use the word "chronotope," I consider Mikhail M. Bakhtin's use of the word. In his essay on the *Bildungsroman,* referring to Goethe's world and mode of visualization, Bakhtin writes that, "Everything in this world is a *time-space,* a true *chronotope*" (42, Bakhtin's emphasis). Here, Bakhtin defines time as "events, plots, or temporal motifs," and space as "the particular spatial place of their occurrence" (42). In this instance, chronotope seems to signify the ways in which a particular location in space determines the direction of an event. Yet more than mere chronological time and geographical place, Bakhtin's chronotope also includes both naturally given and culturally created spaces that are operative in the articulation of new ideas.[5]

February 2001. Hobe Sound, Fla.

While on research leave and spending two weeks in Hobe Sound, I prepare to explore Martin County and its roads, museums, historical societies, libraries, town halls, and people. I begin with roads . . .

To compose a diegesis—an imaginary space and time, as in a setting for a film—that functions as the "place of invention," the field or network I must re-construct has all the qualities of a diegesis in a film. A diegesis involves time as well as space.

> *She who wanders through a building or site acts precisely like a film spectator absorbing and connecting visual spaces. The changing position of a body in space creates architectural and*

cinematic grounds. The consumer of architectural (viewing) space is the prototype of the film spectator.

—Guiliana Bruno
"Site-Seeing: Architecture and the Moving Image"

It so happens that the story of Olympia—Picture City is itself composed around a map. Where is Picture City, exactly?

Stuart Messenger. January 31, 1924. Advertisement.

> "Be our guest. Ride with us to Olympia and see 'A City in the Making'" (11).

February 2, 2001. Hobe Sound, Fla.

. . . Heading towards Hobe Sound Beach, I followed Bridge Road as it dips into a shady gully past the railroad tracks, passes Gomez Avenue, and then crosses the Sound on a thin bridge and enters a dark canopy of native Florida banyan trees. I stopped and took a picture of the banyans. I then continued on and reached the first intersection, Gomez Road. On the 17th of July in 1815, King Fernando of Spain granted 12,180 acres of Florida coastal land to Don Eusebio Maria Gomez in exchange for public services rendered the government of the province. The tract includes Jupiter Island, from the Jupiter Inlet almost to the St. Lucie Inlet and the town of Stuart (from 1893–1896, the burgeoning town was originally called Potsdam, so named by its German settlers). It extends west into the mainland approximately three and three-quarters miles, which includes Hobe Sound and its outlying area.

February 2, afternoon . . .

My mother accompanied me on a visit to the new Hobe Sound Library on U.S. Highway No. 1. Inside, we discovered stacks labeled "Local History," including a few shelves of bound volumes by such authors as Janet Hutchinson and Norah Lind. After visiting the library, we identified the Stuart Heritage Museum and the county historical society as two worthwhile sites to investigate.

Following the library stop we then spent the afternoon perusing the exhibits and archives of the Stuart Heritage Museum, temporarily housed in a branch building of Wachovia Bank off of U.S. Highway No. 1 in

Stuart. We learned that the museum building proper, on S.W. Flagler Avenue and known as the Stuart Feed Supply, is undergoing architectural restoration. At the makeshift museum, we met Caroline Pomeroy Ziemba, the museum's director's and author of Martin County, Our Heritage *(1997).*

As I read Ziemba's and other accounts from the Hobe Sound Library, I quickly realized that no single published "history" concerning the Gomez Grant or, more specifically, Olympia-Picture City, tells quite the same story—a detail missing here, others embellished there . . .

> *History [thus] vacillates between two poles. On the one hand, it refers to a practice, hence to a reality; on the other, it is a closed discourse, a text that organizes and concludes a mode of intelligibility.*
>
> *History is probably our myth. It combines what can be thought, the 'thinkable,' and the origin, in conformity with the way in which a society can understand its own working.*
>
> —Michel de Certeau. *The Writing of History*

History is narrative, a written construction, a verbal play. By synthesizing the information contained in a variety of "histories" found in various locations, here is what a chronological "history" of land settlement and development might look like:

History I: Gomez Tract

In May 1832, the United States Government confirmed the land grant title to Gomez, just 13 years after Florida became a territory of the United States and 11 years after it was received as a state (Hutchinson 199; Ziemba 12–13). In the 1700s, no settlements of long endurance existed on the Gomez Grant, save that of a Franciscan monk's, Padre Torry (in some histories, spelled "Torre"), a man allegedly imported from Cuba during the last reign of the Spanish flag, sent to run a plantation and a mission to bring religion to the Indians of Florida on the Jupiter Island part of what would be the Gomez Grant. For a time, however, Gomez himself apparently lived upon and cultivated a portion of the land (Fleming & Fleming; Ziemba 16). In those days, some of the area's crops were pineapple, coconut, and sugarcane. "In 1821, Gomez sold 8,000 acres, including Jupiter Island, to Joseph

Delespine, for $1.00 an acre ("Abstracts of Title"; "Looking Back" 5). In 1882, The Indian River Pineapple and Cocoanut Grove Association subdivided all of Jupiter Island (Fleming & Fleming). Ten years later, Yorkshire, England developers formed the Indian River Association, Ltd., and purchased as an investment Jupiter Island and the rest of the Gomez Land Grant ("Abstracts of Title"; Hutchinson 200–201; Ziemba 18).

The 1890s were active times in the county later named Martin.[6] In 1894, Potsdam Postmaster Broster Kitching "negotiated with Henry Flagler to bring the railroad through Potsdam—later Stuart. . . . [H]e gave the railroad company land for the right-of-way. . . . The line was brought to the north side of the St. Lucie [River], and the Potsdam Station was established" (Hutchinson 103). One year later, the Stuart depot was moved to the south side of the St. Lucie River. "With the depot came the Stuart name" (151) in honor of Homer Hine Stuart, Jr., an early settler of the town that would grow up on the St. Lucie (Thurlow 11–13). "By the turn of the century . . . [t]he railway was so important to the area that there were stations in Stuart (Potsdam), Jensen, Rio, Salerno, Fruita, Gomez, and Hobe Sound" (Hutchinson 289). Kitching's deal with Flagler would prove instrumental for later county expansion and economic development.

When Flagler, the northern industrialist and Rockefeller Standard Oil partner, put his train track down Florida's east coast, through Hobe Sound the end of 1894, the area was thrown open for development. Northern entrepreneurs like Flagler tried to sell the under-populated and mosquito-ridden parcel of southern Florida as the land of eternal summer and paradise on earth (Sammons 35). The idea was to extend the railways further south and trigger a land boom. After a cold winter in Palm Beach in 1894/95, Flagler decided he would eventually extend his railway (what historian Seth H. Bramson calls the "Speedway to Sunshine") all the way to Miami. Northern land speculators would market south Florida land all over the United States to eager pioneers and developers. In September 1895, Flagler's system was incorporated as the Florida East Coast Railway (F.E.C.). Though north of both the cities of Miami and Palm Beach, the Gomez Grant—conveniently bordering the F.E.C.—became known for its unspoiled natural beauty (Ziemba 18).

Historical narrative strives to offer a type of complete "picture," yet somehow hides, even denies, the act of discovery, the excavation of unexpected details as the historian works.

How is the historian's work similar to the filmmaker's?

Writing in 1926, in "Calico-World" Siegfried Kracauer commented on the enterprise of making films at Germany's UFA (Universum-Film AG) studios in Neubabelsberg in the 1920s:

> Instead of leaving the world in its fragmented state, one reconstitutes a world out of these pieces . . . Life is constructed in a pointillist manner. It is a speckling of images that stem from numerous locations and initially remain unconnected. Their sequence does not follow the order of the represented events. . . . The cells must be formed one after the other. Here and there, pieces of inventory come together. . . .
>
> The director is the foreman. It is also his difficult task to organize the visual material—which is as beautifully unorganized as life itself—into the unity that life owes to art. He locks himself and the strips of film into his private screening room and has them projected over and over. They are sifted, spliced, cut up, and labeled until finally from the huge chaos emerges a little whole: a social drama, a historical event, a woman's fate. (287–8)[7]

Kracauer's formulation for this enterprise is elegant and also an apt description of the historian's program: like the pieces that make up a film, history is ordered, sorted, and spliced into in an even continuum. Walter Benjamin would say, however, history is maelstrom.

February 9, 2001. Hobe Sound, Fla.

Map section

. . . I headed north on A-1-A and took a right on to Palm Street. On the corner of Palm and First, I visited "Lot 135" of the North Hobe Sound Shores subdivision, as recorded in Plat Book 3, page 49, filed 13 July, 1956, Martin County, Florida, public records. On Lot 135 is the home of Hobe Sound residents veteran journalist Eva Campbell and her husband Thomas. From my personal interview with Eva, I learned that

when it comes to Hobe Sound, "in some ways, there are no archives" (Eva Campbell).

February 7, 2001. Hutchinson Island, Fla.

Today at the Historical Society of Martin County and Elliott Museum on Hutchinson Island, the curator handed over a stack of un-catalogued and unorganized documents: dozens of newspaper clippings, a 1980s article penned by an amateur historian, an oversized brochure. I noticed that the oversized piece is a promotional publication. A drawing of Juan Ponce de Leon as "Discoverer of Florida" graces the cover of this elaborate sales brochure for "Olympia-Picture City," a document immediately recognizable as manifesting the hyperbole of the 1920s land boom:

> *[T]he Gomez tract is situated well outside of the frost belt in fashionable, tropical, seashore Florida. Its tropical verdure cannot be excelled. . . . When one can combine a tropical [sic] latitude with a high altitude, the condition must be ideal. The altitude of Olympia—Picture City rivals at least any height along the Atlantic coast in the entire State of Florida. (8–10)*

The sales pamphlet promoted the area as highly accessible: one could easily reach Olympia—Picture City by railroad, boat, and the Dixie Highway (10). "When one combines tropical conditions, seashore, Indian River, wonderful highways, tropical verdure, all forms of pleasure and recreational pastimes, wonderful products of the soil, the value of Florida's pleasure-satisfying and health-giving lands are [sic] beyond present computation" (14). The pamphlet continued, "The entire territory is ablaze with development. There must be one continuous Riviera between Stuart and Miami" (14).

The brochure further promoted the advantage in buying part of Olympia—Picture City's 10,000 acres at initial prices, likening land sales in Florida to the bargain sale of the whole of Manhattan Island and touting the inevitable increment value and appreciation of a timely land purchase. The general plan for development, they claimed, was meant to imitate that of the smartly platted City of Washington, D.C.; a charter, they detailed, was applied to the Florida Legislature for the incorporation of the municipality of Olympia—Picture City. Throughout photographs of Royal Palms, "President Harding on Olympia Golf Links," "A home on the property," "Proposed Picture City Station," and various scenic vistas of the Indian River, the beach, and Gomez Road, among others, gave picto-

rial dimension to the narrative. Two "tentative" maps of the entire area of Olympia—Picture City and a back cover narrative appeal of the Florida peninsula as "the happiest latitude and longitude on earth," indeed, "The Land of Unlimited Opportunities" conclude the piece (Olympia—Picture City).

Aside from the rendering of Picture City Station, I noticed that no mention of the movie colony appeared in the publicity brochure.

Fantasy? Farce? In *City of Quartz,* Mike Davis's 1992 tome on Los Angeles, Davis traces L.A.'s uneven development and writes:

> I begin with the so-called 'Arroyo Set': writers, antiquarians, and publicists under the influence of Charles Fletcher Lummis (himself in the pay of the [Los Angeles] *Times* and the Chamber of Commerce), who at the turn of the century created a comprehensive fiction of Southern California as the promised land of the millenarian Anglo-Saxon racial odyssey. They inserted a Mediterraneanized idyll of New England life into the perfumed ruins of an innocent but inferior 'Spanish' culture. In doing so, they wrote the script for the giant real-estate speculations of the early twentieth century that transformed Los Angeles from small town to metropolis. (20)

Davis might well have been describing Florida, where the overstatement of the land boom also began with the press. A "history" of the promoters:

History II: Boosters, Barkers, and Go-Getters

The fantastic Florida land boom began in 1922 and Martin County was a direct product of the boom. [8] "[It] came into being at the height of the astronomical real estate development when everyone in the state was prosperous and money was the least of all worries" (Hutchinson 305). While during this time period Miami and the Florida Gold Coast underwent tremendous expansion in terms of population, construction, and money in circulation as parameters of rapid economic growth,[9] the effect of the boom was too often to substitute image over substance. Boosters were frequently anxious to incorporate the motion picture into their media arsenal. Studio promotions in the mid-twenties crisscrossed the entire state, from Miami to Orlando and Palatka to Pensacola (Nelson, v I 370). Florida's scenic beauty and variety—be it a rocky coastline, sandy beach, or dense steamy jungle—good atmospheric conditions, mild winter climate, low labor and land costs, and nearness to New York fueled efforts to build a viable motion picture industry in the state. Given the high-rolling economy of the mid-twenties, slick promoters presented "fascinating stories of the 'millions to be made in producing moving pictures in Florida'" (Matlack 54–5). After all, some millions had already been made in Jacksonville.

The once famed "world's winter film capital," Jacksonville had high hopes of becoming a long-term major motion picture headquarters.[10] In addition to being a production center, Jacksonville was Florida's leader in film exhibition: in 1897, the city's Park Opera House was converted to allow the first commercial exhibition of a motion picture in Florida (Nelson *Lights!* 108). In 1904, Jacksonville's Duval Theatre became the first Florida theatre converted exclusively to the showing of photoplays (108). As early as the winter of 1908, Florida's then largest city also had its first ambitious bellwether studio, Kalem, and by 1916, an expanding moving picture industry (Nelson v I, 132). A leading commercial and transportation city and a major southeastern theatrical tour stop, the temperate Jacksonville and surrounding area was a convenient location to New York and also offered a host of scenic backdrops and authentic locations—ideal conditions for moviemaking (133–36). There films could be shot economically, and celluloid could be saved from cold weather damage. According to Terry Ramsaye in *A Million and One Nights,* from 1912–1914, "there were more movie units working in Jacksonville and in St. Augustine than in Los Angeles" (507). Kalem's success with Florida-made pictures soon brought other movie companies to the City (Bowser 154–5; Nelson v I, 144–5). A pre-war local recession stalled development, but by 1916, the city's future as a movie center looked bright (Nelson, v I 64, 173).

Things changed. Even with factions of business and government support and efforts of some enthusiastic boosters, including their production of feature films created to lure California and New York producers to the North Florida city, many different factors—such as local merchant price gouging and lack of local banking support—nonetheless limited long-term growth and eventually led to the demise of Jacksonville as a major film center. These factors included community relations and public consternation about the city's movie people and their practices.

During Jacksonville's mayoral race in 1917, a coalition of reform interests—churches, prohibitionists, and anti-vice crusaders—unhappy with raucous filming practices, helped unseat the city's incumbent "movie booster" mayor, J.E.T. Bowden, thus hampering future development of filmmaking in the city (155–95). Long-time Florida newspaperman Joe Crankshaw insists that the public's cry for reform in Jacksonville contributed to the passing of Blue Laws, prohibiting filming, baseball games, and movies on Sundays.[11] During the 1920s, many Jacksonville film companies headed west to the friendlier political climate, better weather, and more diverse terrain of Southern California. Despite the debacle in Jacksonville, during the late-teens and early 1920s, filmmakers nonetheless remained active in many other Florida cities, including Tampa, Miami, and even Stuart.

February 11, 2001. Stuart, Fla.

After traveling on A-1-A about eight miles north of the Bridge Road intersection in Hobe Sound, I eventually reached the old downtown section of Stuart and stood on SW St. Lucie Avenue and SW Osceola. In front of me was a two-story hollow block concrete structure that in 1912 housed the Bank of Stuart, Stuart's first, which served the era's businesses and hotels in Stuart and neighboring towns. The notorious "Ashley Gang," South Florida's own storied band of criminals, robbed it a time or two. Local booster Harry. C. Feroe donated the lot on which the old bank building stands, and, in 1913, built next door to it another two-story frame building that also still stands. I read a frieze on its roof: "1913 Feroe Building." Turning right, I walked one block east from these buildings, to St. Lucie Avenue, to see where Feroe also erected the twenty five-room St. Lucie Hotel (c1913), conveniently located on the St. Lucie River shoreline next to the city dock and near the post office and F.E.C. depot (Hutchinson 296–97; Thurlow 155). From the teens through the 1950s, the St. Lucie was known for its cuisine and as a rendezvous for sportsmen. Today I rested on its site, now a parking lot, and gazed out at the St. Lucie.

Stuart Messenger. November 19, 1915. "Pretty Hobe Sound Ideal Winter Resort; Picturesque Jupiter Island the Residential Section" (1).

From the high ridge that extends north and south parallel with the railroad on the mainland's business section, "the spectator gazes entirely across palm-covered Jupiter Island" (1).

Stuart Times. November 19, 1915. Advertisement. "The Lyric Theater: A Motion Picture House of Quality" (8).

Immense development was underway and the area's boosters promoted everything: spectacular views, temperate weather, even Stuart's own Lyric Theater.[12] Area publicists became further enthralled with the movies when, in the spring of 1916, a Bostonian named Henry W. Savage led his production company to Stuart. Savage and seventy-five motion picture people, including the accomplished cameraman Carle Louis Gregory, disembarked the F.E.C., checked into the St. Lucie Hotel, and set up headquarters. They proceeded to film what Savage called *Westward, Ho!* ("Movie Actors").

February 8, 2002. Gainesville, Fla.

I began to unpack it: a large carton containing over a year's worth of collected materials.

The metaphor of the archive suggests the simultaneity of the past and present, where events from the past mingle and combine with those from the present.

History III: Newspaper Archives

Stuart Messenger. April 19, 1923. "Jupiter Island Inn and Town."

Malcolm Meacham, a New York real estate developer and Palm Beach winter resident, buys "Jupiter Island Inn and Town and all the holdings of the Indian River Association, Ltd., of England" (1).

Stuart Messenger. July 19, 1923. "Jupiter Island Deal Closed."

A deed is filed in Palm Beach County for the Jupiter Island property and holdings, "including the town site of Hobe Sound," and that these "were purchased by the Olympia Improvement Corporation which was recently incorporated in Florida with a capital stock of $1.5 million" and of which "Malcolm Meacham is president" (1).

In effect, the outfit called Olympia Improvement had purchased a sizable portion of the Gomez Grant (Hutchinson 201; Ziemba 18). The name Hobe Sound was changed to Olympia and Jupiter Island became Olympia Beach. "The name Olympia fit in nicely with the neighboring towns to the south, Jupiter, Juno, and Mars (Mars no longer exists)" (Ziemba 117). Olympia Improvement's officers included Anthony J. Drexell Biddle, Jr. and the brothers Benjamin and Angler Duke, among others ("Jupiter Island Deal"; Reid).

Stuart Messenger. January 17, 1924. "Meacham Starts Olympia Sales Campaign This Week."

Meacham and Olympia Improvement begin selling lots after some improvements made: "All along the [Dixie] highway fronting the town have been erected poles and the electric light and water plant are both owned by Olympia Improvement" (1).

Stuart Messenger. January 31, 1924. Advertisement.

"Olympia has its own electric light and water plants, the water being soft and pure, no bottled water being required. . . . Sites have been reserved for churches, schools, motion picture theaters, and other semi-public buildings." Olympia, with its railroad station and telegraph and post offices, an important a real estate announcement as Flagler's Palm Beach. Departing from their sales offices in the Kettler Theatre building in West Palm Beach, the developers gave daily tours of their city in the making, one they called "not 'just another Florida land speculation'" (4–5).

Stuart Messenger. August 20, 1925. "Olympia-Gomez to be Picture City; New York Picture Men Buy Big Tracts for Huge Development" (1).

"Miami papers yesterday carried the announcement of the founding of Picture City by New York interests led by Lewis J. Selznick, on what is known as the Gomez Grant, which lies eight miles south of Stuart and which adjoins Olympia on the north. The Gomez tract is the last large undeveloped acreage on the tropical east coast of Florida" (1).

The project also reached the New York publicists:

New York Times. September 2, 1925. "Famous Names Among Picture City Buyers."

"McAdoo, Walsh, Dr. George Ryan, Fannie Hurst and Louis Mann Buy in Florida" (39). Prominent politicians, educators, physicians, actors and playwrights—and a Hollywood writer.

New York Times. September 13, 1925. "Plan Big Florida Studio."

"$1,000,000 Motion-Picture Operation for Picture City" (RE28).

New York Times. November 28, 1925. "To Develop Picture City. New YorkersReorganize Florida Concern. J.P. Day Sales Manager" (2).

"Joseph P. Day, Felix Isman, Charles L. Apfel and K. B. Conger, all of New York, have affected, it was learned here today, a reorganization of the Picture City Corporation which will develop Picture City" (2).

New York Times. December 27, 1925. "Joseph P. Day to Sell Florida Development; With Felix Isman He Will Offer Olympia Beach—Picture City."

The one-time holdings of Malcolm Meacham's Olympia Improvement Corporation are to be combined with remaining portions of the famous Gomez Grant (X1).

In addition to being an incorporator of the developer, a company called Picture City Holding Corporation, Apfel was president of its affiliate, the Olympia Holding Corporation (Beales 3; Nelson v I, 370–72) as well president of the New York offices of Picture City Corporation. Starting from the north end of the Grant, plans were mapped out to accommodate a community of some 20,000 residents, using Gomez as the first city in the complex. Next was to materialize Picture City, a haven for Hollywood stars and moguls. Then, the southernmost city in the development would be Olympia, planned to house some of the 20,000 people (Crankshaw, "Stuart, Martin").

On September 29, 1925, a "Special Warranty Deed" between Farmer's Bank and Trust Company out of West Palm Beach and Mar-John Realty Company, Inc. out of New York was filed (Public Records of Martin County). Plots were sold under the personal direction of Joseph P. Day and Felix Isman's Trimount Realty Corporation of West Palm Beach and Miami ("Joseph P. Day"). Apfel's full-page announcements in such papers as the *Miami Daily News* hyped the development to Americans and Canadians ("Our Florida").

Apfel planned, built, and named a series of curving roads.

February 3, 2001. Hobe Sound, Fla.

Just past Bridge Road's right turn for the business district, I followed a curious network of streets bearing the names of Greek gods and goddesses and their Roman assimilations: Apollo Road, Hercules Avenue, Mercury, Mars, Saturn, Athena, and Venus Streets, then Juno Crescent and Plutus, Neptune,and Apollo Streets, among others—all radiating outward from a central geographical point, a park called Zeus, now the home of the Hobe Sound Baseball Diamond. Well-rehearsed mythology has taught us that in ancient Greece, such Olympian gods as Zeus, Apollo, and Athena were named after their dwelling place, Mount Olympus. Zeus, the god of the sky, was its ruler. In Hobe Sound, Zeus Park commands a large open space. A main artery, Olympus Avenue, extends westward from the park while SE Olympus Street runs eastward. The topographical effect of the park and its contiguous streets is an obliquely angled neighborhood, one platted to resemble an Olympic arena.

Commencing from Zeus Park, I traveled all the radiating streets I observed named for the gods. I soon found myself on nearby Apollo. There on a lot stands a mission-style building, its architecture reflecting the influence of early Spanish settlers in Florida and California. An aging cement wall borders the front left of the property, a tangle of weeds and brush on its sandy surface. A large sign erected by the Apollo Street School Foundation stands prominently in front of the deserted building.[13]

Stuart News. August 20, 2000. "Historic Status Sought for Apollo School" (B1+).

Often alleged as erected by the Olympia Improvement Co. in 1924 as Olympia's town hall, the building may have been built on the Olympia town site by the Picture City Corporation and later offered to the county as a school building in 1925 ("Offer of $10,000 School"). After the Olympia Holding Company was forced into receivership, in 1932 the building was purchased by the Martin County School Board, which used it as an elementary school for the next 30 years. In the early 1960s, the Hobe Sound Elementary School closed its doors as a school, and, for a time, the building accommodated a day care center and then a thrift shop (Kiehl).

The Roads and the Dreamers

With the installation of light poles, an underground electrical system along the roadways, and a water plant, Apfel and many others hoped that these infrastructures, flanked by the F.E.C Railroad (with a station promised in each town site), would ultimately support a complete community centered by a burgeoning industry: the movies. In Olympia's subdivision alone, 585 building sites were platted for the land south of Bridge Road, between U.S. 1 and A-1-A (Kiehl). Studio lots and additional housing plats would be designed and designated for the land Apfel called "Picture City"—named so for the area's "picturesqueness" and, later, as double-entendre for the proposed movie capital. Film industry magnates, stars, and personnel would thus reside in tropical style within close proximity to their workplaces.[14]

Apfel's efforts in the twenties were in keeping with overall state development activity; yet with respect to his Olympia—Picture City project, the image over substance argument remains somewhat inconclusive. Olympia—Picture City was certainly conjured by some of the biggest players in the 1920s land boom, tycoons with big dreams. Yet society don Meacham, Olympia Improvement's president (and, according to *Palm Beach Post* writer Paul Reid, also at one time the vice president of the Palm Beach National Bank, a bank in the mid-twenties, like countless other Florida banks, rife with fraud and insider abuse)[15] hired the right architect, Maurice Fatio (1897–1943)—a classically trained designer of public buildings.

Fatio came to the United States in 1920 from Geneva, Switzerland, expressly to create Olympia. As chronicled by Reid, who in the late twentieth century had the rare opportunity to interview Fatio's reclusive daughter, Alexandra Fatio Taylor, Olympia is the very reason Fatio had come to Florida. Fatio Taylor's letters, those written by her father, were "effusive in their praise for Olympia, the architectural plans he was going to provide for homes, the grand hotel, the golden future" (Reid 4E).

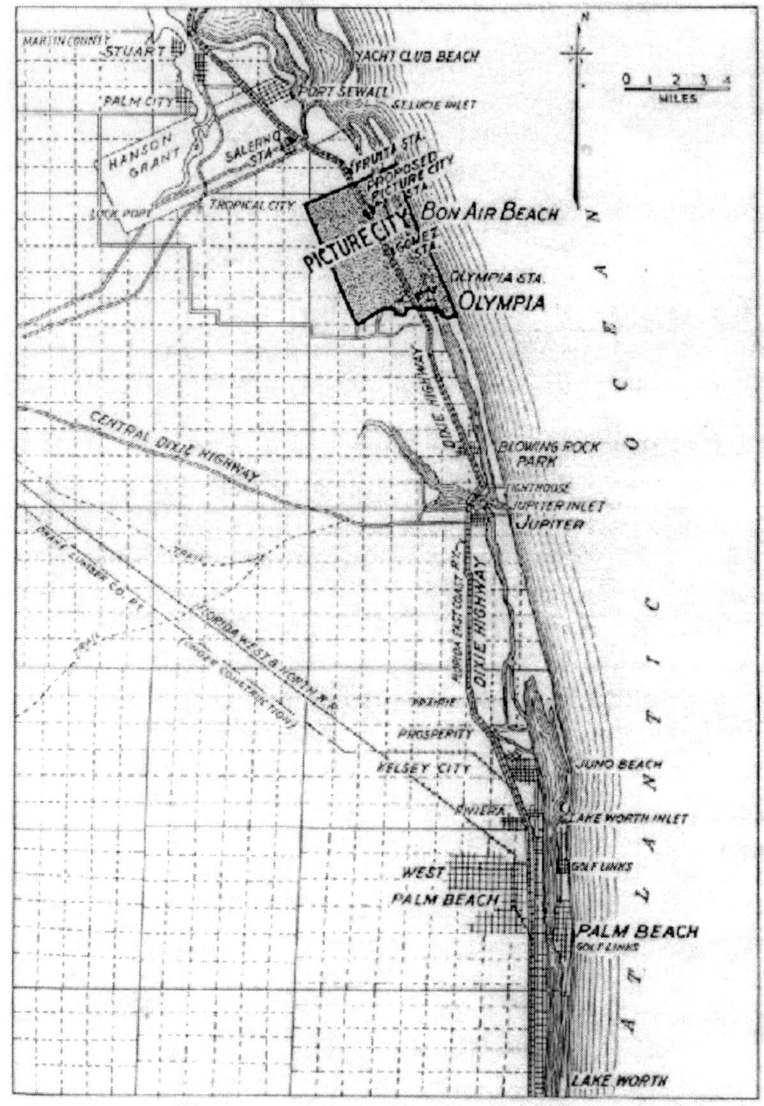

Detail Map Stuart to Palm Beach

Olympia Improvement Corporation's map of the South Florida East Coast, c1925. Original caption: "Detail Map Stuart to Palm Beach."

Letter from Maurice Fatio to his parents, 1925:

> 'I have cut out this map of Florida from the [*Miami*] *Herald* to give you an idea of the location of Olympia;

> it is not an advertisement, and you can see that our city is already considered to be an important resort'" (4E).[16]

February 4, late in the day . . .

After studying a faded newspaper photo of a landmark with a caption indicating "Ridge Road," my mom and I drove past Bridge Road and the Hobe Sound business district and headed south on Highway A-1-A. The road twists through dense vegetation for roughly another mile, and then joins U.S. Highway No. 1. Before that merge, on one curve a right turn off of A-1-A offered an incline leading to the highest point on Hobe Sound. We took that right and started to climb. Just at the crest, a simultaneous shriek: "Look, there's the water tower!"

There at the top, where Water Street and SE Ridge Avenue meet, we found a water facility with an adjacent steel-tone water tower rising dozens of feet into the sky. In the mid-twenties, another tower stood in its place, one nearly identical to the modern replacement barring one notable detail: on its vertical shank the 1920s tower had the painted words "PICTURE CITY"—metonym for big dreams and high hopes.

Miami Daily Tab, August 19, 1925.

"The Olympia section is ready and moving picture people can migrate immediately" (as qtd. in the *Stuart Messenger* on August 20, 1925: 1).

History IV: Zukor, Selznick, and Schenck

Before author Fannie Hurst purchased property in Picture City in the mid 1920s, she had already established herself and was known in 1925 as one of the highest paid writers in the United States.[17] Her stories began coming to the big screen as early as 1918. The first notable film based on any of Hurst's fiction was Frank Borzage's 1920 adaptation of her story *Humoresque,* about a boy who works his way out of New York's slums and into the circles of the wealthy and powerful. The subject matter proved extremely controversial for its producers—according to author Kent Jones, the plot and setting of life on New York's Lower East Side as being far grittier than Adolph Zukor (1873–1976), the head of the distribution company handling the movie, had wanted or expected. Jones quotes a Zukor-authored memo to screenwriter Francis

Marion stating: "If you and Fannie Hurst are so determined to make the Jews appear sympathetic, why don't you choose a story about the Rothschilds or men as distinguished as they?" (Eder). The unflappable Zukor of Famous Players-Lasky Corporation went on to distribute the film, a box-office success (and Fannie Hurst continued her writing career, often producing fairly successful screen treatments).[18]

Like Zukor, Lewis J. Selznick was one among many small tradesmen who had gambled on the movie business in the anarchic first decade of the cinema in the United States, hoping to turn a quick profit.[19] "From penny-arcade showmen and nickelodeon operators they became 'manufacturers' of their own films, then producer-distributors, and finally Hollywood studio chiefs" (Cook 42–3). Selznick, a cavalier entrepreneur and bitter rival of other studio execs, namely Zukor, owned Select Pictures, his own feature film company that successfully produced films from 1917 until 1922. At the height of his powers, Selznick was also the corporate head of World Film Corporation, the most powerful film distributor at that time (Koszarski 66). His Select Pictures was "a painful burr in the side of powerful producer Zukor." Zukor despised Selznick's bold thievery of the slick publicity for his Famous Players, created by B.P Schulberg. Famous Players coined "famous players in famous plays" as the official slogan that was well known to the public. Selznick shamelessly promoted Select with the busier slogan, "features with well known players, in well known plays."

> This obvious theft was made even more galling to the physically diminutive but powerful Zukor because Selznick had put these slogan signs all over Broadway with bigger lettering and more lights than Zukor's. This was only one example of Selznick's propensity for shameless oneupsmanship. When Selznick was sent an ultimatum to cease and desist, he gleefully replied, 'Hell no, Adolph, I'm having too much fun!.' (MacIntyre)

Selznick's blithe business approach and penchant for outrageous publicity, however, cost him. The suicide of Select's actress Olive Thomas in 1920 and the loss of their star attraction, Clara Kimball Young, to Zukor's Famous Players, contributed to Select Pictures' demise (MacIntyre). Selznick would never gain the respect and obeisance of industry ranks. Today, his legacy largely remains in his two famous sons, producer David O.—of *Gone With the Wind* immortality—and agent Myron.

In fact it was David and Myron who, in 1921, encouraged their father to support a proposed movie studio location in Jacksonville, Florida. At that time there were still some who harbored hopes that the North Florida city might regain at least part of what it lost (Nelson, v I 189). Jacksonville's Chamber of Commerce appointed a special film committee and, despite some opposition, plans were soon underway for the new "Fine Arts City," promoted as "the world's largest motion picture production center" ("World's Largest"). Traveling north from Palm Beach on the F.E.C., David and Myron stopped in Jacksonville and made a formal inspection of the city's motion picture facilities.

Florida Times Union. February 13, 1921. "Selznick Brothers Place Stamp of Approval on Cityfor Production" (2:13).

The "entirely favorable" report of their findings led the senior Selznick, called "one of the 'biggest' men in the picture industry" by the *Times Union,* to offer financial support for the project ("Selznick Brothers"). He soon pulled out of the project, however, after ambivalence concerning the site's construction led to the withdrawal of local capital (Nelson, v I 193).

The speculator Selznick apparently had sustained interest in viable money making opportunities. Nelson claims that Selznick began speculating in Florida real estate as a way to recover from his own corporate bankruptcy (Nelson, v I 371). According to Thomas Schatz, in 1923 Selznick was also looking for a way back into the movie business (49).

Stuart Messenger. August 20, 1925. "Olympia-Gomez To Be Picture City; New York Picture Men Buy Big Tracts for Huge Development."

"We have toured the state. . . . The selection of Gomez—Olympia, now Picture City, has been made because we believe it to be finest possible location for a motion picture colony. It is a beautiful and picturesque country," Selznick gushed of the Gomez Land Grant (1).

"A new capital for the industry as whole" was Selznick's slogan (Beales 5). With his sons, Selznick had signed an agreement in mid-July 1925 with a New York real estate syndicate, the one headed by Apfel, to operate the world's largest studio on 250 acres in south Martin County. Upon completion of the studio, the 250-acre site was to be transferred to another corporation and controlled by the Selznicks.

This corporation would conduct the motion picture studio and production business. The Selznicks were to receive jointly $750 a week to cover expenses for six months after the developer corporation's organization. They also got one-fourth of all land sales profits and agreed not to compete in motion picture production in Florida for five years. Financing was provided by a $1.5 million mortgage loan from Sinclair Oil titan Henry A. Daugherty. To account for his loan, Daugherty sent employees Charles C. Kelly, controller, and Davis A. Moore, head bookkeeper, to a West Palm Beach office.[20]

Rumors had Joseph Schenck, movie mogul and husband of silent screen star Norma Tallmadge, involved in the "Picture City" speculation ("Olympia—Gomez"; Beales 1) and, for a brief time, the promised state-of-the-art facility and outlaying residential infrastructure seemed tangible. Throughout the fall of 1925, the South Florida papers ran bold advertisements for the Picture City development, appearing alongside those for other nearby boom projects: Golden Gate, Palm City Estates, St. Lucie Estates. The Picture City advertisements relied heavily on narrative. Apfel appealed:

> The Studio Section of Olympia Beach—Picture City offers the big builder, home builder, investor and speculator, a genuine opportunity to realize their aim. Plans for the first unit of a motion picture studio have already been approved. Florida, in the opinion of those who know, is second to none in possessing at least all advantages for the successful manufacture of motion pictures, with the added advantage of being in close proximity to New York and other large centers of distribution than the present location of this industry. ("An Appeal")

South Florida Developer. February 23, 1926. "Selznick is Coming to Discuss Forming Mortgage Co. Here" (1).

February 5, 2001. Hobe Sound, Fla.

Just a few blocks away from the Apollo Street School and facing the railroad tracks on Dixie Highway, I strolled before buildings that largely comprise the town's business district. At 11970 is the Courtyard Grill, which once housed the Hobe Sound Post Office before it moved in the 1990s to its new expanded facility at 9995 SE Federal Highway (U.S. Highway No. 1). I decided to walk one block north of 11970 Dixie Highway, toward a two-story stucco structure that was known from 1931–1956 as the Mahan Building and during those years housed the Hobe Sound Post Office (Mahan 16–17).

In 1928, the Post Office was housed for a short time further north, in the 18000 block on Dixie Highway. In the mid 1920s, an addition off the rear left of yet another Dixie Highway building, for a time known as Randall's Radio and T.V., housed yet another Post Office (Hutchinson 204; Mahan 15). A photograph in Janet Hutchinson's History of Martin County *reveals the now-gone annex, which depicts a sign on its stucco facade. It reads, "U.S. Post Office Olympia FLA" (Hutchinson 204).*

"Whoopie, let's go!": An Anecdote

On what started as just another routine workday in 1926, twenty-eight-year-old Paul Mahan received a phone call from his boss, Mr. Moore, in West Palm Beach, telling Mahan that he was sending a messenger to Mahan's Olympia Beach office, a two-story frame waterfront building on what is now Jupiter Island one block south of the present public beach at the end of Bridge Road. Under Moore's orders, Mahan was to take a check to the bank in Stuart where they had an account, cash it, and give the money to the messenger who would then bring it back to Moore. The messenger arrived about twenty minutes before bank closing time. Mahan looked at the check and said, "Whoopie, let's go!" Mahan made it to the bank with a few minutes to spare, cashed the check, gave the money to the messenger and saw him on his way. That was the most money Mahan had seen since he quit his Treasury Department job in Washington. The bank did not open the next day (Mahan 12).

Paul Emery Mahan moved from Washington, D.C., to West Palm Beach, Florida in 1924. While living in West Palm Beach, he worked as a real estate salesman out of the Kettler Theatre building office of the Olympia Development Company, the New York firm selling lots in the newly established town site Olympia. Six months later, when lots ceased to sell, he moved to the Hobe Sound field office as bookkeeper-paymaster of the Olympia Holding Corporation. On that fateful day in 1926 when Mahan "cashed the check," the company had changed hands. A week later, Moore paid Mahan severance by matching the sum of Mahan's personal bank account. Moore's boss, financier Henry

A. Daugherty, closed the Olympia Beach office and decided not to loan more to the project. Mahan was out of a job.

As fate would further have it, on August 30, 1928, Mahan was appointed Postmaster of Olympia. The Olympia Post Office was located in an annex, now gone. The town's name changed back to Hobe Sound the following February,[21] and Mahan moved the post office to another location a half-mile away (in the present day 11800 block on Dixie Highway). In 1931 he moved the post office again, two blocks south, to what became known as the Mahan Building. He later built another building on 11970 Dixie Highway that housed the Hobe Post Office until the mid-1990s. Mahan retained his position as Postmaster in Hobe Sound "for the rest of his working years" (he died in June 1986) and lived long enough to write his autobiography, *Hobe Sound: It Could Only Happen in a Small Post Office,* thereby leaving for historical record the only personal account of the business operations of Olympia Improvement Corporation and Olympia Holding Corporation. Mahan confirms that surveyors and their crews were employed, an expensive and large topographical map of the Picture City area was drawn, lots were sold, and a few Spanish-type buildings were constructed. But the project went bust (Mahan 6–7). "Many supposedly level-headed businessmen took up a new sport, that of jumping out of twenty-story office windows. The head of Olympia Development Company was one of them" (6). In March 1929, it was Malcolm Meacham who jumped or fell from an 11th-floor window at his New York apartment. "His enterprise had already plunged financially" (Reid 4E).

According to attorney and amateur historian Walter R. Beales, who interviewed Mahan in April 1986, Olympia—Picture City failed to make its purchase money first mortgage payments beginning in March 1926 (Beales 7). All the while, Mahan claims, wealthy Olympia Beach [Jupiter Island] residents "went on giving their parties and enjoying the Florida Sun" (Mahan 11).

February 21, 2003. Gainesville, Fla.

I could not find data for any film from 1915 titled Westward, Ho! *I consulted the pages of Richard Alan Nelson's detailed history of Florida's motion picture legacy. There was something on page 409 . . .*

Names

Directed by George F. Marion and starring Robert Patton Gibbs, the feature film *Westward, Ho!* was to be the first made in the Stuart and Hobe Sound vicinity. Extras were selected from local talent and filming went from Stuart west to Indiantown and south to Rocky Point, just bordering Hobe Sound (Hutchinson 209; "To Make"). Some of the final editing was performed in Jacksonville (Crankshaw, "Hobe Sound"). Stuart proprietor Stanley Kitching (Broster's nephew) promised to "procure the rights to have this picture presented at the Lyric Theatre as soon as Mr. Savage releases it for exhibition" ("To Make").

. . . there, a detail in Nelson's text confirmed it. I have been misled!

Little did Stuart residents know that Savage duped them with a phony film title. He had wanted to keep other motion picture directors and filmmakers from knowing his true aim. Savage actually filmed *Robinson Crusoe,* which was released and distributed by State Rights and Warner Brothers in November 1916. In Stuart, Kitching delivered: on February 15, 1917, *Robinson Crusoe* was screened in the 250-seat Lyric to such a crowd that shortly thereafter ground was broken for a second, and larger, Lyric (Thurlow 111). Indeed, the film was a nationwide box-office success, despite or because of Director Marion's numerous "realistic" scenes that focused in on the atrocities committed by black cannibals (Nelson, v II 409).

Moving Picture World. December 16, 1916. "'Robinson Crusoe' (Savage)."

"The company had scarcely started to work when the ambition was born in the breast of every colored man for miles around to become a moving picture cannibal" (1667).

The individuals were apparently "willing to appear in a film depicting the least desirable aspects of their racial history" (Nelson, v II 410).

Interest in local movie making, however, was not limited to the ambitions of those of a single race. The newspapers describe a universal and wide-reaching fascination. Savage's stay in Stuart was so well received that soon the newspapers were buzzing.

Stuart Messenger. April 28, 1916. "Picturesque Stuart in Moving Pictures."

". . . there is a probability of making Stuart a permanent place for the production of many high-class pictures" (1).

Stuart Messenger May 12, 1916. "Movie Actors Well Pleased With Stuart."

Stuart residents feel confident that the film's success will draw production studios to the area (1).

While the film's achievement did generate a number of "Crusoe pictures" (Nelson, v II 410), none, however, were filmed in Stuart. In fact, *Robinson Crusoe* was the only dramatic narrative film ever produced near Olympia—Picture City in the first half of the twentieth century.[22]

The film's bogus title *Westward, Ho!* confounds just about as much as does the history of the name "Hobe Sound." The early history of Hobe Sound and Jupiter Island are so closely intertwined that the two were at one time synonymous and their names intimately connected (Ziemba 69). People have tried to untangle the history by attempting to trace the derivation of names.[23]

What's in a name? What do names tell us? To muse: Savage's duplicitous film title *Westward, Ho!* figuratively gestures "west," paradoxically foreshadowing the fate of Picture City—and Hollywood as the center of the movie making industry as destined to be on the West, not East, Coast. And "Hobe Sound has the distinction of being the only post office in the United States with the name" (Mahan 51).

Miami Herald. March 10, 1926. Movie Listings.

". . . Astounding Adventure . . . stupendous story!" (55).

Mortgage Foreclosure. September 23, 1932.

Mary Duke Biddle, Plaintiff

vs.

Olympia Development Corporation, a corporation of Florida, Defendant

"This is a suit to foreclose 6 certain mortgages now owned and held by Plaintiff herein, given to secure notes which have not been paid and are in default. . . ."

Local newspapers went silent. Martin County Public Records specify foreclosures, among them suits filed by Farmers Bank and Trust Company beginning in September 1926; no records indicate that Fannie Hurst's—or any "prominent" buyer's—house was ever built (Public Records of Martin County). The only "Olympia" in Florida to thrive after 1926 was Miami's 2,147-seat grand and highly embellished Olympia Theatre. Designed by renowned theater architect John Eberson, the Olympia opened on February 18, 1926 (Kinerk and Wilhelm 221–4).[24] In March 1926, at the very same month Olympia—Picture City failed to make its purchase money mortgage payments, the Olympia Theatre was screening a film released by First National, fierce competitor of Adolph Zukor's Famous Players-Lasky. Strangely enough, the film's title: *The Lost World.*[25]

Miami Herald. March 10, 1926. "Olympia Beach Sold: 5,000-Acre Tract Figures in Deal; Development is Promised," by B.F. Snyder.

"All holdings of the Olympia Improvement Corporation, original developers of Olympia Beach, Bon Air Beach and Olympia are shown by [a] deed to have transferred to the Olympia Holding Corporation." These holdings included 5,000 acres of beach and river property. "Much of the property is on the west side of Jupiter river, extending southward a considerable distance beyond the southern boundary of the old Gomez grant, and across the Dixie Highway and Florida East Coast Railroad."

"Along with the land the Olympia Holding Corporation also acquired all buildings and equipment of the Olympia Improvement Corporation, including an electric light plant, water works, hotel, cottages, machinery and offices of the company at West Palm Beach and Olympia" (4).

A mortgage given the grantors by the new owners called for $1,166,000 and indicated that the actual amount of cash involved in the deal was $1 million. Mortgages assumed by the purchasers totaled $425,000, raising the total cost of the property to $2,500,000. "The transfer is by far the most important ever recorded in Martin County" (4).

February 10, 2001. Hobe Sound, Fla.

. . . Heading towards Hobe Sound Beach on Bridge Road, I crossed over Gomez Road and, on Jupiter Island, I found Beach Road running parallel to Gomez Road and the Atlantic Ocean. Gomez Road serves the Sound side and Beach Road serves the sea side. Tucked away off the roads, behind a lush forest of pines, palms, sea grape, and flowering trees, are hundreds of houses—"shingled New England clapboard, Spanish arched, crushed-roof Bahama" (Barry 18). Along the roads, visible are small name signs planted beside service entrances and drives for each residence: Duke, Blake, Reed, Burke, Ford, Whitehead, Johnson, Cole, Downing, Bartram, Fentress, Sinclair. . . .

East · West

On the other U.S. coast, the obstacles of development were not groves and the Everglades, but the citrus gardens of Orange County and the San Fernando Valley and "recognition of the desert as simply another abstraction of dirt and dollar signs" (Davis 4).

Miami Herald Tropic Magazine. February 9, 1969. "Hobe Sound Hideaways: Natural Habitat of the Old Line Rich," by Bill Barry.
Front cover: "Even the Money Must be Old."

In the winter of 1969, apparently on the prowl for lifestyle trends, *Tropic's* Bill Barry reported from Hobe Sound that the railroad tracks in Hobe Sound represent the railroad's "Old Line." The tracks dissect the town:

> neatly and cleanly. . . . On the east side of the railroad tracks is the Sound and the sea and Jupiter Island—winter home of Roosevelt, Whitney, Ford, Olin, Whistler, Doubleday; on the west side of the tracks is the town and the shops, and homes of the people who are not Old Line. (14)

When the Olympia Improvement Corporation sold to the Reed Family in the early 1930s (Public Records of Martin County), Jupiter Island became the home for quiet money as opposed to the flashy dollars that had built Miami and Palm Beach. Under the Reeds, Hobe Sound's Jupiter Island became an insulated community. In fact, Jupiter Island and the whole of Hobe Sound remain a *non*-Hollywood, a nice place that is "hard to label" (Filo) versus "Los Angeles (and its alter ego Hollywood) . . . a city of seduction and defeat, the antipode of critical intelligence" (Davis 18).

February 14, 2001. Micanopy, Fla.

On the return trip north to Gainesville, Fla., I took a detour off Interstate I-75 to U.S. Highway 441. In historic Micanopy, on an old book dealer's dusty shelves I discovered Jay Barnes's Florida Hurricane History. I read: A Category 4 hurricane swept across Miami on September 18, 1926, and, in September 1928, another powerful storm moved directly over Palm Beach and the south shores of Lake Okeechobee near Belle Glade. The Miami Hurricane killed 373 people, injured 6,381, and left 43,000 homeless and another 811 missing. 1,836 storm victims drowned in the Palm Beach and Lake Okeechobee Hurricane weather disaster (Barnes 111–42).

(Not quite) out like a light

As the historical accounts and newspaper reports describe it, the height of the fantastic Florida land boom, which started in 1922, began tapering off in the spring of 1926 and went out like a light when the great hurricane of 1926 hit Miami that fall. In the winter of 1929, the name Hobe Sound was restored as the town's official name. Thus despite national trade advertising, the fragmented yet grandiose dream of Olympia—Picture City faded aborning. The '26 and '28 hurricanes and the '29 crash evidently inflicted damage to the ideological and financial capital of the region's boosters. These factors—combined with the embargoes by the F.E.C. on shipments of building materials, failure of local speculation, and the adoption of Blue Laws—have all been held in some part responsible for sealing Florida's movie-making fate in the 1920s.[26] New findings suggest, too, that Florida's banking failures of 1926 played a significant role.

Alas, Hollywood, California prevailed.

> Southern California—meaning Los Angeles, meaning Hollywood—possessed an affinity between me-

> dium and place that would soon attract the entire industry to it like a powerful magnet. Here, [D.W.] Griffith proved, was an environment, social and scenic, that was composed of fragments available for eclectic use. (Starr 293)

Griffith had tried Florida. In November 1919, he took his company to a location near Fort Lauderdale and made two routine productions, *The Idol Dancer* and *The Love Flower.* In 1923, he returned to film *The White Rose.* Ever since his 1915 epic *Birth of a Nation,* however, controversy regarding his treatments of African Americans surrounded his productions. Griffith's work in Florida eventually amounted to only sporadic location shooting. Yet imagine this possibility: the likes of David Wark Griffith and Cecil Blount De Mille—two directors largely responsible for mobilizing Southern Californian movie making in the teens and 1920s (Starr 289–312) and consequently securing that locale as the center of the American film industry—had instead *made all their pictures in Florida.*

February 28, 2002.

Suppose the Selznick's had succeeded? . . .

Socio-cultural critic Mike Davis argues that the turn-of-the-century Southern Californian publicists' "imagery, motifs, values, and legends were in turn endlessly reproduced in Hollywood, while continuing to be incorporated into the ersatz landscapes of suburban Southern California" (Davis 20). Like Los Angeles, Olympia—Picture City may have been planned or designed in a very fragmentary sense (primarily at the level of its trace infrastructure), but, unlike Los Angeles, where celluloid or the electronic screen have remained the dominant media of the region's self-expression, Olympia—Picture City was not infinitely envisioned in quite the same manner. Nonetheless, the grand idea for a utopian space for film production, exhibition, and everyday life at one time it had its own myriad rhetorics—fragments that, if one follows closely enough, make it possible to conceive associative histories far more textured than an old one-dimensional map[27] and, strangely enough, closely resembling the movies.

"[Film] is a mobile map. . . . Film has much in common with [this] traveling geography, especially with regard to its constant reinvention of space."

—Guiliana Bruno,
"Site-Seeing: Architecture and the Moving Image"

January 2003. Winter Break.

When traveling just outside of the Palm Beaches in 2003, I notice bright orange billboards beside the north- and south-bound lanes of the Florida Turnpike. They hype the "new golden age" of living, a planned housing community dubbed "Olympia."

Coda

The intertext is ironic, if largely unnoticed. Olympia, it seems, is being "remade."[28] The new sprawling development "rising in Palm Beach County" promises to "suggest the look and feel and glamour of Palm Beach itself. . . . The atmosphere," it boasts, "is very much Old World. The life style is the very best of the New."

These passages are drawn from Olympia's extensive full-color glossy promotional materials. Olympia, located in Wellington, Florida, is a product of Minto Communities, Inc., a South Florida building company, and architect Mitch Kunick. This collaboration self consciously and heavily borrows from and capitalizes on the designs and name of renowned Palm Beach architect Maurice Fatio. What Minto et al do not share in their promotional literature, nor in their oral representations delivered by sales consultants, is that Fatio came to the United States from Geneva in 1920 expressly to build the city of Olympia. His Palm Beach fame came *later,* after Olympia—Picture City failed to materialize. Although in their sales office Minto proudly displays a book of Fatio's work, those who buy Minto's hype—and houses priced from $283,900 to over $1,000,000—may still have little idea, if any at all, that the developer borrowed the site name and, more significantly, in the process of doing so elided a tiny bit of remarkable history about their development's namesake. Strikingly, this new Olympia's "Old World" speaks not to the promise of Olympia—Picture City and Florida in the 1920s, and not even to the obvious referent, the Mediterranean; rather, it refers to society architect Fatio's Mediterranean-*inspired* Palm Beach houses of the 1930s.

The new "Olympia" marks a reinvention, but only through an imaginative revisiting of the forgotten city, exploring a path not taken, is this revealed.

Less than a few dozen miles north of this new and monstrous simulacrum, the light standards for Picture City still stand forlornly along A-1-A, the remains of an alternative future.

July 20, 2004. Gainesville, Fla.

As I edited this essay for publication, I decided to conduct another on-line search of the Historical New York Times, *on this occasion for display ads. Apfel, Day, and Isman, I found, ran a bombastic full-page ad for Olympia Beach—Picture City dated December 25, 1925.*

Subsequent full-page ads (bearing the same above names) appeared on January 3, 17, and 31, 1926. In a startling new research development, I recognized that Picture City Studios was speculated locally and promoted in advertisements only in the South Florida papers, for the New York Times' advertisements make no mention of a utopian space for film production, exhibition, and everyday life.

Notes

I warmly thank Eva Campbell for our afternoon interview in February 2001, and for sharing her personal collection of primary source documents and photographs regarding the history of Picture City as well as Hobe Sound's history under the management of the Reed family and the Hobe Sound Company since 1933. I also thank journalist Joe Crankshaw for lively e-mail exchanges about Florida's movie production history. I am particularly grateful to Susan Duncan, former Curator of the Historical Society of Martin County, and the late Caroline Pomeroy Ziemba, of the Stuart Heritage Museum, for sharing their knowledge of Martin County's past and guiding me to many useful people and sources. I am indebted to Susan Duncan for her continued assistance and encouragement.

I appreciate, too, the staffs of the Elliott Museum, the Martin County Historical Society, the Stuart Heritage Museum—especially Sally Stuart Glassburn—and the Hobe Sound Public Library. I also thank Roma Thornton for joining the research journey and Jeff Rice for his stimulating comments—and cajoling—over the years of this enterprise. I dedicate this essay to my parents, Joan Cummings Noto and Edward Ronald Noto. Without them, I would not have experienced the thrill of discovery and the pleasure of invention with respect to this project. *"Look, there's the water tower!"*

1. *Webster's Seventh New Collegiate Dictionary.* Springfield, MA: G & C Merriam Company, 1971: 839.

2. In 2002, public works re-paved and, in 2003, added signals at this four-way intersection.

3. In September 1696, the Englishman Jonathan Dickinson and his British Barkentine ship, the *Reformation,* ran ashore on Jupiter Island while en route to Philadelphia. In his *Journal,* also known by its formal title *God's Protecting Providence,* Dickinson penned the earliest written accounts concerning Jupiter Island. The park is named in his honor. See his "Narrative of a Journey from Port Royal in Jamaica to Philadelphia, August 23, 1696 to April 1, 1697" in *Jonathan Dickinson's Journal or God's Protecting Providence.* Stuart, FL: Southeastern Printing Company, Inc., 1981. Also, see Janet Hutchinson's *History of Martin County,* page 199 and Douglas Waitley's *Roadside History of Florida,* pp. 250–51.

4. The development of Olympia and Olympia Beach predated Picture City, though the names "Olympia," "Olympia—Picture City," "Olympia Beach—Picture City," and "Picture City" are used interchangeably in various historical records.

5. See "The *Bildungsroman* and Its Significance in the History of Realism (Toward a Historical Typology of the Novel)" in *Speech Genres and Other Late Essays.* Trans. Vern M. McGee. Ed. Caryl Emerson and Michael Holquist. Austin: U of Texas P, 1986. 10–59.

6. Janet Hutchinson records that in Tallahassee on May 29, 1925, Governor John W. Martin signed the legislature bill creating the County of Martin. See *History of Martin County.* Comp. Janet Hutchinson. Ed. Emeline K. Paige. Stuart, FL: Historical Society of Martin County, 1998: 67–73. In 2003, "Martin County consists of the City of Stuart [County seat], and the Towns of Jupiter Island, Ocean Breeze Park, and Sewall's Point. Respectively, they are 5.5, 2.6, .1, and 1.2 square miles in size. It also includes the communities of Hobe Sound, Hutchinson Island, Indiantown, Jensen Beach, North River Shores, Palm City, Port Salerno, Rio, South County, and Tropical Farms." See "About Martin County." *Martin County, Florida.* 15 June 2001 < http://www.martin.fl.us/about.html>.

7. See Siegfried Kracauer, "Calico-World: The UFA City in Neubabelsberg." Levin, Thomas Y., ed., trans., intro. *The Mass Ornament: Weimar Essays.* Cambridge, MA and London: Harvard UP, 1995.

8. See Anne O'Hare McCormick, "Miracle Men on Florida's Gold Coast." *New York Times* 8 Mar. 1925: SM3. McCormick characterizes the proponents of the land boom, calling their undertakings "the latest violent form of winter sport."

9. Important to mention is the other "Hollywood," Hollywood, Florida, founded by planning visionary Joseph Wesley Young. Hollywood, Florida, located between Palm Beach and Miami, was incorporated as a city on November 28, 1925. Having formerly lived in California, Young chose as the name of his "Dream City" the name of the Southern California town that had once been so attractive to him (thus, in name only, the correlation with Hollywood, California). See Roberts, Richard. "A Brief History of Our City." *City of Hollywood, Florida.* 2002. <http://www.hollywoodfl.org/html/brief_history.htm>.

10. For a detail-rich portrait of Jacksonville's colorful film history, see Richard Alan Nelson's third chapter in *Florida and the American Motion Picture Industry 1898–1980* Volume I. For my brief account I draw from Nelson's account in his 1983 volume, his 1987 publication *Lights! Camera! Florida!,* Terry Ramsaye's *A Million and One Nights,* Eileen Bowser's *The Transformation of Cinema,* and newspaper stories.

11. In his November 8, 1992 feature article for the *Stuart News*'s "Treasure Guide," Crankshaw insists that, "The Blue Laws did the most damage because the film makers liked to use the deserted city streets on Sundays for their scenes." See "Hobe Sound Wasn't Always a Peaceful Place," page 124.

12. In 1915, the existing Lyric Theater was actually the first of three with the same name. John C. Hancock built this first Lyric Theater in 1913. A second Lyric was replaced by the third Lyric built in the same locale as the second, near Stuart's downtown (in fact, just near the old Feroe buildings), and which opened its doors on March 15, 1926. The third Lyric still exists today (Hutchinson 96; Ziemba 142–3).

13. The Foundation hopes to raise funds to refurbish the historic site as a local cultural center and, because of its architectural style and former use as a two-room schoolhouse, list the property on the National Register of Historic Places. See McCue, Dan. "Historic Status Sought for Apollo School." *Stuart News* (20 Aug. 2000): B 1,9.

14. A full-page advertisement in the *Miami Daily News* was titled "Our Florida Selection Olympia Beach–Picture City," along with a sub-heading, "Named for its Picturesqueness" (22 Dec. 1925): 37. A January 20, 1926 full-page spread in *The Miami Herald* promoted the "Studio Section of Olympia Beach—Picture City" (23-E).

15. In 1994, an attorney and adjunct assistant professor of history at Florida State University, Raymond B. Vickers, published a groundbreaking account of Florida's bank loan failures during the Florida land boom of the mid-twenties—the years preceding the stock market crash of 1929. Using bank records that had been legally sealed for almost 70 years, Vickers' offers a comprehensive study revealing previously untold—and unknown—accounts of Florida's massive insider abuses and conspiracies to defraud. His account sheds new light on all 1920s South Florida land speculation ventures and the

ensuing panic that befell the public. See Raymond B. Vickers. *Panic in Paradise: Florida's Banking Crash of 1926.* (Tuscaloosa and London: U of Alabama P, 1994). In particular, see pp. 17–77 regarding Palm Beach banks.

16. At the University of Florida in 1977, Robert J. Ceravolo published his voluminous master's thesis entitled "Maurice Fatio: Palm Beach Society Architect." Ceravolo's biography of Fatio makes no mention of those years in the early 1920s when Fatio prepared designs for Olympia, and specifically for the planned Olympia Beach Hotel. In fact, there is no mention of Olympia. Ceravolo, however, apparently had no access to Fatio Taylor's letters, those that confirm her father's early 1920s business in the area now called Hobe Sound. Ceravolo instead reports that Fatio arrived in Palm Beach in 1927, where he found "a fantasy land dominated by the Spanish castles of Addison Mizner" (37). There, Fatio began designing homes for the Palm Beach set. Fatio's Palm Beach work is as well known today as is Addison Mizener's.

17. Seymour "Sy" Brody reports that, "by 1925, she [Fannie Hurst, (1889–1968)] and Booth Tarkington were the highest paid writers in the United States." "Fannie Hurst," <http://www.us-israel.org/jsource/biography/hurst.html>. For a complete account, see Brody, Seymour. *Jewish Heroes and Heroines of America: 150 True Stories of American Jewish Heroism.* Hollywood, Florida: Lifetime Books, Inc., 1996.

18. For a brief time, author Zora Neale Hurston (1891–1960) worked as Hurst's secretary. In the early 1940s, Hurston worked as a story consultant to Paramount Pictures—the studio once led by Adloph Zukor and, for a time, employing David O. Selznick (Schatz 69–81). Hurston died in obscurity in Fort Pierce, St. Lucie County, FL, which was, ironically, at one time part of Martin County (Hutchinson 173–4).

19. Film historian David Cook locates Selznick (and his Select Picture Company) among a group of men who, by 1914, controlled independent companies and who would come to dominate the American film industry. Among them were "Carl Laemmle of Universal Pictures, Adolph Zukor of the Famous Players Company and Jesse L. Lasky of the Feature Play Company (both later merged with several smaller production companies and the Paramount Distribution Exchange as the Famous Players-Lasky Corporation), Samuel Goldfish (later "Goldwyn") of the Goldwyn Pictures Corporation, Louis B. Mayer of the Metro Picture Corporation, Marcus Loew and Nicholas and Joseph Schenck of Loew's, Incorporated, Lewis J. Selznick [1870–1933] of the Selznick Picture Corporation, William Fox of the Fox Film Corporation, and, after the war, Harry, Abe, Sam, and Jack Warner of Warner Brothers Pictures, Incorporated" (42).

20. These details appear in several contexts, i.e., an article entitled, "Olympia-Gomez to Be Picture City; New York Picture Men Buy Big Tracts for Huge Development," in the *Stuart Messenger;* amateur historian Beales's "Once There Was Picture City," 1–7; and public records.

21. *A Chronology of Florida Post Offices* (1962) dates Olympia's Post Office from 1923–1929. See Bradbury, Alfred G., and E. Story Hallock. "Olympia Post Office 1923–1929." *A Chronology of Florida Post Offices.* Sewall's Point FL: The Florida Federation of Stamp Clubs and the Sewall's Point Company, 1962.

22. In the second half of the century, the areas today known as "The Treasure Coast" and "The Gold Coast" had some interesting film activity. Robert Alan Nelson reports that out-of-state filmmakers used the area for location shooting. For a list of films, see Nelson's Volume II, p. 508, n20.

23. One account claims that before Gomez, Indians called Jobi had lived on the land. The water between the mainland and the island was called Jobe Sound. Jobe was like Jove, thus the island became Jupiter, named for the god of mythology. Much later, the Spanish J in Jobe was displaced by the Anglo H (Barry 18). Another account—interpreting various travel narratives such as the 1696–97 writings of Jonathan Dickinson, the reports of Don Pedro Menendez de Aviles of 1565, and those by Bernard Romans in 1775—asserts that the Indians of the area were the Jobses (Crankshaw, "Hobe Sound Wasn't Always . . .").

Of the claim that between 1763 and 1783 the English tried to establish the colony of Hoe Bay, *Jonathan Dickinson's Journal* confirms "Hoe-Bay" (19), and Paul Mahan corroborates with the slight spelling variation "Hobay" (Mahan 5; Ziemba 69–70). Moreover, the prefatory narrative to the Abstracts of Title for all land and lots in Martin County, prepared by the Law Offices of Fleming and Fleming in1916, traces the derivation of the name Jupiter Island to this latter account, citing that the English "Hoe Bay" was spelled by the Spanish as "Jove" on an old map in the room of the Florida Historical Society. "When the British came into possession of Florida, it would be easy to transform the word Jove in Jupiter, the two names being synonymous for the same heathen diety" (Fleming & Fleming). Thus the derivation of the present day names "Hobe Sound" and "Jupiter Island" is, indeed, enmeshed. Accounts vary, as well, with respect to how Hobe Sound got its "last name." It seems likely that it may have come from the inlet, or sound, at Jupiter.

24. The building was listed on the National Register of Historic Places in 1984, and survives today as The Olympia/Gusman—named for philanthropist Maurice Gusman who saved it from proposed demolition. See Kinerk and Wilhelm, page 224.

25. For movie listings for mid-March 1926, see the *Miami Herald* [Miami] (10 Mar.1926): 55.

26. Florida journalist Joe Crankshaw maintains the Blue Laws were responsible. In an email correspondence he writes, "The movie industry was once big stuff in Florida, that is why the Hobe Sound people wanted to develop Picture City as a major movie making center. They failed when church

ladies in Jacksonville enforced the Blue Laws and drove the fledgling industry out of the state" (correspondence with author, 30 Jan. 2003).

27. Though there are, indeed, old maps of Picture City. In addition to the "tentative" maps created by the developer and included in the mid-twenties Olympia—Picture City promotional materials, there is also a very large map, circa 1926, hanging on a wall in the Stuart Heritage Museum in Stuart, FL. The map includes Picture City. Several areas of the Picture City development are clearly visible, such as those for "Picture City Gardens" (near present day Hobe Sound Beach), "Picture City Ter." (near the light standards on A-1-A), as well as "Picture City Manors" and "Picture City Estates," depicted on the map as just above the northern border of the Gomez Grant. The map also shows Gomez Station, no longer in existence. The map, titled "East Half of Martin County, FL 1926," was compiled by The Roat Concern, Inc., Stuart, Martin County, FL Engineers and Surveyors. The map also reads, "Revised to November 1929."

28. In his essay "Kubla Honky Tonk: Voice in Cyber-Pidgin," Greg Ulmer tracks the hybrid voice of the technologies we inhabit and that inhabit us. "My ambition is to compose a remake" he writes, and the idea that the remake is, for Ulmer, a 20/21st century form of writing too often ignored. Through the concept of the film remake, Ulmer illustrates what he calls the composite diegesis of Xanadu. Similarly, Olympia can be read as a type of composite diegesis. See Gregory Ulmer, *Language Machines: Technologies of Literacy and Cultural Production.* Ed. Jeffrey Masten, et al. New York and London: Routledge, 1997. 252–71.

Works Cited

"About Martin County." *Martin County, Florida.* 15 June 2001. 20 Apr. 2003 <http://www.martin.fl.us/about.html>.

"Abstracts of Title and Title Insurance to All Land Lots in the County of Martin in the State of Florida No. 7329." Stuart, FL: Florida Abstract & Title Insurance Co. of Florida, 1956.

"An Appeal—Studio Section of Olympic Beach—Picture City." Advertisement. *Miami Herald*20 Jan. 1926: 23-E.

Andrews, Evangeline Walker and Charles McLean Andrews, eds. *Jonathan Dickinson's Journal or, God's Protecting Providence. Being the Narrative of a Journey from Port Royal, In Jamaica to Philadelphia between August 23, 1696 and April 1, 1697* [sic]. Stuart, FL: Southeastern Printing Company, Inc., 1981.

Bakhtin, Mikhail M. "The *Bildungsroman* and Its Significance in the History of Realism(Toward a Historical Typology of the Novel)" in *Speech Genres and Other Late Essays.* Trans. Vern M. McGee. Ed. Caryl Emerson and Michael Holquist. Austin: U of Texas P, 1986.

Barnes, Jay. *Florida's Hurricane History.* Chapel Hill: U of North Carolina P, 1998.

Barry, Bill. "Hobe Sound: Natural Habitat of the Old Line Rich." *Tropic: Miami Harold Magazine* 3.6 (9 Feb. 1969): 14+.

Beales, Walter R., III. "Once There Was Picture City." Unpublished Paper. Stuart, FL: Martin County Historical Society Archives, 1987.

Bowser, Eileen. *The Transformation of Cinema: 1907–1915.* Berkeley, Los Angeles, andLondon: U of California P, 1990. Vol. 2 of *History of the American Cinema.* Ed.Charles Harpole. 10 vols. 1990–2003.

Bradbury, Alfred G., and E. Story Hallock. "Olympia Post Office 1923–1929." *A Chronology ofFlorida Post Offices.* Sewall's Point FL: The Florida Federation of Stamp Clubs and the Sewall's Point Company, 1962.

Bramson, Seth H. *Speedway to Sunshine: The Story of the Florida East Coast Railway.* Boston : Boston Mills Press, 2001.

Brody, Seymour "Sy." "Fannie Hurst." *Jewish Virtual Library* 2003. 23 Feb. 2003 < http://www.us-israel.org/jsource/biography/hurst.html>.

Bruno, Guiliana. "Site-Seeing: Architecture and the Moving Image." Ed. Clark Arnwiner and Jesse Lerner. *Wide Angle* 19.4 (Oct. 1997): 8–24.

Campbell, Eva. Personal interview. 9 Feb. 2001.

Cook, David A. *A History of Narrative Film.* New York and London: W.W. Norton & Company, 1981, 1990, 1996.

Crankshaw, Joseph. "Historic Gomez Grant is Steeped in Memories of Florida's Past." *StuartNews* (1960).

—. "Hobe Sound Wasn't Always a Peaceful Place." *Stuart News "Treasure Guide"* 8 Nov.1992: 6, 12, 14, 124.

—. "Stuart, Martin Celebrate." *Miami Herald* Nov. 1 1985: 1TC ("Treasure Coast"), 5TC.

—. Email correspondence with author. 30 Jan. 2003.

Davis, Mike. *City of Quartz.* New York: Vintage Books, 1992.

"Day's Daily Drive." Advertisement. *New York Times* (31 Jan. 1926): RE6.

deCerteau, Michel. *The Writing of History.* (1975) Trans. Tom Conley. New York: Columbia UP, 1988.

DeYoung, Bill. "Almost Hollywood." *Stuart News.* 19 Apr. 2004: 1+.

Duncan, Susan L. Personal interview. 7 Feb. 2001.

East Half of Martin County, FL. Map. Stuart, Martin County, FL: William H. Roat and the Roat Concern, Inc., 1926.

Eder, Bruce. "Fannie Hurst Biography." MSN Entertainment *All Movie Guide.* 2003. 27 Feb.2003 <http://entertainment.msn.com/celebs/celeb.aspx?mp=b&c=342659>.

Eisenstein, Sergei. "Montage and Architecture." *Assemblage* 10 (1989): 111–31.

Filo, Edward. "Hobe Sound Defies Labels." *Stuart News* 10 Sept. 1998: "Inside South County."

Fleming & Fleming. "Prefatory" to *Abstracts of Title.* Jacksonville, FL: 29 Feb. 1916.

"Famous Names Among Picture City Buyers." *New York Times* 2 Sept. 1925: 39.

Fuller, Walter P. *This Was Florida's Boom.* St. Petersburg, FL: Times Publishing Company, 1954.

"Heywood Broun, World Famous Columnist." Advertisement for Olympia Beach—PictureCity. *New York Times* 17 Jan. 1926: RE3.

History of Martin County. Comp. Janet Hutchinson. Ed. Emeline K. Paige. Hutchinson Island,FL: Gilbert's Bar Press, 1975. Stuart, FL: Historical Society of Martin County, 1998.

Humoresque. Dir. Frank Borzage. With Gaston Glass and Vera Gordon. Cosmopolitan Productions and Famous Players-Lasky Corporation. 1920.

"Joseph P. Day to Sell Florida Development; With Felix Isman He Will Offer Olympia Beach—Picture City." *New York Times* 27 Dec.1925: X1.

"Jupiter Island Deal Closed." *Stuart Messenger* July 1923:1

"Jupiter Island Inn and Town." *Stuart Messenger* Apr. 1923:1.

Kiehl, Steven. "Old Apollo School May Get a New Life." *Palm Beach Post* 8 Aug. 1999: 1B+.

Kinerk, Michael D. and Dennis W. Wilhelm. "Dream Palaces: The Motion Picture Playhouse in the Sunshine State." *Journal of Decorative and Propaganda Arts* 23: Florida Theme Issue. Florida: The Wolfsonian—Florida International University, The Wolfson Foundation for Decorative and Propaganda Arts, Inc., and the Florida Department of State, Division of Historical Resources, 1998: 208–37.

Koszarski, Richard. *An Evening's Entertainment: The Age of the Silent Feature Picture, 1915–1928.* Berkeley, Los Angeles, and London: U of California P, 1990. Vol. 3 of *History of the American Cinema.* Ed. Charles Harpole. 10 vols. 1990–2003.

Kracauer, Siegfried. "Calico-World: The UFA City in Neubabelsberg." *The Mass Ornament: Weimar Essays.* Ed., Trans., and Intro. Thomas Y. Levin. Cambridge, MA and London: Harvard UP, 1995. 281–88.

Lind, Norah. "The Hobe Sound Story: Boom, Bust, Steady Growth." *Island: Through the Years.* Hobe Sound, FL: Jupiter Island Publishing Co., 1988. 40–45.

"Looking Back." *1997 Preferred Business Guide.* Hobe Sound, FL: Hobe Sound Chamber ofCommerce, 1997. 5–7.

Lost World, The. Dir. Harry O. Hoyt. With Bessie Love, Lewis Stone, and Wallace Beery. First National Pictures, Inc. 1925.

Lyric Theater, The. Advertisement. *Stuart Times* 19 Nov. 1925: 8.

MacIntyre, Diane. "Lewis J. Selznick." *The Silents Majority.* 2003. 15 Jan. 2003<http://www.silentsmajority.com/BTC/prod9.htm>.

Mahan, Paul. *Hobe Sound: It Could Only Happen in a Small Post Office.* Self Published (1978). Printed in Port Salerno, FL: Florida Classics Library, 1978.

Matlack, Shelton S. "Miami a Second Hollywood." *Suniland* 1.1 (Oct. 1924): 54–55.

McCue, Dan. "Historic Status Sought for Apollo School." *Stuart News* 20 Aug. 2000: B1+.

"Meacham Starts Olympia Sales Campaign This Week." *Stuart Messenger* 17 Jan. 1924: 1.

McCormick, Anne O'Hare. "Miracle Men on Florida's Gold Coast." *New York Times* 8 Mar.1925: SM3.

Minto Communities, Inc. *Olympia: Minto Ushers in the New Golden Age of the Palm Beaches.* Wellington, FL: Minto Communities, Inc., 2001, 2002, 2003.

"Movie Actors Well Pleased With Stuart." *Stuart Messenger* 12 May 1916: 1+.

Nance, Ellwood C. *The East Coast of Florida: A History 1500–1961.* Delray Beach, FL: The Southern Publishing Company, 1962.

Nelson, Richard Alan. *Florida and the American Motion Picture Industry 1898–1980.* Volumes I and II. New York and London: Garland Publishing, Inc., 1983.

—. *Lights! Camera! Florida! Ninety Years of Moviemaking and Television in the Sunshine State.* Tampa, FL: Florida Endowment for the Humanities, 1987.

Noto, Edward R. Letter to the author. 26 Oct. 2000.

"Offer of $10,000 School Building is Made to County." *Stuart Daily News* 9 Oct. 1925: 1.

"Olympia-Gomez To Be Picture City; New York Picture Men Buy Big Tracts for HugeDevelopment." *Stuart Messenger* 20 Aug. 1925: 1.

"Olympia Improvement Corporation, The." Advertisement. *Stuart Messenger* 17 Jan. 1924: 4–5.

—. Advertisements. *Stuart Messenger* 31 Jan. 1924: 4–5; 11.

Olympia—Picture City. Publisher unknown. c1925.

"Our Florida Selection: Olympia Beach—Picture City." Advertisement. *Miami Daily News and Metropolis* 22 Dec. 1925: 37.

"Picturesque Stuart in Moving Pictures." *Stuart Messenger* 28 Apr. 1916: 1+.

"Plan Big Florida Studio." *New York Times* 13 Sept. 1925: XII: 28.

"Pretty Hobe Sound Ideal Winter Resort; Picturesque Jupiter Island the Residential Section." *Stuart Messenger* 19 Nov. 1915: 1.

Public Records of Dade County, Florida. Plat Book "A" (1893): 17.

Public Records of Martin County, Florida. Deed Book No. 20 (1928): 116.

—. Deed Book No. 23 (1930): 238.

—. Deed Book No. 25 (1932): 524.

—. Lis Pendens Book No. 1 (1926): 59.

—. Mortgage & Loan Assignment Book No. 1 (1929): 435.

—. Mortgage & Loan Assignment Book No. 1 (1932): 558.

—. Mortgage Book No. 4 (1925): 26; 330.

—. Mortgage Book No. 6 (1925): 294.

—. Plats of Picture City, Plat Book No.1.

Public Records of Palm Beach County, Florida. Mortgage Book No. 65 (1923): 138.

—. Plats of Picture City, Plat Book No.1 (1925): 80.

Ramsaye, Terry. *A Million and One Nights: A History of the Motion Picture Through 1925.* New York: Simon and Schuster, 1926. London: Frank Cass & Company, 1964.

Reid, Paul. "Lost City of Olympia." *Palm Beach Post* 2 Oct. 2000: 1E+.

Roberts, Richard. "A Brief History of Our City." *City of Hollywood, Florida.* 2002. 12 Feb. 2003 <http://www.hollywoodfl.org/html/brief_history.htm>.

Robinson Crusoe. Dir. George F. Marion. With Robert Patton Gibbs. Henry W. Savage, Inc., State Rights, and Warner Bros. 1916.

"'Robinson Crusoe' (Savage)." *Moving Picture World* 30.11 (16 Dec. 1916): 1667.

Ray, Robert. "Mystery Trains." Rev. of *Reinventing Film Studies,* eds. Christine Gledhill andLinda Williams. *Sight and Sound.* Nov. 2000. 16 Feb. 2002 <http://www.bfi.org.uk/sightandsound/2000_11/mysterytrains.html>.

"St. Lucie Hotel." Advertisement. *Stuart Times* 20 Oct. 1916: 8.

"St. Lucie Hotel Opens for Season." *Stuart Messenger* 2 Jan. 1924: 1.

Sammons, Sandra W. *Henry Flagler: Builder of Florida.* Lake Buena Vista, FL: Tailored Tours Publications, 1993.

Schatz, Thomas. *The Genius of the System: Hollywood Filmmaking in the Studio Era.* New York, New York: Henry Holt and Company, 1988, 1996.

"Selznick Brothers Place Stamp of Approval on City for Production." *Florida Times Union* 13 Feb. 1921: Sec 2: 13.

"Selznick is Coming to Discuss Forming Mortgage Co. Here." *South Florida Developer* 23February 1926: 1.

"Selznick Sons May Take Over Motion Picture Project at Camp Johnston is Report." *Florida Metropolis* 12 Feb. 1921: 13.

Snyder, B.F. "Olympia Beach Sold: 5,000-Acre Tract Figures in Deal; Development is Promised." *Miami Herald* 10 Mar. 1926: 4.

Starr, Kevin. *Inventing the Dream: California Through the Progressive Years.* London: Oxford UP, 1985.

Stuart, Hix C. *The Notorious Ashley Gang; A Saga of the King and Queen of the Everglades.*Stuart, FL: St. Lucie Printing Co., 1928.

"The Lyric Theater: A Motion Picture House of Quality." Advertisement. *Stuart Times* 9 Nov. 1915: 8.

Thurlow, Sandra Henderson. *Stuart on the St. Lucie: A Pictorial History.* Stuart, FL: Sewall's Point Company, 2001.

"To Develop Picture City." *New York Times* 28 Nov. 1925: 2.

"To Make Movies at the St. Lucie Inlet: Henry W. Savage to Produce Feature in This Vicinity." *Stuart Messenger* 21 Apr. 1916: 1.

Vickers, Raymond B. *Panic in Paradise: Florida's Banking Crash of 1926.* Tuscaloosa and London: U of Alabama P, 1994.

"What Palm Beach and West Palm Beach Were Five Years Ago Olympia Beach—Picture CityShould be in a Few Years!" Advertisement. *New York Times* (3 Jan. 1926): RE5.

Waitley, Douglas. *Roadside History of Florida.* Missoula, MT: Mountain Press PublishingCompany, 1997.

"We Have No Competition." Advertisement for Olympia Beach—Picture City. *New York Times* 27 Dec. 1925: RE3.

"World's Largest Motion Picture Production Center Will Be Built at Camp. Jos. E. Johnston." *Florida Times Union* 1 Jan. 1921: Sec. 2, 13+.

Ziemba, Caroline Pomeroy. *Martin County, Our Heritage.* Stuart, FL: Stuart Heritage Inc., 1997.

8 Serial Logic: Meditations on *Homesick: FemTV Remembers the Gainesville Murders*

Elizabeth Coffman and Michelle Glaros

"To what extent is serial killing an effect of serial television, of its imprinting on our national unconscious?"

—Avital Ronell

First, there was one body. Then there were two. And then two more. In August 1990, a small town in Florida was rendered apocalyptic while the world's media watched, waiting for the next small interior space to be brought to narrative life by the macabre game playing of a serial killer. For two weeks, the town barely breathed. We spent our days calling the rumor hotline. We spent our nights watching images of our collective story flash by on television. Daniel Rolling, a transient who was camping in some woods close to student housing, stalked and mutilated five students that summer. He dismembered the bodies and "arranged" them within their apartment spaces so that upon entering the space the "viewer" would see the bodies posed and reflected in mirrors. The media coverage of the gruesome murders continued for several months, until Rolling was identified as the killer. During this same period, "camera-ready" bombs dropped for the first time on the city of Baghdad while the country watched and waited for the moment of impact to occur live on television again and again.

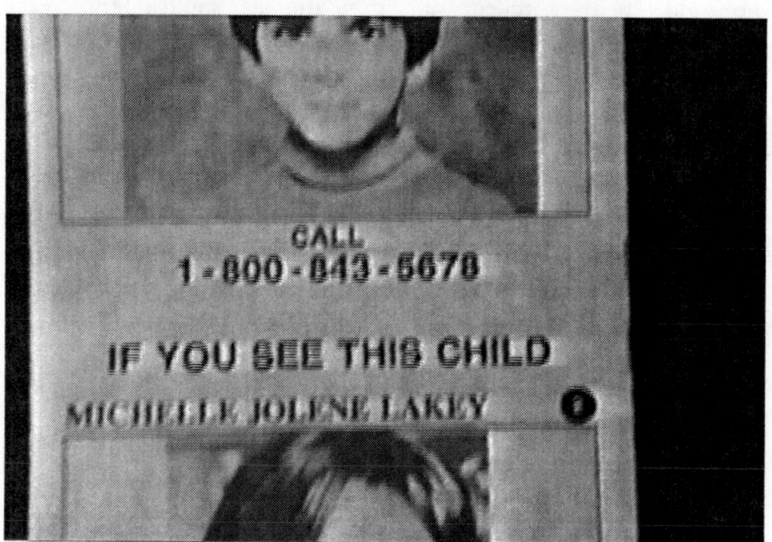

Michelle Glaros 2002. All subsequent images are used from this film and used by permission of Michelle Glaros.

With this experimental essay we would like to unearth the theoretical connections between serial killing and serialized media by simultaneously digging up an historical artifact—a video short produced by the collaborative FemTV-shortly after the serial killer Danny Rolling came through a Florida university town in 1990 and committed the "Gainesville Student Murders." We hope to use this "old media" as a divining rod that will show us *'the way,'* (or at least a way), to think about the migration and adaptation of what we are calling *serial logic* from television to new media. The video *Homesick* (FemTV, 8 min., 1993) retells neither the story of the victims who died, nor the detection process that catches their murderer, but rather, it presents impressions of our fragmented memories and our attempts to understand narratives that endlessly reproduce their own casualties/causalities. This is not so much an essay about a video, but rather an attempt to articulate a rhetoric for a media culture that is increasingly, and perhaps disturbingly, defined by serial violence. Thus, our writing surfs through a complex of ideas, visiting one before jumping to another while often circling back again. Its tangential, looping nature loosely mimics the organizational patterns of experimental video and the rhetorical logic of new media.

Ten years ago, FemTV used videotape and analog editing to explore the viewer's relationship to the serial gaming of both the killer and the media during those terrible weeks in 1990. Now, more than a decade later, it is increasingly easy to see how the gap defines the story. Seriality, perhaps the dominant logic that interfaces with new media, is most easily recognized by the intermittent structure of commercial television, with its repeated bits of narrative information, and its frequent interruptions of advertising spots and company promotionals. This logic of seriality also proliferates through the Internet, both in paradigmatic terms (repetition of forms-templates, layouts, gaming pathways) and syntagmatic "realities" (real-time narrative or informational interactions broken by periodic breaks, gaps, or hypertextual linkings).

The stories that most spectacularly repeat these interrupted patterns of "being" and "time" are contained in narratives of the serial killer and in the media's serial production of violence. Serial killers are found in countless adaptations on film and television and in mass cultural obsessions with more indirect narrative applications, such as in broadcast news reports of wartime bombings or in the repetition of killing patterns in video games. In most of these serial killing narratives, a particular taxonomy starts to emerge: questions of motive, detection, intuition, and profiling circulate around the mysterious absence of the killer. Death is never an end in these stories; it is merely a *shocking and awful* pause before the story/game continues.[1]

But why stir up trouble now? What can the genre of experimental video tell us about the permutations of serial logic and of the ways media artists must insert themselves into this logic in order to turn it on its head? As in any good series, we'll start at the beginning of our story:

Our video collaborative, known as FemTV, formed in the late 1980s, when a group of graduate students and local artists transformed a reading group into a video production collective. We wanted to answer the call we found in so much feminist film theory—to experimentally apply activist-oriented critical ideas to newly emerging forms of media technology, and to do so in noncommercial and interventionist ways. We completed several short videos that screened in museums and at conferences on topics circulating around women, technology, beauty, racism, and then serial killing. In 1990, FemTV became intrigued by the media coverage of the Gainesville student "event" and with, as Avital Ronell suggested to us, the similarities between serial murder and serial television. We found ourselves held hostage and then mesmerized by our roles as witnesses to the media's narrativizing of "events" in a small, university town, and by Danny Rolling's own specific and meticulous acts of murder. Between 1991 and 1993 we collected found footage and filmed/taped scenes in and around the sites of the Gainesville murders for *Homesick*.

Loosely divided into five parts, *Homesick* recreates images, spaces, and sounds that televisually imprinted themselves in our popular memory. Like the serial imprinting of the image of a plane hitting the World Trade Towers over and over again in 2001, the repeating video images of body bags being carried out of apartment complexes in 1990 constructed for us unseen, but imaginary, narratives of violently dismembered female bodies. Now, viewers watch body bags being moved to helicopters in Iraq, while their virtual witnessing is digitally reframed by blogs, cell phone images, and the absorption of fragmented bits of news. Absorption of repeated violence leads to alienation from the community, digital or not.[2]

During the incubation period for *Homesick,* the first Gulf War, known in history books and encyclopedias as the first "televised war," shattered our domestic spaces in ways eerily similar to Rolling's serial killing. The streaks of light and resulting blasts that flashed across our television screens daily interrupted soap operas and game shows with reckless disregard for their structures, as did the Gainesville Student Murders. We didn't think about these repeating patterns at the time, but now that we find ourselves playing this game again, we recognize ourselves oscillating between the positions of killer and audience. We watch live as the evidence of our country's technology in the Middle East flashes across our screens once again without emotion. We read online voices from the desert, while bloggers upload unsanctioned reports of military actions—illicit readings that remind us of what it felt like to be a community held hostage by violence.

Above all else, this essay is a retrospective of our entry into the rhetoric of new media. Fifteen years ago, as we cut *Homesick* on our analog editing system, we were struck by new media theorists' prophecies about the democratization of artistic production—production that soon got actualized by the computer's agile, non-linear combinations of image, sound, and text. These prophecies resonated with the manifestos of those artists who advocated producing guerilla video in essays of the 1970s and who inspired our own turn to video.[3] With this resonance in mind, we direct our attention toward an exploration of serial logic as both the legacy and the link that connects "old media" to new media. Years after the final cut, we discern a parallel between the rise of our interest in seriality and the rise of new media. Through this act of re-visioning FemTV's work, we see *Homesick* as an expression of our early attempts to negotiate the interactive narratives of violence that were then coming to life on other screens.

Physiognomy

Most writing about serial killing seeks to unveil the identity of the serial killer. For example, in *Serial Killers: Death and Life in America's Wound Culture,* Mark Seltzer focuses on the connections between the killer's mind and his desire to mimic (as a means of negotiating identity) what the author calls "machine culture," a culture of addictive violence and spectacle. Seltzer employs Walter Benjamin's theory of mimesis when considering the nature of the serial killer's identity formation. We rejected this approach to serial killing, adopting instead

Benjamin's theories of habit and memory and a broader consideration of what happens to the audience, once the "aura" of individuality is shattered by reproduction. Whereas Seltzer is interested in the serial killer's identity formation and the public perception of serial murder, we are more interested in the effects of seriality on its audience and in seriality's rhetorical connections to "old" and new media. What does serial violence do to us?

Benjamin's ideas of tactility and the media explore the phenomenological experiences of the audience as well as how those experiences are structurally mediated through media. As Michael Taussig points out about Eisenstein and his relationship to film, the Soviet director realized early on "the interdependence of montage with the physiognomic aspects of visual worlds"(28). Film is the closest thing we have to consciousness—its tactility is connected to its meaning with audiences. Eisenstein worked out the dialectical politics of film in the graphic perspectives within shots, between shots, in the slowing down of shots, and through an analogous understanding of Kabuki theatre. After working in film, (and reading Eisenstein), the members of FemTV also carried a tactile understanding of the visual world around with them which was only heightened by the murders and the pervasive media coverage of primarily young, female students in Florida. We remember viscerally what it felt like to be working and teaching in a university town that shut down for fear of a killer. It was not just fear that we felt; it was, more importantly, a structural and metaphorical sense of containment.

Homesick investigates the manner in which the structural formation of media representations informs our popular memory and then, less clearly, how these memories inflect our understanding of and interaction with the world. Our interest in the experience of women in televisual culture reflects those areas of reception theory that move beyond the passive receiver model of communication to include models that consider how popular memory informs our habits, especially our visceral responses to situations (e.g., how we feel in the shower after watching Hitchcock's infamous "shower scene" in *Psycho* or swimming in the ocean after viewing *Jaws,* both casualty-producing narratives that quicken the heartbeat and shorten the breath). In his "Work of Art in the Age of Mechanical Reproduction" essay, Walter Benjamin suggests that the distracted reception of film has more in common with a kind of "tactile appropriation" of art than with concentrated "optical reception," and that this tactility is "accomplished not so much by attention as by habit" (240).

Voiceover from *Homesick: FemTV Remembers the Gainesville Murders*

> I remember . . . sitting in my house . . . and hearing a noise.
>
> I remember sitting in my house and hearing a noise. I remember sitting in my house and hearing a noise. I remember sitting in my house and hearing a noise . . . (http:// www.archive.org/details/HomesickTheGainesvilleStudentMurders).

Homesick's use of varying image qualities, textures, and resolutions explores the relationship between memory, liveness, and realness. For those who lived during the 1950s and 1960s, the aesthetic of the Super-8 image is nostalgic. Even for those born much later, the simulation of this image on television dramas such as *The Wonder Years* creates a memorable association between its grainy, jumpy aesthetic and the notion of childhood memory. During the 1980s, the bright, high-contrast video image distinctly came to mean both "real" and "unstaged." Most often viewed on broadcast television or in documentaries, these video images suggested the idea that what was recorded had been or was "live" and that thus it was "real." In contrast, the filmic or cinematic image came to mean "highly constructed" and "staged," a distinction which explains the shaky, handheld camerawork and video look of the successful horror film, *The Blair Witch Project* (1999)—its texture made it seem *live.*

Today, the ultra-high-resolution animated images of digital games suggest an other-worldly quality that is increasingly labeled "realistic." In *The Language of New Media,* Lev Manovich calls the reader's attention to the cultural values associated with varying image qualities or textures. Manovich argues that our notion of what looks real is not real at all, but photographic, and that programmers' and designers' pursuit of more and more realistic or real-looking digital worlds and games has actually resulted in what he calls hyper-real images, images whose resolution is in fact higher than that produced by the human eye viewing the natural world. Our repeated exposure to these digital images, notes Manovich, has conditioned us into recognizing photo-reality as "reality."

By sequencing together in slow motion a news image of a Gainesville police detective, Super 8 film footage of Rolling's campsite, and then audio from a 1990 *Phil Donahue* talk show, *Homesick* questions the visual and aural codes of the media's serial killer formula. Structurally, serial killing stories represent a crossroads between the paradigmatic and syntagmatic elements of narrative meaning.[4] Each serial killing story includes formulaic elements: woods, houses, dark corners, POV shots, body bags, police photos, eroticized female bodies, a heightened sense of sound. *Homesick* varies the quality and texture of images and sounds to foreground the paradigmatic qualities of the serial killing narrative and to investigate, using Benjamin's term, the "tactile" nature of our memories.

Homesick's delivery is more contemplative and less political than other alternative media approaches such as Eisenstein's. But FemTV shares with him the impulse to distract from mechanical conformity and to question paradigms that formally shape institutions, whether they are police investigations or capitalist markets. Differently textured images in *Homesick* are presented multiple times, separated by the appearance of extended black screens and an assortment of music, sound effects, and voiceovers, ultimately landing within the paradigm of a "stylized" art documentary. Video suggests the televisual image, Super 8 film represents a home movie aesthetic, a slowed, video image evokes the surveillance camera, and Fisher-Price "pixellated" images suggest the imaginar, provoking a deconstructive space for 'woman-to-camera' interaction. The audio track is a similar collage of news announcers, police detectives and psychics—disembodied voices describing memories, and original and found music.

The paradigm for serial killing on film and television becomes syntagmatic for the public in its inherent connection to time and repetition; corpses are produced almost as quickly as meaning, and subject positions oscillate as if in an endless hall of distorted mirrors, magnifying our sense of dread. *Homesick* considers multiple sites of identification in the serial killer formula, and deliberately tries to undermine the distinctions between victim, detective, witness, and killer in order to create a visceral sense of fragmentation and confusion over boundaries.

Standing in this crossroads, our project means to press some urgent questions: to what extent is popular memory composed of the different textures of images and sounds, of, for instance, the whine of 747's overhead? Does the serial repetition of these textures reinforce their currency in the iconography of our popular memory bank? What is the physiognomy of the past?

Being Live

Historically, the logic of seriality is introduced as a medium matures and develops a mass market because serials are remarkable tools for establishing and then developing a consuming public. Serials set up delays across narrative breaks that are often marked by the device of the cliffhanger. Unlike the classical narrative text, serials give the appearance of being never-ending. Indeed, it is the suggestion of the never-ending story that defines soap operas, one of the most popular and familiar forms of serial television. As Roger Hagedorn notes in his brief study of serial narrative "serials are distinguished as a narrative form by the discourse they trace between the producing industry and the readers/spectators/listeners who consume them" (27). In the breaks between episodes and temporary resolutions, fans endlessly speculate in office lunchrooms, fan magazines, and themed chat rooms about possible narrative trajectories.

One of the most striking characteristics of electronic seriality, as opposed to earlier forms, is the relationship it maintains with its audience. In the gap of meaning that opens up after trauma or horror occurs, repeating images of the event offer small comfort to the viewer. They operate on the viewer's open wounds but eventually numb them with repeated exposure. Yet, by watching repetitive television we experience a communal commingling with dreadful anticipation—the emotional state that most signifies the serial—a leery expectation of what is yet to come. These repetitions point to television's predictable attempts to patch over the gap with graphics, music, and serial imagery. The whole process plays like a bad pop song or a reality game show gone wrong. Says Ronell, "TV acts as a shock absorber to the incomprehensibility of survival, and views being 'live' or outliving as the critical enigma of our time" (*Finitude's Score* 308).

The recent appearance and reappearance of shocking photographs of sado-masochistic torture from the Abu Ghraib prison in Iraq remind us of our role as audience to the serial killer's performance and invoke the defining question of serial logic: what next? Television and the Internet reframe the images of the soldiers documenting their digital "fun" in powerful ways. For many viewers, a soldier giving a 'thumbs-up' next to a dead or humiliated Iraqi becomes one of the most damning images of the U.S. military in decades. In her essay, "The Photographs are Us," Susan Sontag suggests that the Abu Ghraib photographs, "reflect a shift in the use made of pictures—less objects to be saved than messages to be disseminated, circulated" and we are reminded of Gainesville police spokeswoman and detective Sadie Darnell's statement that the Gainesville killer seemed to be sending their audience messages through his staging of the killing scene (27). The Abu Ghraib images were not necessarily controversial for conservative supporters of the "occasional" use of torture to extract information, nor for the listeners of Rush Limbaugh's radio show, who, Sontag notes, suggested that the photographs simply portray what happens at college fraternity parties. In light of these last examples, another reading of Ronell's comments about the psychological role of broadcasting serial death might be: We (the photographers) deserve to live. The dead (and the photographed) do not. The Iraqi photographs get replayed, cropped and recontextualized with historically different presentational methods on television and the Internet.[5] (Death is broadcast on the Internet, not on U.S. television.) In both places, though, once the images are released from the confines of military censorship, their content guarantees both their circulation and their invocation of immediate local reaction—the decapitation of a U.S. citizen by angered and horrified Iraqis. What Next?

Serial murder rearticulates these patterns of shock. It is at once fascinating and terrifying because it demands a relationship between the "community," which is defined by the patterns of the crimes rather than by more familiar or traditional boundaries, and the killer. We, as the killer's audience, make his crimes legible by reading their pattern back to him; together, we produce an interactive narrative. Serial logic requires just this sort of relationship. As Gilles Deleuze suggests in "Mediators," "If you're not in some series, even a completely imaginary one, you're lost. I need my mediators to express myself, and they'd never express themselves without me: you're always working in a group even when you seem to be on your own" (125). We, the killer's audience, function as his mediators. Perhaps, as Ronell suggests, our memories of popular television (its structure and content) prime us as mediators. We watch ourselves from virtual distances—the empty spaces of television and now the Internet—as we become historical. In *Homesick,* we find ourselves mediating in serial fashion between representations of ourselves and the killer, with the uneasy knowledge that our expression somehow also participates in his own.

Mind the Gap

During the making of our video, a new rhetoric for research, drawn from the taxonomy of serial killer narratives, began to emerge—first, an identification of serial gaps or interruptions. This structural recognition is accompanied by "shocking" and repetitive violent content; the use of profiles to characterize or identify both victim and killer; the use of surveillance technology for detection, protection, and sometimes self-expression on the part of the killer; and the use of intuition, hunches and other "irrational" turns in the detection process (psychics), all of which lead to an ambivalent understanding of motives or causality when explaining violence and its representation.

New media theory and criticism of the last decade highlight the rhetorical importance of the gap as a meaningful space or phenomenon. Notably, the history of inscription technologies is littered with concerns about gaps. The development of print technology raised questions about how to use gaps effectively between letters and words. As print habits standardized, printers called readers' attention to gaps in an effort to increase reading and comprehension rates. Early filmmakers struggled to standardize the rates at which film moved through the camera and the projector in order to successfully distract viewers' eyes from the gaps between frames. Classical Hollywood cinema developed strict rhetorical guidelines for shooting and editing film to divert the viewer's attention away from the gaps between shots. So powerful is the continuity system that most casual viewers of film and video remain consciously unaware of the edit or suture points in the films and videos they watch every day. Experimental filmmakers, new media theorists, critics, and authors continue to be transfixed by the thoughtful possibilities that lie fallow in the in-between space/time of the film/video frame or the hypertextual link.

The term *link*, in fact, covers over what so many theorists find productive about hypertextual organization: the gap. Perhaps we should rename the link 'the gap' so as to call more attention to the possibilities that lie therein. Link derives from the word *glink,* meaning joint, which suggests both a joining together of the limbs and the potential for tearing them apart. In their exploitation of the link, hypertext theorists herald this gaping space as a device that opens texts up to readers and opens readers up to texts (putting readers in the position of also having to be writers—writers of/in the gap). While the continuity systems of most "old" media work to produce classical narrative structures (defined in part by the closing/closure of the text), the gaps of "new" media produce open structures suggesting that new media might more readily be considered a label that suggests *a way of working* rather than *a state of being* (digital). As we produced *Homesick,* we struggled to understand the differences between old and new media, as anyone who has worked with film or video in the last decade is likely to have done. Though film and video are, technically, old media (pre-computer media) they are also new media in the sense that they are being completely transformed by computing that converts analog to digital signals and digital to analog signals at the press of a button. The key features of new media production—copying and looping—are alive and well in contemporary film/video production, but they are often used to produce classical or closed texts. Consider the work of tweening. Lead animators produce key frame images that serve to "outline" a figure's movement while others goad computers into "tweening" those images to fill in the gaps between them. The goal is to produce a final animation that represents fluid, hyper-realistic movement and imagery. Perhaps a more useful way to differentiate old from new media is to consider the ways gaps are toyed with. Old media is a way of working that produces closed texts that cover over gaps while new media is a way of working that produces open texts that revel in gaps.

How, then, do the gaps and interruptions of the broadcast medium and, increasingly, the Internet, construct our consciousness? Do the gaps affect the ways in which we produce knowledge about ourselves and those *events* that surround us? How many of us play in that momentary suspension of meaning? One section of our video evokes such questions by weaving together Super 8 home movie footage of young girls dancing with Barbie dolls, notices of missing children that appear on milk cartons, and repeated images of body bags excerpted from local television news footage, all separated by black. One of the defining tropes of a certain experimental style seems to be a refusal to explain or make too obvious transition points. 'Deliberate on the gap' might be a motto for guerilla video. The video artist chooses black as a challenge to comprehensibility and an incitement to mysterious musings. To this end, fragments of Avital Ronell's question repeatedly appear as onscreen text in intermittent spaces of black in *Homesick:* "To what extent is serial killing an effect of serial television—of its imprinting on our national unconscious?"(71).

When Ronell asks this question, she invokes the concept of serial logic. Rather than pose the familiar question—To what extent is RL (Real life) violence caused by VR (Virtual reality) violence?—she calls attention to the role of *effect.* We read Ronell's twist of the familiar logic of cause/effect as a directive that tunes attention to the reader's role in detecting or reading serial violence. One way to read her query is to ask: Are we epistemologically predisposed to read certain events-as-texts serially? Serial logic differs from the more familiar predicate logic. Predicate logic is a logic of identity: if A is B and B is C then A is C. Predicate logic is *to be* something. Alternately, serial logic is a logic of intermittence, of the interval, of endless deferral. It is an aggregate logic: and, and, and . . . articulated by the gap between events.[6] Rather than transfer identity (A is C), serial logic repeats a pattern. Ronell suggests that our ability to recognize serial killing is an effect of our televisual training, of our learned ability to make sense of the repeating patterns of the television series.

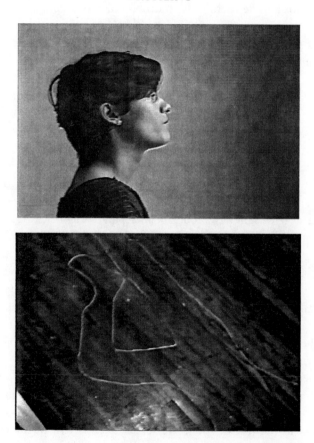

Profiling

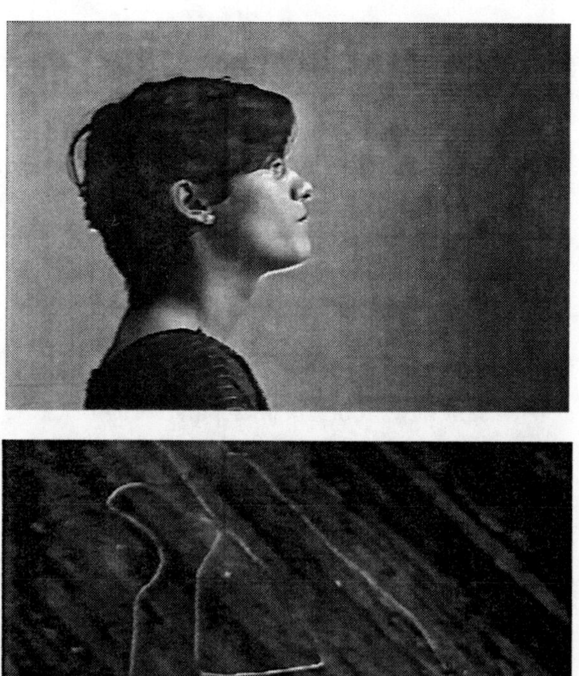

Found Audio

The profile is gained from a psychological study of past offenders.

—Sadie Darnell, spokeswoman and detective for the Gainesville Police Department

A serial killer tends to be a white male . . .

—Criminologist and television commentator

Not a few citizens are self-conscious about the efforts of a talk show to share information about something this horrible . . .

—Phil Donahue during his taping in Gainesville the week after the murders.

. . . and that made people feel incredibly vulnerable, because you didn't know, of course, who it was, and you didn't know whether it was going to end.

—Sadie Darnell

Audio from Homesick

The format of *Homesick* is not a docu-drama, but rather a series of sketches or profiles, modeled, in part, on the "counter-cinema" of Godard and the French New Wave , and a documentarian's response—our narrative need to understand trauma. "Profilare," the root of profile, means to draw or trace an outline of an object. Our video and now this essay try both literally and figuratively to "trace" the connections: between profiles, catalogues, surveillance, detection, identity, old media, new media, and televised war. We question the logic of the official term that proposes an identifiable set of characteristics. We never "see" the fragmented body of the female (or male) victim, only a yearbook photograph or an abstracted body bag. We never "know" the killer, only his FBI profile. Profiling turns humans into acts of metaphor—how many shared characteristics does one need to become a match? Olive skin? Dark eyes? Middle Eastern origin? He looks *as if* he were a terrorist. For both killer and victim, profiling is used as a means of containment.

Profiling the killer allows the authorities (and, vicariously, the watching audience) to imagine the killer as a character; the act of profiling turns an otherwise flat character into one that is round, or has the potential for being rounded out. We imagine that if s/he is a round character, s/he then can be interpreted and thereby diffused, if only we can come to *understand* them. In this case, the authorities use the profile to identify the killer; in doing so, they attempt to convert the logic of the series into predicate logic. The recipe for the serial killer is formed: sexual abuse in childhood plus medical training equals serial killer. Of course, this information proved incorrect in the case of Danny Rolling (and many other serial killers). No known history of sexual abuse. No advanced medical training. Just a childhood spent hunting in Louisiana. Like Jeffrey Dahmer's biography—an oddball son of a chemist and a "loner"—no other unusual or traumatic history was found for the press to name as cause. Serial killer Eileen Wuornos, however, provided the press (and Hollywood) with her abusive history as a prostitute. Despite her "deviant" femininity, she fit the profile (before Wuornos's series, the FBI profiled all serial killers as male).

The victim's profile is used in a similar manner—to delineate who is at risk and thereby contain the spreading panic. If we are not petite, white brunettes (the profile of Rolling's victim), we are not at risk. But then came the muscular male victim, whom we explain away as an aberrance. And so the logic of the *and, and, and* continues, despite the desires of the media and the investigative community to force the story into a classical structure.

In *Homesick*, we use profile shots, silhouettes, and chalk outlines to question the existence of one truthful or representative "profile." Chris Coates, our composer, determined parts of the musical score by outlining the profiles of the victims' yearbook photographs, superimposing these profiles onto staff notation paper and reading the high points as notes. Through this method we explored how these photographs could be both iconographic and indexical—how, in other words, they haunted us by pointing to the traces of their existence. The repeated broadcast of these culturally staged images (the yearbook pose, a pose most of us have struck with our own bodies) burned them simultaneously as icons into our television screens and into our collective memory. With our score, we wanted to think of ways to mark the victim's presence and absence. Even though *Homesick* is not a eulogy, we also wanted the music to provide an emotional and metaphorical connection to the experience of loss.

Serial killing similarly perverts the "normal" relationship between detection and the production of knowledge. Most strikingly, serial killing twists traditional understandings of motive, which are fundamental to understanding any profile. The serial killer's motives often appear abstracted and symbolic. If portrayed, they are often betrayed by the technology of new media. For instance, in the opening credits of Ridley Scott's *Hannibal (2001),* the piazzas of Florence are shown as timecoded surveillance video. Is someone watching, or being watched? The digital camera, whose image resolution degrades before our eyes, searches the space for something. Suddenly, morphing technology allows for the dreadful discovery of Hannibal Lecter's face in the architecture of the square. His pattern appears everywhere and nowhere, emerging from the digital murk, obscuring its code in a nightmarish moment of video mysticism. His motivation with the camera, as it is with the police, is to watch. It is finally, though, low-grade surveillance video that identifies and captures Hannibal as he shops in a store for a rare, elitist product, one of the trademarks of his profile. But his capture via video (and the Internet) occurs in essentially non-performative spaces, the 'downtime' of the serial killer. Guerilla detection sifts through the digital traces we all leave via new media, creating a profile from the smallest of moves.

Serial producers recognize motive in the continual production of the series. They produce to continue the series; killings are merely a means to a continuous end, a way of maintaining the series—a fragmentary, repetitive form of story-telling with room for surprises. New media applications that most readily employ this continuing structure may be found in the wildly popular digital games that focus scoring on body count—first-person shooter and role playing games.[7] The serial killing that is the object of many of these games again and again brings the motivation to continue the series into our living rooms, replacing cinematic and televisual representations of serial killing with hyperreal images and sounds. When engaged with such games, players become the creative Hannibal Lecters of the new millennium—serial activists for narrative excess.

Lecter fascinates, in part, because he refuses to take up the classical characterization that cinema and television traditionally assign serial killers. Lecter is intent on uncovering the motives of others around him, dissecting his victims verbally before he dissects them physically, or even talking them into taking the knife to their own bodies. *Silence of the Lambs* gleans its title from Clarice Starling's motives for justice, not from Lecter's, and in *Hannibal,* we get even less information about why he does what he does. Hannibal Lecter is the narrator of his own mystery and, in this second film, he becomes pure fugitive. He dismisses any personal motives with a kind of perfunctory common sense logic—his desire to kill is the most rational in the world—we should all be so enlightened. Clarice's attempts to profile Lecter unravel in the face of his own unraveling of her. Lecter stumps us all; he is the successful fugitive, the sacrificial savior of embattled femininity, a chosen member of the FBI's ten most wanted list, who will, no doubt, run and then return.[8]

Our video questions the function of motive (and its inevitable return) through the manipulation of found audio from events surrounding and following the serial killings in Gainesville. In these audio excerpts, the Gainesville community, which included citizens, the police, "experts," and the media, speculate as to what the killer's series might mean, revealing through their speculations their desire (and the community's) to convert serial events from open narrative events into classical narratives with a defined end. One track includes a public statement made by Gainesville police officer, Sadie Darnell, that the killer may have been leaving "messages" at the crime scenes. The media speculated that the murder scenes were "staged" as in a theatrical set. Was the killer communicating with his "audience," through his careful arrangement of a demented mise-en-scene? Were these messages part of an elaborate syntax? Could we answer him (and therefore satisfy him) by decoding his messages? Defining a crime as serial depends on an audience (the police, the community, etc.) reading both the crimes and the gaps between them as meaningful, as a sign of the coming apocalypse.[9] According to Philip L. Simpson, the serial killer "longs for the deliverance of such an apocalypse in order to embrace its transcendental energies, and so attempts to will it into being. His apocalyptic performance attempts to reforge, through rote performance of a murderous ritual whose origins lie in antiquity, a lost link between language and underlying warrant of meaning. The repetitive performance becomes being and meaning, not just a substitution for it" (121–22). Motive, in this case becomes both predicate and aggregate in form. Performance requires some premeditated plans, but the act of performance itself suggests a suspension of time, an ongoing exercise in being.

We interrupt this apocalypse. . . .

Domestic Surveillance

"Two weeks after the murders I had a friend over for dinner. When he came over for dinner he told me about a sound that he heard in his house, a sound like a muffled heartbeat, or a sound that was coming from underground." (Voiceover)

"What we're dealing with is a person who has an insatiable need for power and dominance and control. Someone who knows what they're doing, who enjoy not only terrorizing their five victims, but may also be enjoying the terror that he's played upon this community." (Voice of Criminologist and Television Commentator)

"Step forward. Turn right, please. Turn left, please. Step forward. Turn right. Turn left. Step back in line." (Voiceover)

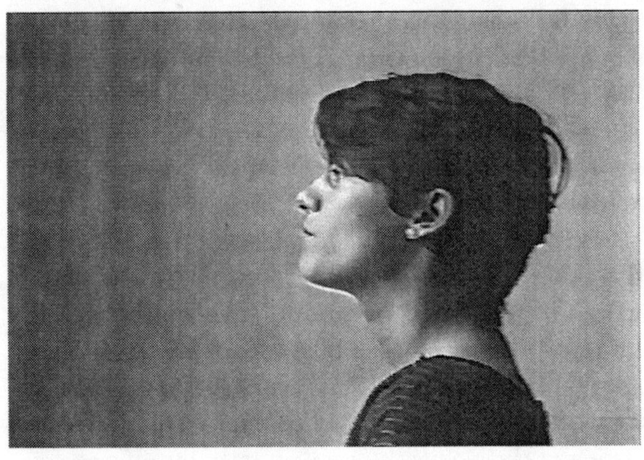

Because so much of FemTV's memory of the Gainesville murders involved scenes of women (like ourselves) at home alone, afraid that someone might be watching as we waited for the next murder to occur, we felt that visually these memories could be represented through images of the interior of the home as shot through a surveillance-like camera perspective. We begin *Homesick* by juxtaposing exterior shots with Super 8 film of the woods (where Rolling allegedly camped during the murders) with a narrative voiceover that recalls the paradoxical transformation of our familiar domestic spaces into spaces of alienated terror. The video track opens with an intermittent black screen. Three images interrupt the black screen: black and white Super 8 shots of the woods, a woman turning on lights as she enters a doorway, and a sheriff's deputy repeating a 'chopping' gesture in slow motion. The audio track begins several seconds into the first black screen. A woman's voice is heard repeating: "I remember, sitting in my house, and hearing a noise." A woman's voice is heard repeating: "I remember, sitting in my house, and hearing a noise." Images of a woman leaving a kitchen and turning off a light are repeated. This layering of sound and image, of exterior and interior, sets up the spatial and sexual differences between the home and the woods. It also demonstrates, perhaps, our own traumatized, narrative drive to visit a space where the killer had camped. As Mary Anne Doane has suggested in *The Desire to Desire: The Woman's Film of the 1940s,* the home represents both architecturally and theoretically a feminized space that acquires, in certain narrative mise-en-scenes, characteristics of the Freudian *unheimlich* or the uncanny (139–140). Familiar space is made strange and threatening through acts of visual perception. The threat of femininity and the danger of the domestic space are brought together in the perceptual space of the serial murderer just as they are in the Gothic drama, the 'woman's film,' or most contemporary horror films. *Homesick*'s use of the anecdotal voiceover in conjunction with images of domestic space refers back to the strategies of these 1940's women's films. The video also disembodies the voices of the experts—police, psychics, criminologists—as a distancing strategy that we hope resonates with a sense of the uncanny.

Of particular interest in *Homesick* is the role that the television set, a piece of domestic furniture, played in the transformation of our living spaces. Our televisions became the conduits through which the media's fragmented bits of information on the murders flowed into our homes. Rather than taming the images of the murders as the domesticated box usually does, the television became the portal that suddenly made our homes *unheimlich*. We were able to watch ourselves being watched simultaneously by the killer and the media. Today, our new media technologies only heighten the sense of surveillance and invasion we first felt when the television made our homes uncanny. With new media, the stakes in this game are much higher; the transformation of the home into a portal (a term frequently used in new media to describe the flow of information) is made quite literal. The unregulated Internet opens our homes to all sorts of unsanctioned text, images, and sounds while the machines is our midst can be goaded into reporting our activities to their corporate sponsors. Meanwhile, our very identities, our abilities to be, are now at stake as thieves glide into our homes to steal our credit, the very definition of being robbed in the new millennium.

In *Homesick* we evoke rather than represent these vectors of surveillance by including images of the media documenting a live telecast of Phil Donahue and his local Gainesville audience. The audio track provides commentary from one of Donahue's guests, an 'expert' criminologist who specializes in serial killers. The voiceover suggests that the "killer's insatiable need for power" is fed by media representations of his crimes and the community they create. Text informs the viewer--an anonymous spectator cut the cables during the live, Donahue broadcast, abruptly ending it. *Homesick* addresses its viewer directly, situating her/him within a complex geometry of surveillance that, we hope, provokes an active response—more cutting of the cables.

Detection/Intuition

Sadie Darnell: *"The killer may be leaving messages or giving us messages. That's different than leaving notes."* (Voiceover)

Answering machine recording: *"Hi. It's Michelle. It's after five and we hadn't heard anything. We were wondering what happened. We were kind of worried about you. O.K. Talk to you later. Bye."* (Voiceover)

"Hi. Are you there? Pick up. Hmm. I guess you're out or sleeping or something. We haven't heard from you in a while and we were just wondering what was going on, so give me a call when you get in. O.K.? Bye." (Voiceover)

"Hello? This is the Sheriff's office. Answer the door." (Voiceover)

The information that flowed through our old media machines into our homes was an interesting mix of fact and fiction, including gossip and rumor. In *Homesick*, we contrast the production of (a body of) "legitimate" knowledge with knowledge or information that remains outside the bounds of accepted institutional forms. In the video crime solving methods of profiling, deductive reasoning, and classical narrative align with legitimate forms of knowledge while intuition, visions, and seriality align with outsider knowledge. What is the relationship between deductive methods of crime solving and other strategies that involve the "irrational" and "feminine" modes of intuition, dream logic, hunches, and psychics? What is the role of these alternative strategies in a rhetoric for new media?

Sadie Darnell was the spokeswoman for the Gainesville police during the murder investigation; she was also a detective on the Gainesville police force and an activist for women's issues in the community (and Tom Petty's cousin). She represents the female crime-solver in popular culture, as well as the voice of an "official" who appreciates intuition and the irrational. The character of the female detective typically has to make sense out of violent representations of the female body while simultaneously negotiating for power and respect in the work place. The female detective often finds herself in a contest between intuitive, outsider knowledge and the more "legitimate" knowledge of detection. In the Hannibal Lecter films, we find a more complex type of interaction between predicate and aggregate forms of logic in the characters of Starling and Lecter. In an opening scene of *The Silence of the Lambs,* Jonathan Demme directs multiple camera perspectives at Clarice Starling (Jodie Foster) while she gazes at the graphic photos of the dead females' bodies, foregrounding the double play of watching the female look at the female victims and subtly suggesting that she might have a different way of looking at the crimes. Demme's version shows us how to read the visual representations of serial violence back to ourselves; in this case, through the eyes of a young, female detective navigating an overwhelmingly masculine work environment. Starling's interchangeable use of deductive logic, small town pragmatism, and womanly intuition allows her, with Lecter's assistance, to access the sadistic logic of Buffalo Bill by discovering the elusive clue—one that only someone with access to feminine or alternative knowledge would grasp—Buffalo Bill likes to sew.

Representations of the female detective have become prevalent in the intervening years since we produced *Homesick.* For example, the BBC production of the *Prime Suspect* series, which stars Helen Mirren as smart, solitary, work-obsessed Detective Chief Inspector Jane Tennison, also uses the alternating plot themes of serial killing and serial sexism. The show was immensely popular in England, not least because one of the repeated themes involved Tennison's confident handling of attempts to undermine her authority. Another theme, though, focused on her deductive logic and thinking skills, her assertiveness, her impatience—all traits stereotyped as masculine, which may have helped her in the police station, but seemed to fail her at home and in her personal life. In this case, the mixing of the stereotypes carried a cost with them. In a more successful mix-up of stereotypes, the character of scientist Dana Scully (Gillian Anderson) on the Fox network's highly successful *X-Files* represents an interesting reversal of the feminine/intuitive and masculine/logical detective types. A large part of the show's interest has to do with Scully's ability or, rather, her inability to believe in the "truth" that's "out there." Her partner, Fox Mulder, is the intuitive detective whose role seems to be, in part, the feminization of Scully; he is the source of outsider knowledge. An integration of the two ways of knowing seems to be one of the elusive and pleasurable goals of the show. Many of the *X-Files* episodes focus on capturing serial murderers, frequently of alien origin, and an overall theme of the show is the (sometimes campy) presentation of alternative forms of knowledge. There also existed, first on ABC and then on A&E Home Video, a fairly popular series called *Profiler,* starring Ally Walker as a female detective with a psychic ability that allows her to enter into the serial murderer's mind and to envision his/her point of view. Her unusual intuitive powers allow her to compose a profile of the killer. She is a much more predictable but not completely uninteresting version of the intuitive female detective catching the serial killer. Whereas the *X-Files* aligns legitimate and outsider (or masculine/feminine) modes of knowledge with two highly differentiated characters, *Profiler* marries the two in one character. Walker uses her feminized/outsider psychic ability to understand the killer's pattern in masculinized/legitimate terms of containment; she uses her psychic ability to produce the profile, the paramount form of knowledge heralded by the show's title (it isn't called *Visioner*). In the end, she always presents a classical narrative of the killer to her bosses. Nevertheless, the degree to which these female characters face conflicts surrounding the issues of femininity, intuition, and power demonstrates our popular media's obsession with testing the limits of female detection and alternative forms of knowledge.

By introducing the issue of intuition as an alternative form of knowledge or knowing in *Homesick, FemTV* hoped to accomplish two things: first, to reappropriate the cliché of feminine intuition as a source of power; second, to suggest that intuition should not be a gendered category of knowledge at all, but open to anyone who seeks to disrupt or play with the conventions of deductive reasoning.[10] Because the theme of detection is tied clearly into questions of logic and narration, our video sets up the contradictions within the "scientific" model of crime-solving logic by drawing attention to the use of psychics in investigations. The not uncommon use of psychics during police investigations is rarely mentioned in the mainstream press. Psychics, who are stereotyped as female in most media representations, belong to an important form of underground knowledge, a popular mythology of crime-solving techniques. We question the ways that scientific logic, and the "official" detection process tend to classically narrativize "facts" by denying other kinds of information. For the video, we sought out a number of alternative perspectives, such as Theresa Hayes, a psychic who was contacted regularly by the Gainesville Police Department to assist with crime solving. We interviewed Ms. Hayes in her home, and included her voiceover when she spoke of the quality of her visions. We were interested in the texture of her hallucinations. "They are not like dreams," she said, "but more like visions" that you can see and walk into. She solved crimes with the help of "Jesus" and her visions. The police force never asked her for proof, they just followed up on her descriptions.

In *Homesick,* the psychic's voice alternates with comments by Sadie Darnell about how we have "let go" of our intuition because of our dependence on "technology" (as heralded by the recent television franchise *CSI: Las Vegas, Miami,* and now *New York*). On the image track *Homesick* accompanies the voices of the detective and the psychic with low grade Fisher-Price pixellated video that shows a woman in a bathing suit playing in the water and "hamming it up" with the camera. The associations with water were meant to resonate with a sense of an imaginary and playful space—one in which a woman's representation in front of the camera is more clearly interactive and perhaps intuitive, although not without an awareness as to its constructed nature.

As FemTV continues to cut and write, the collective's search for meaning in *Homesick* has not been organized through a classical narrative process, but, like those "irrational" and "feminine" strategies noted in the video, through chance, coincidence, intuition, resemblance, repetition, and an accumulation of seemingly unrelated "facts." The deconstruction of narrative and visual continuity seems one way to represent the serial killing narrative without simply repeating it. We did not want our work to "feel" safe; absence and interruption disrupt continuity while they also refer back to the serial disruption of televisual consciousness. According to Ronell, the "monumentality" or "singularity" of history has been replaced by technologies that "we associate with rapid turnover, substitutional acceleration, seriality, and the erasures which these imply" (*Finitude's Score* xi). As radio journalist Jeremy Scahill suggests in an episode of *Shocking and Awful,* the Pentagon spends 350 million dollars on 'Hollywood-style' recruitment videos that provide "a movie image of what it means to be a soldier." Scahill then asks alternative media to interrupt certain channels:

> How about splicing into that [movie], the U.S. soldier who comes back missing his right leg? How about splicing into that, the U.S. soldier who gets shrapnel in his spine because he had inappropriate body armor? How about splicing into that, the guy who is poisoned from depleted uranium in munitions? Let's splice that and see how many people want to sign up for the Army of 1? ("Dance of Death," Program 5, *Shocking and Awful*)

The televisual dilemma results from paradigmatic boredom and predictability—'Oh, there go those hippies, complaining about the government again . . . ' But the challenge is to make the gap visible, to splice into that movie, to somehow stifle that yawn. Ronell acknowledges that this technology has the potential to turn on itself, to provide evidence in unpredictable or non-performative moments, to oppress the oppressor, to catch the killer. Guerilla media, whether old or new, video or blogging, disrupts the narrative profiling of the clever, white, educated monster—the regressive, patriarchal fantasy of the Hannibal Lecters. The rhetoric for new media we are exploring calls for an alternative mode of thinking to make meaning or intuit the gaps in these stories. The tangential, non-linear, or multilinear nature of such expression resonates with those feminized rhetorical modes that have long been disdained and disregarded by the patriarchal grounding of old media. As *Homesick* tries to demonstrate in visual and aural ways, the tactile memory of the body produces an intuitive, non-scientific, if not wholly psychic way of knowing; a way of knowing that finds a home in new media.

"How much do you think intuition comes into solving crimes?" (Voiceover)

Sadie Darnell:

> *"I'm so glad you asked that. I'm a firm believer in intuition. I really am. . . . I think it also enters into not only someone in the law enforcement function, but when you're out as a citizen in the community or at home, that you may get a sense of 'this is isn't quite right.' You're just not able to figure it out or whatever. And we need to all get better at trusting our intuition . . . And we have let go of it because of technology or whatever . . . Let me give you some advice. The thing to do is trust your gut. Absolutely trust your instincts, and if you feel like you're in a situation and something's kind of tugging at you, something's wrong, chances are it is a situation that's going to escalate and get out of hand."*

Theresa Hayes, psychic consultant for the Gainesville Police Department:

> *"Dreams and vision is two different things. Mmm hmm. A vision is just like if God right now show me something about you, you know, I'm wide awake, this is an open vision here. But a dream, it goes on and I just dream, you know."*

Sadie Darnell:

> *"But the majority of times we get . . . people who say, 'I don't know why I had this dream. I don't know why I thought this. I just had this . . . basically this vision. And I don't want you to think I'm crazy.' And I'm really trying to diminish people in law enforcement from thinking their crazy . . . we don't."*

Theresa Hayes:

> *"Yeah they* [Gainesville Police Department] *called me one time. And he was asking me, how was his dad. No one ever told me that he was shot. But I told him on the phone, I said, 'Well, the only thing that I can tell you is in the dream that I had,' and I had this vision, I said 'this guy was shot in the neck one time.' He said, 'Well, that's what we're looking for now, the gun.' Well he didn't say he was shot, but he said, that's what we're*

> *looking for . . . I know I would see things happening before they happened, and I would keep it to myself. I wouldn't share with no one, because they would always say, 'You're crazy.' They'd always say 'you're losing your mind.'"*

Psychics produce knowledge in part by engaging alternative reading strategies, ones that veer away from literal engagements of the sign and steer toward mysterious, abstract readings. The psychic recognizes patterns many of us cannot see and accepts that these patterns are meaningful, a narrative approach on which the Psychic Network has capitalized. For this essay, we have approached our tape looking for patterns of meaning that we did not initially notice while producing the *Homesick*, meanings we had, until now, been unable to recognize.

Our re-visioning has illuminated connections between seriality, interactive narratives, televised war, and new media production—connections that remained latent in what we took to be the final cut fifteen years earlier. Rather than suggesting that hindsight is 20/20, we have tried to define various ways of knowing, presenting and re-membering events of violence through the tools of new media—through tactile images and sounds, gaps and loops, dreamlike visions and intuitive tangents. FemTV does not believe that our video has "explained" seria logic; our contemporary experiences suggest that, more likely, we are haunted by it [9].

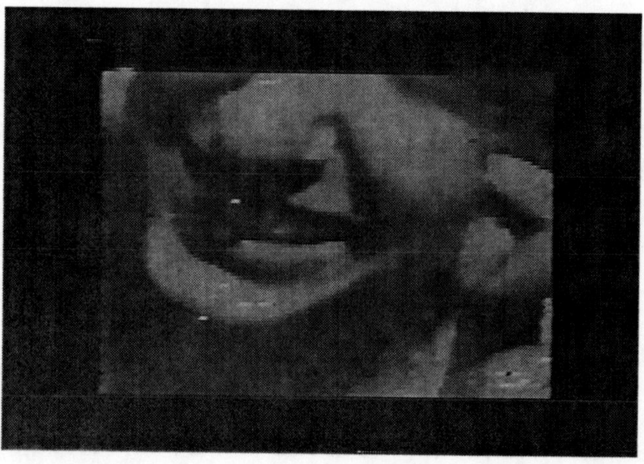

Notes

The other members of FemTV who participated in this video are Lesley Gamble, Aeron Haynie, Leslie Henson, Donna Mitchell, Laura Ogden, and Rose Stasuk. Special thanks to the University of Florida, University of Tampa, Loyola University Chicago, and Centenary College of Louisiana for support and use of equipment, to Lynne Joyrich and other members of the Center for Twentieth Century's Knowing Mass Culture/Mediating Knowledge conference, to Juliet Davis, Ted Hardin, and Michael Laffey for their comments, suggestions, and editorial advice.

1. Since the 1990 University of Florida serial killings, there have been two shooting massacres at universities—Virgina Tech, 4/16/2007, and Northern Illinois, 2/14/2008/, as well as the Columbine high school killings, 4/20/1999. In the Virginia Tech and Columbine cases, there was media speculation and testimony about the killers' video game "habits" and viewing of serial killing films. In the Northern Illinois University case, the killer mailed his girlfriend a textbook on serial killers prior to the murders. The serial logic of shooting massacres is necessarily different from serial killing, but both demand different forms of narrative preparation.; *Shocking and Awful: A Grassroots Response to War and Occupation* (DV, 2005) is a 13-part series on the Iraqi war and military invasion., available for free download at www.DeepDishTV.org.

2. In James Glass's *Private Terror/Public Life: Psychosis and the Politics of Community,* the author interviews a group of extremely mentally disturbed patients to uncover their stories of alienation, instability and community. He comments on how when talking to these alienated and isolated patients, the interviewer "encounter[s] images that place consciousness on the 'edges' of a common humanity" (pg 12), such as the dramatic image of a mother murdering her child. The interviewer's encounter of this otherness, Glass argues, is similar to the Lacanian desire to walk the "rim," or a way to safely play with the 'edges' of accepted community behavior.

3. In her essay "Watch Out, Dick Tracy! Popular Video in the Wake of the Exxon Valdez," DeeDee Halleck, one of the producers for *Shocking and Awful,* decades ago called for a leftist, guerilla intervention into the production and broadcast of grassroots video. Citing the religious right's domination of "alternative" (non-industry based) forms and uses of video technology (including satellite distribution), she challenged the pubic interest community to intervene in what had previously been the exclusive domain of the military/industrial complex and the religious right.

4. Semiotic theory refers to paradigmatic elements as those belonging to a vertical axis of options from which a representative element is selected. Syntagmatic elements belong to a horizontal access to which paradigmatic selections are continually and repeatedly added. Film and television represent the serial killing story paradigmatically—as a particular modus operandi se-

lected from a list of possible m.o.'s applied to a geographic region selected from a host of possibilities, and detected by applying a certain knowledge or method of thinking to the puzzle at hand. Serial killing is terrifying, even apocalyptic, because of its syntagmatic qualities, the ongoing (seemingly never ending) series that defines it and suggests that sooner or later we all may be caught by its insatiable accumulation.

5. Sontag also wonders whether the sexual nature of the torture was "inspired by the vast repertory of pornographic imagery available on the Internet." It is the new media technology of the digital camera and the immediate and democratic access to the Internet that allowed for the rapid distribution of these pictures and their subsequent controversy.

6. In her essay "Understanding the Act of Reading: the *WOE* Beginners' Guide to Dissection," Jane Yellowlees Douglas refers to Michael Joyce's hypertext narrative *WOE* as an Ecoian Open Work and as "The genuine post-modern text rejecting the objective paradigm of reality as the great 'either/or' and embracing, instead, the 'and/and/and.'" Douglas argues that the reader takes pleasure in hypertext's call to interactivity as the reader is forced to fill in the proliferating blanks generated by the endlessly deferring text while savoring the anticipation of having his/her fantasies of the narrative fulfilled or rejected.

7. *America's Army* is a multiplayer, online FPS game produced and released for free by the U.S. military. See www.americasarmy.com. Talmadge Wright, in "Creative Player Actions in FPS Online Video Games Playing Counter-Strike," observes that First Person Shooter games "reproduce and challenge everyday rules of social interaction" while also promoting "verbal dialogue" and non-verbal forms of creative expression.

8. In a bizarre and uncanny moment in *Hannibal,* an Italian detective is shown hunting for images of Lecter on the FBI's Most Wanted site on his computer. Before Lecter's face emerges from the digital gloom, the camera focuses briefly on the computer image of Osama bin Laden-soon to be identified as a different kind of serial killer, but only after the release of the film.

9. HBO's recent series *The Wire* (2006-08) turns the audience's desire for understanding motive on its head with the storyline of a cop and a reporter who both 'fake' the existence of a serial killer of homeless men in Baltimore by dropping repeated clues at the site of homeless who die on the street. The cop wants the mayor to give the police more money for solving 'real' crimes, and the reporter wants to sell papers. No serial killer exists—just a city's collapsing infrastructure. But fear sells papers and forces mayors to distribute funds.

10. John Waters' *Serial Mom* critically underscores the humor surrounding the excessiveness of serial killer narratives. The existence of his parody is a testament to commercial media's dependence on this rhetorical paradigm. Kathleen Turner's character is both prescient and intuitive, in a laughable, ghostly sort of way. Humor interrupts intuition here . . .

Works Cited

Benjamin, Walter. "The Work of Art in the Age of Mechanical Reproduction." *Illuminations.* Ed. Hannah Arendt. Trans. Harry Zohn. New York: Schocken Books, 1968.

Deleuze, Gilles. *Negotiations.* New York: Columbia UP, 1990.

Deep Dish TV. *Shocking and Awful: A Grassroots Response to War and Occupation* (DV, 2005)

Doane, Mary Ann. *The Desire to Desire: The Woman's Film of the 1940s.* Bloomington: Indiana UP, 1987.

Glass, James. *Private Terror/Public Life: Psychosis and the Politics of Community.* Ithaca, NY: Cornell U P, 1989.

Hagedorn, Roger. "Doubtless To Be Continued: A Brief History of Serial Narrative." *To Be Continued . . . Soap Operas Around the World.* Ed. Robert C. Allen. London: Routledge Press, 1995.

Halleck, DeeDee. "Watch Out, Dick Tracy! Popular Video in the Wake of the *Exxon Valdez.*" *Technoculture.* Ed. Constance Penley and Andrew Ross. Minneapolis: U of Minnesota P, 1991.

Ronell, Avital. *Finitude's Score: Essays for the End of the Millenium* (Texts and Contexts, Vol. 8). Omaha: U of Nebraska P, 1998.

Ronell, Avital. "Haunted TV: Rodney King/Video/Trauma." *ArtForum*31, no.1 (September 1992).

Simpson, Philip L. "The Politics of Apocalypse in the Cinema of Serial Murder." *Mythologies of Violence in Postmodern Media.* Ed. Christopher Sharrett. Detroit: Wayne State UP, 1999.

Taussig, Michael. *Mimesis and Alterity: A Particular History of the Senses.* New York: Routledge Press, 1993.

Sontag, Susan. "The Photographs Are Us," in *The New York Times Magazine,* May 23, 2004 (pp 24–29).

Wright, Talmadge, Eric Boria, and Paul Breidenbach. "Creative Player Actions in FPS Online Video Games Playing Counter-Strike." *Game Studies* 2.2 (Dec. 2002). 11 April 2008 <http://www.gamestudies.org/0202/wright/>.

Part 4

Pedagogy: Teaching and Learning (in) a New Academic Apparatus

9 Nietzsche at the Apollo: An Experiment in Clipography

Barry Mauer

Introduction

"Clipography" is a neologism for a subgenre of Gregory Ulmer's "Mystory," a research method that links self-knowledge and disciplinary knowledge (*Internet Invention* 79). Clipography uses the poetic "dream logic" of pop-music video clips as its formal paradigm for doing academic research. It draws the materials of the "popcycle" (*Heuretics* 195)—family, entertainment, school, and discipline—into contact and circulation using music video poetics as an analogy for its form. Clipography is distinct from argumentative writing, with its single authorship, consistent "voice," continuity, logical progression, and unity. In contrast, it borrows from rock'n'roll to offer polyvocality, discourse crossing, fragmentation, and pattern formation in a collage form of writing. The clipographer cites materials from the four discourses of the popcycle and juxtaposes them.

As a method for doing textual research, clipography uses the researcher's identifications to produce knowledge. Roland Barthes initiated identification-based research in *A Lover's Discourse;* by finding correspondences between his life and scenes from Goethe's epistolary novel, *The Sorrows of Young Werther,* Barthes gained self-knowledge and knowledge about the objects of study in the humanities—literary texts. He did not treat the literary text as an autonomous object; he used it as part of a collage text he created.

The term "clip" is relevant to this work in several ways. The definition of the term includes cutting and trimming, and holding loose things together. As a noun, it means an extract, a news story cut out of a print publication, any of numerous devices that grip or clasp loose things together, and a container for bullets, slotted directly into an automatic firearm. The implications of these terms resonate with clipography by emphasizing the collage nature of the work as well as its striking effects (many of the insights it produced struck me like bullets).

In this article, I present the poetics of clipography and then offer my own example of clipographic writing, "Pythagoras at the Apollo Theater."

Why Clipography?

Clipography is my answer to the following question: what genres are appropriate for conducting humanities research and writing in electronic media? Roland Barthes demonstrated that there is no incompatibility between identification and critical thinking and that one can do textual research through identification. As Barthes discovered, closeness to textual materials combined with the appropriate research methods can produce knowledge and motivate critical examination. Clipography, which uses identification as its starting point, allows the writer to make a "self-portrait" out of the materials of entertainment and the discipline, showing the writer her points of identification. These elements constitute what Ulmer calls the writer's "premises": " . . . the inventor's ideological *premises* do not determine in advance the outcome of the process but constitute the field, place, diegesis, or *chora* of its genesis" (84). Ulmer posits that we reason with, and through, our premises and that only by making them explicit, by putting our premises into the writing apparatus and thus external to our minds, can we perceive how they function.

In *A Lover's Discourse,* Barthes refers to *The Sorrows of Young Werther* as a map for his identifications; he points to correspondences between figures from the novel and figures from his life. *A Lover's Discourse* also includes citations from theorists whose work holds great significance for the humanities, including Freud, Bettelheim, Nietzsche, Lacan, Leibnitz, and Brecht. Barthes' method produces knowledge about literature, language, ideology, and the self. Yet *A Lover's Discourse* is a performance of discourses rather than a conclusive proof or truth claim about a particular text. As such, it marks a shift from traditional academic methods; it is an open intertextual form of writing, one that allows for a dialogue among multiple discourses.

The Poetics of Clipography

Clipography responds to the need for new research strategies for computer media. It poses an alternative to long narratives, expositions, and arguments; because computer screens can display only a limited amount of information at one time, it is more appealing to use shorter "beats" in composition—no more than a few key ideas in one unit—and to link these beats hypertextually.

Clipography arose from the insight that the structure of *A Lover's Discourse* is very similar to that of a music video. In fact, Barthes' description of his project uses terms that are musical and visual; each scene of *A Lover's Discourse* is a "figure," a "kind of opera aria" (5) that brings Barthes' "image repertoire" into view. Furthermore, Barthes organized his bits of discourses into a series of two-to-three page fragments (like two-to-three minute videos) resembling the "thought beats" in music videos. Stephen Johnson, director of videos for Talking Heads and Peter Gabriel, explains his notion of the thought beat as a means of "cramming information" for videos that must "bear up under repeated viewings and still have something to offer" (Goodwin 62).

Like the music video, Barthes' writing features "hooks" to gather knowledge. The musical "hook" in a pop song is a repetitive chorus or refrain, "that is designed to compel the listener to want to hear the song again and again" (Goodwin 91). In music videos, visual hooks include "routine close-ups of pop stars' faces . . . images of women that employ the classic techniques of objectification, fragmentation, and (occasionally) violation . . . and a set of (visual) associations that connects with a musical motif" (90–94). Barthes' hooks include memorable anecdotes about authors, literary characters, emotional situations, clichéd analogies and significant places that shaped his identity. Clipography by no means includes the objectification and violation of music videos, though it does include the idea of "hooks."

Both *A Lover's Discourse* and clipography depict fragmentary scenes of language to help the writer gain access to his constitution as a subject. In Scholes, Comley, and Ulmer's discussion of mystory (243–4), they note that institutions position their subjects; they refer to this subject positioning as "education" because the subjects must learn their "proper" position within the institution:

> Identification is at the heart of this education in that one becomes who and what one is by internalizing an

> image of the nurturing authority figures encountered in one's world. According to the theory, this act of identification with parent figures in the family—extended to the authority figures encountered in other institutions that constitute the interpellation process as one matures—is a "mis-recognition," a necessary "mistake" that implants alienation at the core of selfhood as an experience. To be a "self," that is, is to carry internally an image acquired from "outside." Identity is "extimacy," as psychoanalyst Jacques Lacan put it, coining a term that combines in one word "external" and "intimacy." An individual subject is not autonomous and self-identical, but is dependent upon an effect of language into which he or she has entered." (243)

The encounter in which one internalizes the values and behaviors of the nurturing authority figure is called the "scene of instruction." Barthes calls the catalogue of images that from these scenes of instruction the "image repertoire." The purpose of clipography is to bring our "image repertoire" into view so that we better understand the cultural apparatus we inhabit. (20) The figures from his image repertoire arise from a turn of phrase:

> For instance, if the subject awaits the loved object at a rendezvous, a sentence-aria keeps running through his head:"All the same, it's not fair . . .": "he/she could have . . ."; he/she knows perfectly well . . ." knows what? It doesn't matter, the figure "Waiting" is already formed. (6)

These phrases convey an emotion: for the lover, "even the mildest bears within it the terror of a suspense" (6). Barthes follows the lover's discourse by shaping his writing to the form of the lover's "plots and plans" (3). Most of Barthes' fragments establish a place—a café, a hotel—and each place has a dominant mood. In these places, Barthes connects his thoughts to scenes from *The Sorrows of Young Werther*. The references to *Werther* and other texts, Barthes writes, are " . . . not authoritative but amical: I am not invoking guarantees, merely recalling, by a kind of salute in passing, what has seduced, convinced, or what has momentarily given the delight of understanding (of being understood?)" (9).

Clipography is like a research collage that uses musical principles to select and assemble research materials. Collage writing requires that we abandon some long-held assumptions about what constitutes good academic writing. One such assumption is that originality is of high value. But the value of originality arose with print literacy. Barthes writes:

> . . . in ethnographic societies the responsibility for a narrative is never assumed by a person but by a mediator, shaman, or relator whose "performance"—the mastery of the narrative code—may possibly be admired but never his "genius." The author is a modern figure, a product of our society insofar as, emerging from the Middle Ages with English empiricism, French rationalism and the personal faith of the reformation, it discovered the prestige of the individual, of, as it is more nobly put, the "human person." It is thus logical that in literature it should be this positivism, the epitome and culmination of capitalist ideology, which has attached the greatest importance to the "person" of the author. ("Death of the Author" 142–43)

Collage puts into question the primacy of the author. Anyone can juxtapose two ready-made things and thereby produce new meanings. Do these meanings emerge from an inner truth known only to the author or are they imminent to the materials? If, as Barthes suspected, meanings are imminent, can we justify calling the collage artist a genius?

Barthes, in "Death of the Author," argued that no 'author' can fully 'express himself' because our only power as language users is to mix writings. Thus anyone who speaks or writes is by definition a collage artist:

> We know now that a text is not a line of words releasing a single "theological" meaning (the 'message' of the Author-God) but a multi-dimensional space in which a variety of writings, none of them original, blend and clash. The text is a tissue of quota-

> tions drawn from the innumerable centres of culture. . . . the writer can only imitate a gesture that is always anterior, never original. His only power is to mix writings, to counter the ones with the others, in such a way as never to rest on any one of them. Did he wish to express himself, he ought at least to know that the inner 'thing' he thinks to 'translate' is itself only a ready-formed dictionary, its words only explainable through other words, and so on indefinitely . . . (146)

Music videos and pop songs frequently employ collage as "sampling," a means of directly incorporating found audio and visual materials into new compositions. Sampling technologies have disrupted notions of "authenticity" and originality in popular music. Sampling is but one form of intertextuality traversing music and video. Andrew Goodwin finds several ways in which music videos incorporate "other" texts for a range of purposes including:

> 1) Social criticism—incorporates others' words or images in order to critique or attack them. 2) Self-reflexive parody—refers parodically to the video clip form and/or to the music industry. 3) Parody—refers parodically to other forms (TV ads, news shows) and/or institutions (television, advertising, cinema etc.). 4) Pastiche—a potpourri of styles blended for various effects. Removes objects from their original context and recontextualizes them for other purposes. 5) Promotion—typically used to sell a film or other product. 6) Homage—pays tribute to a particular artist, artwork, or cultural form. (160–64)

While Barthes practiced many of these forms of citation, his work avoided parody and self-parody in favor of pastiche and homage. Parody implies a position "outside" discourse; Barthes argued that there is no position outside discourse, only dialogue across discourse networks.

Clipography does not synthesize these collage elements. Rather, it separates elements, like Brecht did with the elements of theater. Goodwin ascribes such Brechtian aesthetics to the pop song; he refers to this separation and layering of elements in the pop song as "stacking up,"

> a phenomenon that creates a multilayered text that can be heard in a variety of ways, depending on where we place our aural attention (with the rhythm, the voice, the backing, the lyrics, and so on). This structure implies a separation of elements common to Brechtian aesthetics, rather than the hierarchy of discourses identified as central in the classic realist text. (94)

Goodwin does not ascribe Brechtian *effects* (such as distancing and alienation) to this stacking up because it is now an accepted convention. In academic research, however, the separation of elements is not an accepted convention and probably would have Brechtian effects.

Traditional academic writing stresses unity of style and the avoidance of ambiguity. By contrast, many media artists, including pop musicians, value polyvocality and open-endedness in their work. In fact, a major objection to music videos amongst musicians and critics is its supposed "fixing in the mind's eye of a set of visual images, which, it is sometimes assumed, closes off the options for listeners to construct their own imaginative interpretation of songs" (Goodwin 7). Goodwin argues that because music videos rely on montage principles for their construction, the relationship of the image to the music and lyrics is often polysemic, like collage:

> It may be that music functions like the newspaper photograph: as a code that is framed by its context (in this case, visual imagery). But it can equally well be the case that the visual images are framed by the network of interpretation suggested by words and music on the soundtrack that would function as aural "captions," in this instance, in just the manner identified (and explored more thoroughly) in another essay by Barthes. ("The Photographic Message" 2)

In music video, the images can comment on the music and the music can comment on the images. Each term or citation in collage writing may comment upon or shift the meaning of the other materials around it. In fact, pop musicians and video artists frequently employ mixed modes to avoid fixing the meaning of music videos: "The three codes of popular music (music, lyrics, iconography) do not always constitute a unified address, and this conflict routinely spills over into video clips" (Goodwin 86).

Clipography takes advantage of the reversibility, multiple address, fragmentation, and discontinuity of rock 'n' roll by practicing a collage form of writing. The clipographer cites materials from several discourses—popular music, family, school, and discipline knowledge—then fragments and juxtaposes them. In clipography, the disciplinary materials do not function as objective commentary on the other discourses but are as much a part of the collage as the other discourse materials.

Step-by-Step Instructions

Just as video artists use the musical figure as a pattern for arranging disparate visual materials, Barthes, in *A Lover's Discourse,* uses a musical figure, a "kind of opera aria," to arrange his disparate materials. Similarly in clipography, the pop song, with its hooks, emotions, and recurrent themes, provides the pattern that the writer uses to arrange the collage of materials drawn from various discourses: those of family, entertainment, school, and academic disciplines. *Step one:* The clipographer begins a clipography project by asking a burning question: "What is my situation in regards to X?" X can be a love problem, a career problem, a disciplinary problem, a community problem, or any other problem in which the writer faces a dilemma. The burning question is an aporia, a problem that requires judgment and cannot be "solved" using positivist research methods. The burning question provides the frame of self-knowledge that the clipography will address. In my clipography, I am interested in determining my relationship to a group of bohemian and radical artists who gathered in Uptown, Minneapolis.

Begin by writing anecdotes about the situation that gave rise to your burning question. The anecdotes need not be complete stories with conclusions or resolutions. In fact, stories without clear resolutions work better since they represent an open set of tensions that clipography can address.

Step two: The clipographer identifies her habits in relation to popular music in order to find points of identification, using them as entry points for exploring the self and the culture.

Select music that reflects your state of mind about the situation you identified in step one; include lyrics of the songs and any relevant information about the music and performer. These songs provide the "figures" upon which the collage will be made. The collage materials chosen should correspond, however obliquely, to the hooks and motifs of the songs. In my clipographic experiment, I chose to work with songs by Prince and Soul Asylum, music from Minneapolis that reflected my state of mind at the time I was asking my burning question.

Step three: The clipographer gathers and assembles research materials from the four areas of the popcycle (family, school, entertainment, and the disciplines), by tracking the signifier (using puns and homonyms), rather than signifieds, as the principle method for research.

Select key words, places, or images from the anecdotes and songs used in the first two steps. Using a keyword search program (like Google or a library search engine), find references to these terms across a variety of texts. It does not matter whether the references are to texts in seemingly "distant" domains. I used the term "Apollo" as a key term and followed references that took me to Pythagoras and to James Brown. The clipographer makes a collage from these materials and the meaning follows from the collage.

Clipography links materials by way of synaesthesia, the evocation of one sense impression from the stimulation of another. Synaesthesia is a type of aesthetic reasoning, and as such, is a much looser way to link information than argumentative reasoning. The keyword works like a pun; it appears in different domains and means different things depending upon the domain in which it appears. The clipographer writes with many or all the meanings of the keyword. Punning is the linguistic analogy for synaesthesia (the poetic form of music videos), in that both are associative rather than linear. Marshall McLuhan, in *The Gutenberg Galaxy,* argued that print media made information conform to visual and spatial parameters, anaesthetizing the other senses. In *Understanding Media,* McLuhan notes that electronic media, unlike print, activates the other senses; "By imposing unvisualizable relationships that are the result of instant speed, electric technology dethrones the visual sense and restores us to the dominion of synesthesia, and the close interinvolvement of the other senses" (*Understanding Media* 111). Synaesthesia allows one to connect disparate materials using poetic principles:

> . . . examples of synaesthesia suggest a number of sources for the iconographies stored in popular cul-

> ture memory: (a) personal imagery deriving from the individual memories associated with the song; (b) images associated purely with the music itself . . ., which may work through either metaphor or metonymy; (c) images of the musicians/performers; (d) visual signifiers deriving from national-popular iconography, perhaps related to geographical associations prompted by the performers; and (e) deeply anchored popular cultural signs associated with rock music and that often link rock with a mythologized "America" (cars, freeways, beer, beaches, parties). (Goodwin 56)

Following McLuhan's observation that electronic media supports synesthetic forms, James C. Morrison also notes how synesthetic forms also thrive in oral cultures; " . . . there are other cultures, notably non-Western, in which synesthesia seems to be more integral to the culture and is even expressed in the morphology of the language." According to the *Encyclopædia Britannica Online* (2000, May 31), in the Austroasiatic languages,

> Expressive language and wordplay are embodied in a special word class called "expressives." This is a basic class of words distinct from verbs, adjectives, and adverbs in that they cannot be subjected to logical negation. They describe noises, colors, light patterns, shapes, movements, sensations, emotions, and aesthetic feelings. Synesthesia is often observable in these words and serves as a guide for individual coinage of new words. The forms of the expressives are thus quite unstable, and the additional effect of wordplay can create subtle and endless structural variations.

The *Encyclopædia Britannica*'s reference to Austroasiatic languages contains several qualities of the mystory form in general: its use of wordplay, its emphasis on aesthetics and pattern, its construction of inventive textual passages based on resemblance that cannot be negated, and its structural instability.

Synaesthesia provides the poetics for clipography by providing the linking terms among personal narratives, entertainment, and the materials of the humanities. The key to makings a clipography is to motivate these links. Clipographers should have a working knowledge of puns, homonyms, figures (textual, musical, and pictorial), metaphor, and metonymy before attempting a project in clipography. Without this knowledge, they will not understand how to link their research materials by means of synaesthesia.

In this remainder of this essay, I provide my own example of clipography. Below is a brief overview of my clipography showing the series of steps I took to construct it. Some of these steps would be valid in a traditional academic paper (i.e. an examination of Harlem might include a discussion of the Apollo Theater, which is in Harlem). But some of the steps (i.e. linking the Apollo Theater in Harlem to the Temple of Apollo in ancient Greece) are loose associations made possible by puns and chance associations. The point of clipography is to find meaning or make meaning from these associations. The following list is a condensed overview of the links in my clipography:

- Establishing a problem: about the difficulty of maintaining alternative communities and my position and mood in relation to these alternative communities.
- A link from Prince's song "Uptown" to a personal anecdote about my teenage years in Uptown, Minneapolis (site of an alternative community of artists).
- A link from Uptown Minneapolis to Uptown, New York (AKA Harlem) because both places are called "Uptown" and both places were sites of a cultural renaissance. Additionally, the music of Prince is, in part, homage to James Brown, who performed in Harlem.
- A link from Uptown, New York to the Apollo Theater, which is a site in Harlem.
- A link from the Apollo Theater to the Temple of Apollo in ancient Greece.
- A link from the Temple of Apollo to Pythagoras, who was a priest of Apollo.
- A link from Pythagoras to Socrates, who drew his philosophy from Pythagoras.
- A link from Socrates to Nietzsche, who critiqued Socratic thought and called for a return of the Dionysian sphere to offset the dominance of the Apollonian sphere in 19th century Europe.

As a result of my clipography, I drew insights that led to greater self-knowledge, knowledge about both ancient about contemporary cultures, and knowledge about humanities texts.

Clipography: "Pythagoras at the Apollo Theater"

The Problem

The problem I address in my clipography is the difficulty of establishing and maintaining alternative communities and my position and mood in relation to these alternative communities. To help me understand this problem, I present anecdotes about an alternative community of artists and bohemians in Minneapolis that was defeated both by its own logic and by the forces of "progress."

Prince's "Uptown"

In 1979, I transferred to Central High School in Minneapolis, a "magnet" school in the center of the city, surrounded by housing projects and multiracial neighborhoods. About one-third of the students, myself included, were bussed in from predominantly white, more-affluent neighborhoods. I was no longer a suburbanite, but I wasn't quite a city kid either because I had not yet learned the habits of city life. Additionally, I was an adolescent—I was no longer a child, but I had not yet learned the habits of adult life. I chose this period to use in my clipography project because it was during this time that I learned my adult behaviors through the negotiations and adjustments I made with different parts of the culture.

When I arrived in high school, the only music I liked was classical music and I detested other kinds of music. Perhaps this preference for classical music reflected a rejection not just of pop culture on my part, but also of modernity in general, which I found oppressive. One day, in 1981, a student came to the classroom door and said, "Prince is downstairs." I had no idea who Prince was, but someone told me he had been a student at Central High School and had since made several albums. The classroom emptied to meet him but I stayed, refusing to participate in the glorification of a pop star. Later, I heard conversations about Prince's visit; he had worn platform shoes, a trench coat, and a purple g-string. The description of his bizarre appearance intrigued me.

I couldn't stand not knowing what I had missed in school and what all the excitement had been about, so two weeks later I bought a copy of *Dirty Mind,* which had a picture of Prince in trench coat and g-string on the cover. When I got home, my parents were having dinner with their friends. I went for the headphone and put on the record. The drum flourish and keyboard bursts at the beginning of "Uptown" had an immediate effect on me; it created one of the most powerful releases I had felt in my life.

Prince's funk sound and look was highly erotic; for me, it was about the release of pent up energies. Another kind of music, punk rock, was exploding in Minneapolis at the same time. Punk rock changed the way I saw the world. Local punk bands included Husker Dü, The Replacements, and Loud Fast Rules (who later changed their name to Soul Asylum). This music did not *release* my energy as much as it charged me with emotional tension. I learned my social habits, which constituted my behavior as a city person and a young adult, from funk and punk. Two songs, Prince's "Uptown" and Soul Asylum's "Voodoo Doll" became emblems of my new identity.

Uptown, Minneapolis

Why this song? Admittedly, the lyrics do not seem particularly good when I read them now, although they do capture some sense of the liberation I felt at the time. Undoubtedly, the song helped me make sense of the social interactions I had with other adolescents. More specifically, "Uptown" helped me make sense of the real Uptown in Minneapolis (at Lake Street and Hennepin Avenue) where my friends and I used to meet. Uptown had an old movie palace called "The Uptown Theater" where films like Renoir's *Rules of the Game* and Bunuel's *Un Chien Andalou* and *Los Olvidados*—my favorite movies—used to play. In addition, Uptown had a coffee shop, one of the first in the city, called "The Uptown Café," where an eclectic bunch of artists and activists gathered. It also had a small bar called "The Uptown Bar," which was a neighborhood hangout and later a nightclub where Soul Asylum, The Jayhawks, and other local bands played.

The neighborhood around Uptown was a place where artists, young people, gays, blacks, and punks gathered together. When I discovered it, I felt as though I had happened upon a cultural explosion. Nothing like it had existed in the suburbs where I grew up. In Uptown, bands played in the street, people gathered in the cafés and talked about art, music, and politics. I discovered, however, that the people who gathered in Uptown did not think of themselves as belonging to a special community; probably they felt it had always been there because they had grown up there. But I had the sense of a chance encounter of great significance; I had found a special intersection of time and place, a sense of joining an extended family, and I wanted others to have that sense too. Prince's lyrics to "Uptown" were key; when he sang "White, black, Puerto Rican, everybody's just a freakin,'" I believed that a community could be formed precisely at the point of a tremendous release from taboos and social boundaries.

Uptown was the site of all that had been banished from my suburban life—sexuality, difference, madness—and I was held to it by an almost magical force of attraction. Particular places, words, and people in Uptown became "sacred" for me (in the sense that Leiris describes in "The Sacred in Everyday Life"). These sacred places and people would soon disappear.

Louis Aragon describes a condemned region of Paris, the *Passage de l'Opera,* in his novel, *Paris Peasant,* a book that inspired Walter Benjamin's "Arcades Project." The people, places, and objects in this region of Paris gained significance for Aragon because the government had marked it for destruction to make way for the Boulevard Haussmann. Uptown in Minneapolis was similarly marked for destruction. Developers built a mall on the corner of Lake Street and Hennepin Avenue, the center of Uptown. They planned to transform the entire area into upscale shopping for wealthy consumers, and this meant that all others had to leave. The most disappointing change was the building of a McDonald's Restaurant across the street from the Uptown Theater and The Uptown Café. The café lost business and closed. The cultural variety that existed in the area became reduced to a few pathetic punks who hung out in front of McDonald's and became known as "McPunks." The McPunks served as a curious freak show for the consumers who invaded the area to shop. Uptown, as I knew it, disappeared.

As in Aragon's story of the *Passage de l'Opera* region of Paris, the local inhabitants in Uptown organized too late to save their way of life. Lacking both a sense of community and a sense of impending doom, they realized what they had lost only after they had lost it. In 1987, about five years after the Uptown Mall opened, a group of anarchists, including myself, organized a '"Bash the Rich" tour of Uptown, modeled on similar actions by the group "Class War" in England. The tour was also inspired by the success of an anti-war demonstration in Uptown a few weeks earlier that had developed in response to the U.S. sending troops to Honduras. On that occasion, hundreds of demonstrators took over the streets, put up flaming barricades, played live music and acted in defiant joy while the police watched. The Uptown experience was similar to the Paris Commune. The "Bash the Rich" tour, like the Paris Commune, ended with the police bashing our heads.

I link my songs and personal anecdotes via Uptown, Minneapolis. At this juncture of my clipography, two songs play alternately. One is "Uptown" by Prince; the other is "Voodoo Doll" by Soul Asylum.

The songs' lyrics express the contradictions and tensions that pulled on me at that time—school pressures, work pressures, and pressures to conform—and made the "release" represented by Prince's "Uptown" more dramatic. The experience of that release made my tension over the stressful conditions of my life more dramatic also. My encounters with these songs showed me the power music had to change my life.

Uptown, New York (Harlem) and the Apollo Theater

From Uptown Minneapolis, I link to another site: Uptown, New York, also known as Harlem. Harlem includes a key site in America's cultural history, the Apollo Theater. The Apollo, which opened in 1935, draws together numerous associations in my clipography: the Harlem Renaissance, with its melding of popular forms (including music) and intellectualism, the Dionysian tradition in soul music, the Apollonian tradition of reason which Socrates used to the exclusion of the Dionysian, and the life and ideas of Pythagoras, an influence on Socrates. Harlem was a center for the creation of hybrid cultural forms, particularly in the music of Duke Ellington, Bessie Smith, Cab Calloway, and Louis Armstrong, who all played in Harlem. Ellington composed "three-minute symphonies," orchestral pieces that had several movements—"Black and Tan Fantasy" is a case in point—yet also had room for soloists to improvise. Generally, these pieces were three minutes long because they had to fit onto one side of a 78-rpm disc. Ellington's music fused European and African-American forms.

At the Cotton Club in Harlem, where Ellington's orchestra played, blacks were not allowed in the audience. His music was publicized to white American audiences as exotic entertainment, "jungle" music. To European critics, however, Ellington was a serious composer whose compositions ranked with those of Debussy and Stravinsky. To many black listeners, Ellington's music was a complex message about the lives of blacks in America. Even though many of his pieces, like the collage-styled "Black and Tan Fantasy," had no lyrics, many blacks heard in the opening and closing funereal strains—and in the title (a reference to small number of "black and tan" clubs in which blacks and whites could mix)—a story about the status of their race in America.

The Apollo Theater in Harlem, despite its name, has been a source for Dionysian culture in the United States. It was the site of a classic live recording, *James Brown Live at the Apollo,* which was a key inspiration for Prince. The event recorded a titanic release, a kind of controlled frenzy, in the audience. Here are some notes on Brown's classic recording from a fan website called "Northern Soul Circle":

> "From the first note things would be jumping." said Ray, "He'd come on stage with his red tails and white bucks and start dancing, and the crowd would go wild. The minute they'd see us in town they knew it was gonna be excitement." It was precisely that excitement that Brown hoped to capture when he decided to record his October 24 1962 Apollo show. The idea to do a live soul album was new at the time, but Brown believed it would be the best way to represent his sound—especially at the Apollo. "Sid Nathan, head of King Records, said 'You gotta be crazy to do that,'" according to Danny Ray. James replied, "Sometimes it makes sense to do something crazy." Brown had to put up his own money to make the record. The resulting album . . . was released early in 1963, and rocketed up the charts.

Pythagoras at The Temple of Apollo

Many Greeks in ancient times believed that Pythagoras was Apollo incarnate. Pythagoras was the first mathematical theorist (and thus a key figure for Plato, the inventor of method), and he was the first musical theorist. Legend has it that he invented the diatonic scale by dividing a string in two and producing the harmonic octave, thus connecting science and music.

Although Pythagoras is important to my clipography project for the reasons stated above, I discovered another correspondence. Pythagoras was a vegetarian, as am I; he supported the ethical treatment of animals because he believed they bore the souls of dead people. One day, Pythagoras admonished a man who was hitting a puppy. "'Stop!' he said, 'don't hit it! It is the soul of a friend! I knew it when I heard its voice'" (Beavers).

One week before I discovered this anecdote about Pythagoras, I had written an "automatic" poem using the cut-up words of a magnetic poetry kit. The poem was the result of my choosing words at random from the kit and inserting words that would produce a grammatical utterance. The poem read:

> I hit a tiny puppy with a club the skin & hair I beat it
> sings essential screams soaring sweetly gorgeously my
> language is drunk

Automatic writing was a new experience for me. I had previously thought of writing as a professional activity, with all the notions of mastery associated with it. Automatic writing, by contrast, is an amateur activity, something anyone can do. Little did I know when I wrote this poem that it was part of a dialogue with Pythagoras. When I wrote the poem, I had not yet investigated the Apollonian and Dionysian aesthetics, elements that were to become essential to my project. The most curious, and to me, aberrant, part of my poem was the last line, "my language is drunk." In hindsight, the line perfectly illustrates a Dionysian message; it suggests that language operates without the will or intention of an author, but manifests itself under some *influence.* Pythagoras answered my Dionysian challenge with an Apollonian reminder about boundaries and self-control. Such correspondences are key elements of mystorical writing, because they indicate the emergence of pattern: the dominant of the form.

Nietzsche's *The Birth of Tragedy*

My research into the Apollonian and Dionysian modes led me to Nietzsche's book, *The Birth of Tragedy.* Nietzsche argued for pleasure in education at a time when Western cultures had repudiated it in favor of the values associated with utility, production, and practicality. Nietzsche called for the return of the Dionysian to offset the influence of the Apollonian. He identified a period in Greek culture when the Apollonian and Dionysian impulses in art were fused into a unity left largely unexplored before or since. This period of Greek culture is vital to me since it serves as a prototype for an aesthetic-analytic pedagogy, of which clipography serves as a method. For Nietzsche, art evolved from its Apollonian-Dionysian duality. Nietzsche explained that Apollo inspired the plastic arts, and most poetry, and that Dionysus inspired the non-visual arts, especially music. The Apollonian is the realm of the ordered dream and the Dionysian the realm of intoxication.

Nietzsche's project, the reunification of the divided Apollonian and Dionysian spheres, depended upon restoring the place of the "subjective" in inquiry. He pointed to the lyrical poets' use of "I" and to "the entire chromatic scale of his passions and appetites" as being reasons to dismiss the lyric poet as *non*artistic, since Homer (the ultimate "artist") did not resort to these devices. Nietzsche asked, "How, then, are we to explain the reverence in which he [Archilochus, a lyric poet] was held as a poet, the honor done him by the Delphic oracle, that seat of "objective" art, in a number of very curious sayings?" (411)

Nietzsche argued that a "musical mood" underlies the compositions of the lyric poets. This compositional foundation made sense to Nietzsche because, as he noted, of the ancient "union—nay identity—everywhere considered natural, between musician and poet."(411) In Nietzsche's discussion of this identity between musician and poet, he concludes that the "Dionysiac artist" (such as the lyric poet) *sees* music. It becomes visible to him; the lyric poet practices a form of synaesthesia.

> . . . a Dionysiac artist become[s] wholly identified with the original Oneness, its pain and contradiction, and produc[es] a replica of that Oneness in music, if music may legitimately be seen as a repetition of the world; however, this music becomes visible to him again, as in a dream similitude, through the Apollonian dream influence. That reflection, without image or idea, of original pain in music, with its redemption through illusion, now produces a second reflection as a single simile or example. The artist had abrogated

> his subjectivity earlier, during the Dionysiac phase: the image which now reveals to him his oneness with the heart of the world is a dream scene showing forth vividly, together with original pain, the original delight of illusion. (411–2)

According to Nietzsche, the unity of the Apollonian and Dionysian spheres briefly flowered in Attic tragedy and lyric poetry before being destroyed by the rationalist anti-Dionysian thought of Socrates and his followers. Yet Nietzsche identified a moment at the end of Socrates' life when his awareness about the limits of reason became acute, a moment that leads Nietzsche to ask "whether there is really anything inherently impossible in the idea of a Socratic artist?" (407)

> It appears that this despotic logician had from time to time a sense of the void, loss, unfulfilled duty with regard to art. In prison he told his friends how, on several occasions, a voice had spoken to him in a dream, saying, "Practice music, Socrates!" Almost to the end he remained confident that his philosophy represented the highest art of the muses, and would not fully believe that a divinity meant to remind him of "common, popular music." Yet in order to unburden his conscience he finally agreed, in prison, to undertake that music which hitherto he had held in low esteem. In this frame of mind he composed a poem on Apollo and rendered several Aesopian fables in verse. What prompted him to these exercises was something very similar to that warning voice of his daimonion: an Apollonian perception that, like a barbarian king, he had failed to comprehend the nature of a divine effigy, and was in danger of offending his own god through ignorance. These words heard by Socrates in his dream are the only indication that he ever experienced any uneasiness about the limits of his logical universe. He may have asked himself: "Have I been too ready to view what was unintelligible to me as being devoid of meaning? Perhaps there is a realm of wisdom, after all, from which the logician is exclud-

> ed? Perhaps art must be seen as the necessary complement of rational discourse?" (407)

I hardly find it surprising that Nietzsche wrote this account and evaluation of Socrates' revelation at a time when Europe was gripped by a fanatical enthusiasm for positivism. Nietzsche was perhaps the most virulent opponent of positivist philosophy, which abandoned all inquiry that did not lend itself to rational explanation. He attacked Socrates repeatedly in his writings, yet he finds a moment in Socrates' life in which he identified with Socrates, to the point of imagining Socrates' thoughts and likening them to his own. To Nietzsche, the idea of Socrates taking up music must have seemed as strange as if August Comte had taken up ballet. Nietzsche noted that Socrates' daimon (inner voice) had until this moment functioned only as a warning voice, which he heard exclusively when he was about to take a course of action, and which always responded in the negative; when Socrates was about to do something the daimon did not like, the daimon said "no." In this case, the daimon issues a positive injunction: "Practice music, Socrates!"

When I discovered that Socrates turned to music before his death, I confirmed my belief that Apollonian tendencies lead to judgments lacking in holistic wisdom. But I also reevaluated my relationship to artists and bohemians, seeing their purely Dionysian tendencies as destructive of community in the long term because they turn continuity into chaos. I sought to bring the Dionysian and Apollonian realms into contact; I became both a scholar and a musician in order to experiment with the crossing of these realms. In short, I chose Apollo; but I need my James Brown too.

As an investigator, I gained some personal benefit from clipography. But clipography should not be seen as an elaborate self-help exercise; its primary function is to conduct cultural studies research using interdisciplinary, hybrid forms of discourse. Clipography brings the subject into the investigation as part of the object of study; as a "machine" for yielding judgment, it relies on non-standard practices such as aesthetic production and associative reasoning to produce expert knowledge. Clipography continues the tradition of imminent critique, of knowledge arising from inside the world, and as such it is consonant with other methods described in this volume.

Works Cited

Aragon, Louis. *La Paisan de Paris.* Paris: Gallimard. 1966.

Barthes, Roland. "Death of the Author." *Image-Music-Text.* Ed. S. Heath. New York: Hill and Wang. 1977.

—. *A Lover's Discourse: Fragments.* New York: Hill and Wang. 1978.

—. "The Photographic Message." *Image-Music-Text.* Ed. S. Heath. New York: Hill and Wang. 1977.

Beavers, Anthony F. "Pythagoras and the Pythagoreans." *Exploring Plato's Dialogues: A Virtual Learning Environment on the World-Wide Web* . The Internet Applications Laboratory at the University of Evansville. 1998. 15 June 1998. <http://plato.evansville.edu/commentary/beavers/pythagoras.htm>.

Goodwin, Andrew. *Dancing In The Distraction Factory: Music Television and Popular Culture.* Minneapolis: U of Minnesota P, 1992.

Leiris, Michel. "The Sacred in Everyday Life." *The College of Sociology 1937–39.* Ed. Denis Hollier. Minneapolis: U of Minnesota P, 1988.

McLuhan, Marshall. *The Gutenberg Galaxy.* Toronto: U of Toronto P, 1962.

—. *Understanding Media: The Extensions of Man.* MIT Press. 1994.

Morrison, James C. "Hypermedia and Synesthesia." *Media Ecology,* Volume 1. 11 April 2004. <http://www.media-ecology.org/publications/proceedings/v1/hypermedia_and_synesthesia.html>.

Nietzsche, Friedrich. "From The Birth of Tragedy from the Spirit of Music." Ed. D. Richter. *The Critical Tradition: Classic Texts and Contemporary Trends.* New York: St. Martin's Press. 1989.

Northern Soul Circle. 4 August 2003. <http://www.northern.soulfans.co.uk/apollo3.htm>

Prince. "Uptown." *Dirty Mind.* Warner Brothers Records, 1982.

Scholes, Robert, Nancy Comley and Gregory Ulmer. *Textbook: Writing Through Literature.* Boston, MA: Bedford Books, 2002.

Soul Asylum. "Voodoo Doll." *While You Were Out.* TwinTone Records, 1985.

Ulmer, Gregory. *Heuretics: The Logic of Invention.* Baltimore: Johns Hopkins UP, 1994.

—. *Internet Invention: From Literacy to Electracy.* Pearson Education, Inc., 2003.

10 Deleuzian Strolls, Wordsworthian Walks, and MOO Landscapes

Ron Broglio

A man is walking through nature. How is one to describe such a walk? This is the problem posed by Romantic literature and particularly the poetry, tour guides, and art of the 18th and 19th century picturesque tradition, which will serve as my content and means of departure into the field of digital humanities. The walk is an event, a performance that actualizes various possibilities from within the environment and the pedestrian. A stroll through a landscape can help us realize the goals and means of new media performances. This essay will take up two sorts of strolls: the Wordsworthian and the Deleuzian. The two walks are in themselves the same. One wanders and wonders amid the elements of nature. But how Deleuze and Wordsworth think about these strolls and how they represent walking makes all the difference. For the romantic poet, rambling through the Lake District is about creating meaning through a resonance between the inner landscape of the mind and the outer landscape of nature. For Deleuze, the inside-outside distinction collapses into lines of flight that unsettle both objects and subjects within the terrain. Deleuze and his vagrant companions unsettle and then set in motion what it means to mean. Translating the Deleuzian stroll to an online environment will provide an open system of play as a heuristic strategy for understanding literature. More specifically, this essay will explore Deleuzian strolls in MOO spaces as a means of reading Romantic period texts.

Perhaps most fundamental to taking a walk is what one is obliged to notice. I sit down to write this essay in a cabin atop a mountain. It is my father's cabin, and I have just returned from a walk with him through the woods. We walked along a trail he made that illustrates the problem of observation. Walking the trail, he points out property lines, boulders, views from overlooks, and strategically placed large sticks that serve as markers along the path. He has cut down small, scrappy trees and cleared underbrush to make the path passable. The trail has an objective. At its end is a large rock with a view of a lake below. The whole experience is quite pleasing, and is designed to please. Along the way, his dog begins chewing, wrestling with, and otherwise moving the sticks meant to mark the path. The dog has begun a game, and I wonder what would happen if we let him have his way. What sort of trail would be made by the dog dragging sticks where he chooses? My father would lose his trail; and by walking along the dog's seemingly random path, I would have to fashion new observations and goals. As yet another exercise in orienteering, think of what would happen were there no trail. The first problem would be orientation—where am I, and where do I need to go? Of course, I do not *need* to go anywhere but feel more comfortable having a sense of purpose that provides meaning to the walk. The goal sets a task, and gives a sense of accomplishment. Next is the problem of what one is to do while walking. Making observations along the way remains requisite for a walk. Yet, what am I to take notice of? The goal helps here. In the walk with my father, I am to notice the new trail itself, his selection of turns and choice of boundaries. Most walks include notice of rocks, trees, and animals, and a perspicuous view. One also observes objects that are less easily thought of as objects in their own right: the weather, the feel of the air, the give of the ground, and the density of vegetation. Fundamental to a stroll is orientation and what counts as objects for observation (Burnett 119-65).

These same fundamentals apply to the picturesque tradition and Romantic walking. The tour guides of Nathaniel West, William Gilpin, and William Wordsworth provide detailed instructions of paths to take, places to stop and make observations of picturesque prospects, and what objects to observe along the way. So, for example, in Thomas West's guide, "The design of the following sheets, is to encourage the taste of visiting the lakes, by furnishing the traveler with a Guide; and for that purpose, the writer has here collected and laid before him, all the select stations and points of view, noticed by those authors who have last made the tour of the lakes, verified by his own repeated observations. (West 6) True to the picturesque tradition, West's viewer is instructed to stands at a specific observation point while using his or her imagination to form nature into a picture "calculated for the pencil," thus meeting the terms of the picturesque aesthetic—nature that can be made into a pleasing picture (West x). Gilpin, in his guide to the Lake District, spends several chapters explaining what objects to observe and how to observe them. He then places the objects together and instructs the view how to compose a scene with a lake as the central object around which the rest of nature is organized: "We have now made a considerable advance towards a landscape. The sky is laid in; a mountain fills the offskip; and a lake, with its accompaniments, takes possession of a nearer distance. Nothing but a fore-ground is wanting; and for this we have great choice of objects—broken ground—trees—rocks—cascades—and vallies" (Gilpin 103). Because nature offers an overabundance of stimuli for the viewer, a system for viewing provides a necessary filter for making nature intelligible. Throughout the picturesque—in painting, poetry, and touring—the land becomes framed and reduced to a calculable sum, a particular objectification of nature that makes the land useful to the viewer and his or her aesthetic interests (Heidegger 318-20). Nature becomes what is intelligible and representable by human culture.

Think back to the sticks that mark my father's trail. These bits of wood mean differently for him than they do for his dog, Abe. For old Abe, they are judged by their playworthiness—are they chewable, will they be the right weight and size to carry or tug at? For my father, Abe's values are less than helpful; in fact, they tug and tear at his own. The sticks can not both serve as markers of a human path and things to be chewed and moved. Nature is intelligible for man and dog differently. For the man, the sticks are removed from nature to serve as signs of culture, signs by which to orient oneself in nature. The sticks are not just any brush, but markers of a trail through and around the woods. For the dog, amid the overabundance of branches, logs, and twigs, the sticks are those selected as worthy of play. Different filters provide different meaning and objectives.

Wordsworth applies to nature a series of traditional 18th century filters about touring and the picturesque. He adds to these his own innovations of interior resonance with the landscape and thus he produces his own signature Wordsworthian Romanticism. The poet becomes known in generations after him as author of the "egotistical sublime" (Keats). His landscape will be that of the poet's mind, as the Prelude indicates, "The preparatory poem is biographical, and conducts the history of the Author's mind to the point when he was emboldened to hope that his faculties were sufficiently matured for entering upon the arduous labour which he had proposed to himself" (Wordsworth 494). Time and again the poet who embraces nature also keeps it at a distance as in the stock Romantic claim from the Preface to the *Lyrical Ballads* in which poetry is defined as "the spontaneous overflow of powerful feeling . . . recollected in tranquility" (740). It is at such tranquil distance that Wordsworth contemplates dancing with the daffodils "when on my couch I lie/ In vacant mood" ("I wander lonely as a cloud" ln 19–20). The same interest in, but remove from, nature can be found in his 1812 tour guide. His guide to the Lake District maintains a basic distinction between observer and the objects in nature to be seen. Each object is considered on its own for its own merit; he includes a chapter on lakes, rivers, and lesser bodies of water and another on mountains, hills and valleys, and still another on trees and other vegetation. Then, like Gilpin, Wordsworth places these individual objects together to compose a typical picturesque scene where the whole softens and harmonizes the parts into a unity. He provides information on where to stand and where to halt the touring of the tour so as to properly frame and compose picturesque scenes in the Lake District. Like a military post, these observation "stations" serve as strategic points that allow the tourist to make advances upon nature while remaining at a safe distance. When the poet is actually confronted with objects or people that will not remain beyond arm's length—such as the Leach Gatherer of "Resolution and Independence" and a fisher in "Poems on the Naming of Places"—Wordsworth turns the subjects into mirrors, through which the poet reflects upon himself and his state of mind. At this point, it is worth noting several characteristics of the poet's representation of nature. While the land is experienced through a bodily walk, the representation of the space always removes the poet from the scene. Objects are clearly demarcated and any that threaten to impose themselves upon the wanderer get appropriated into objects for self-contemplation.

How different Deleuze's meanderings are from the Wordsworthian stroll. A meandering walk first appears in the opening pages of *Anti-Oedipus*. There, the schizophrenic's motion through space is juxtaposed to the neurotic on the couch—think here of Wordsworth contemplating daffodils "when on my couch I lie" (227). There is a shift from what is happening in the mind to what is happening to bodies. *Anti-Oedipus* works against the Oedipal machinations in Freud. One of the major 20th century critiques of Freud has been his inversion of the political. For Freud, power gets played out in the psyche rather than on the streets:

> Oedipus says to us: either you will internalize the differential functions that rule over the exclusive disjunctions, and thereby "resolve" Oedipus, or you will fall into the neurotic night of imaginary identifications. Either you will follow the lines of the triangle—lines that structure and differentiate the three terms—or you will always bring one term into play as if it were one too many in relation of identification in the undifferentiated. But there is Oedipus on either side. And everybody knows what psychoanalysis means by *resolving* Oedipus: internalizing it so as to better rediscover it on the outside, in the children. (79)

Deleuze and Guattari move from the interior to pure exteriors—a body without organs. Furthermore, *Anit-Oedipus* takes aim at the symbolic of Lacan by siding with the schizophrenic. For Lacan, the schizophrenic disavows the Oedipal and so refuses to enter the symbolic; instead, everything that happens takes place on the surface of the real: "The true difference in nature is not between the Symbolic and the Imaginary, but between the real machinic (*machinique*) element, which constitutes desiring-production, and the structural whole of the Imaginary and the Symbolic, which merely forms a myth and its variants" (83). Contrasting the neurotic stuck within the symbolic to the schizophrenic operating on the real serves as a useful distinction for Romantic criticism since much of Wordsworth's self-fashioning and a good deal of criticism afterwards leaves the poet on the couch where his theater of the mind can be examined. By contrast, for the schizophrenic, "Everything is a machine. Celestial machines, the stars or rainbows in the sky, alpine machines—all of them connected to those of his body. The continual whirr of machines" (2). The schizophrenic gets out into the world. Whereas the Wordsworthian walk is designed to reflect the inner workings of the mind and the mind in relation to language, the schizoid stroll as described by Deleuze and Guattari is meant to show relations between bodies. Each body acts as an assemblage that gets defined by how it is hooked up to other assemblages. As Brian Massumi explains, a brick is used for constructing a building, but when coupled with hand and smashed window, a brick is part of a machine of political protest (Massumi xiii). So, an object is not defined by an interior, a property of identity and self-reflexivity (A = A), but by its difference, by what it gets connected to and aligned with.

Because the schizophrenic is not "properly" hooked up to the Oedipal machine of imaginary desires and symbolic values, he is free to roam outside of predictable social paths and create new arrangements of objects:

> we are all handymen: each with his little machines. For every organ-machine, an energy-machine: all the time, flows and interruptions. Judge Schreber has sunbeams in his ass. *A solar anus.* And rest assured that it works: Judge Schreber feels something, produces something, and is capable of explaining the process theoretically. Something is produced: the effects of a machine, not mere metaphors" (*Anti-Oedipus* 2–3).

We will return to the implications of machine as other than mere metaphor later in discussion of MOOs, but for now suffice it to say that the schizoid stroll allows new connections between diverse entities in the real. The schizophrenic's fascination and paranoia over wires, tubes, plugs and outlets is not an interest in internal organs as psychoanalysis insists but rather a fascination with couplings and assemblages in the real.

Working outside accepted social relations of the symbolic, the schizophrenic stroll serves as what Deleuze and Guattari call a line of flight. The term appears in their book on Kafka where K., who is out of sorts with the world around him, opens doors and passageways that are meant to stay closed. He forces connections and plies relationships for ways into Klamm or out of the trial, "The problem is not that of being free but of finding a way out or even a way in, another side, a hallway, an adjacency. . . . the discovery of another dimension, a sort of adjacency marked by halts, sudden stops where parts, gears, and segments assemble themselves (*Kafka* 7-8)." Schreber and K. are figures for what Deleuze in *Difference and Repetition* calls the aleatory point and the dark precursor (118-20). Ronald Bogue explains this wandering figure as "an unfixable element from which determinate elements arise (26)." That is, at no one time can we fix the value of an aleatory point within an equation, yet its presence defines and differentiates all the other points whose values we can find. It is, as Bogue succinctly calls it, "a self-differentiating (i.e. generative) differentiation (through divergent determinations) differing from itself (nowhere itself fixed, stable or possessed of a single identity)" (26). For Deleuze, then, the schizophrenic stroll literally makes all the difference. This nomadic wanderer connects disparate elements without committing to a single series of relations, as in the example of the wasp and the orchid:

> The orchid deterritorializes by forming an image, a tracing of a wasp; but the wasp reterritorializes on that image. The wasp is nevertheless deterritorialized, becoming a piece in the orchid's reproductive apparatus. But it reterritorializes the orchid by transporting its pollen. Wasp and orchid, as heterogeneous elements, for a rhizome. . . . not imitation at all but a capture of code, surplus value of code, an increase in valence, a veritable becoming, a becoming-wasp of the orchid and a becoming-orchid of the wasp. (*Thousand Plateaus* 10)

Placing the wasp assemblage in relation to the orchid assemblage sets off elements of each to form a new wasp-orchid series. The aleatory gathers elements from various groups and like the handyman, cobbles together new relations and creates temporary fixes till the next project, the next event. Taking a Deleuzian stroll means taking a chance. There is no guarantee how things will turn out. The walk is an event, and the one moving through space may well get caught in unpredictable relations not sanctioned by common sense or social sense. We may end up following sticks tossed about by dogs rather than those placed by men.

The return for such meanderings is a chance to see and interact differently. In relation to digital humanities this difference takes place at three levels: the land, language, and the screen. To be a bit more precise the levels are the real land, the mediated landscape as in Wordsworth's poetry and tour guide, and the landscape of the computer screen. The problem that started this conversation is "how does one describe a walk through nature?" The problem becomes more complex by now asking how one remediates a walk using the computer screen. For the sake of this essay, I would like to talk about how MOOs can be used to think through the land, language, and the screen.

For those unfamiliar with MOOs, they are robust chatroom spaces that allow users to modify the rooms, describe their player characters, and introduce into the space programmable objects. Most MOOs used in academic settings are web-based. They use the old text-based MOO platform and build on top of that the enCore web interface designed by Cynthia Haynes and Jan Rune Holmevik at the University of Texas, Dallas.[1] The interface represents Haynes and Holmevik's work in LinguaMOO as a long history and continued formative development in new possible MOO interactions. With its web interface, anything possible in a web page is also possible in a MOO, including image mapping, pop-ups, Quicktime movies, and Flash games. The MOO adds to the web page the chance to chat and the opportunity to introduce programmable objects. The objects are programmed by users in a MOO computer language similar to C and can run fairly elaborate scripts.

What the MOO provides for Romanticism is a remediated environment that forces the MOO player to think about how the land is made present by the poet as a walker in the field then as a poet writing about the experience. Each step in this series is another level of mediation. First, the land serves as content to the body that moves through the space and selects content from the land for interaction and expression. The body, now as a recording device that bears on it the relationships from the walk, serves as content for the poem which expresses aspects of that which has been experienced. The next stage is a digital space such as a MOO that recreates the poem as a series of rooms and objects. The poem is content for the MOO site. The site is the player-programmer's expression of the poem. Finally, the challenge for the MOO player is to create an experience for other MOO players visiting and interacting with the digital space. The visiting players' interactions work as yet another level of expression with the MOO room functioning as content.

At each level, the form of expression is both a performance of relation to the content *and* interpretation of that content. For example, the walker in the woods selects elements for consideration, interaction, and comment. This could mean pointing to a particular tree, looking at a lake, or standing on a precipice to gain a better view. Pointing, looking, and standing are all physical acts, and at the same time interpretive gestures that select objects from the surrounding landscape and single them out for special treatment. The bodily gestures make the land a more human place by adding our physical relatedness to the elements in the environment. Our pointing, looking, and standing are both physical acts and gestural signs that mean not only physically, but also linguistically. At the next stage of expression, the bodily gestures and their physical-linguistic meaning get selected and translated into words. In the case of Wordsworth's poems, the words are meant to harmonize an experience. In Coleridge's famous definition from *On The Priciples of Genial Cricitsim* (1814), beauty lies in the ability to harmonize and create a "multeity in unity" through the power of the mind. Wordsworth's poetry filters the diversity of experience into a theme. Early drafts of poems and his sister's diaries are useful for understanding the selection, filtering, and crafting process. Finally, a MOO space that re-represents the experience of the narrator in the poem provides yet another layer of interpretation. The player-programmer must decide what words in a poem he will make into objects, what actions from the poem warrant programming into interactive verbs, and how to divide the poem into "rooms" or spaces. Each design element functions as a level of interpretation. As the player-programmer creates digital spaces from the poem, his interpretive moves function much like the poet's gestures in the wilderness. The programmer is pointing out and highlighting elements from within the poem much as the person on a stroll points, looks, and stands with his body. The programmer is also like the poet who picks from his walking experience and crafts select moments into words. The event of interaction and interpretation arises from moving through the space of land, poem, or screen.

At each level, space becomes architectured; that is, space is organized and ordered to provide meaning. The architectural structure of space, as created by gesture and navigation, is not always evident in the wilds of nature. Later, the poem refines and shapes this space, yet still the constructedness of the environment is not always evident. Using the poem to build a MOO space forces interpretive decisions about how the land becomes an organized and poetic landscape. The very object-ness of object-oriented programming means the programmer must think of the land and poetic landscape as objects. Additionally, the ability to program verbs on MOO objects means the creator of the space must select particular activities to highlight and must consider what the result of these actions will be. Each decision in building out the landscape represents one virtual or "compossible" world among many.

Victor Vitanza in his essay on MOOs, Deleuze, Leibniz, and folds, explains that MOO spaces provide the opportunity for branching choices and with each choice is another world. [13] Some of these worlds can co-exist and are compossible, while others are radically exclusive of each other and so are called incompossible. Vitanza presents us with the first and most violent of acts, the choices necessary to build a world exclude other possible worlds. Choice creates the violence of interpretation and the possibility of meaning. Each choice, fold, and world resonates with or denounces others along a wide surface of forking paths. Each world—virtual or real—is a stick dropped to mark a path. While Vitanza himself withdraws from providing examples of what such (in)compossibility would look like in MOOs, I would like to take up his "gift" of worlds and provide a few of my own.

Consider, for example, a MOO space designed around the Wordsworth poem "Point Rash Judgment" from his "Poems on the Naming of Places." [2] The MOO space is divided into three "rooms." The division of rooms is an interpretive decision about different spaces within the poem. The first room looks like an ideal landscape for a picturesque walk, with flowers, a lake, and a slight breeze. The decision to include these elements is part of the programmer's interpretation of which objects are important in the poem. If a player is interested in the flowers, he is asked if he would like to pick some. The players decision to pick flowers or not will result in commentary by the programmed flowers about the temporality of beauty and about ecology and Romantic love and use of the landscape. The other two rooms proceed in similar fashion. In the second room the MOO player is introduced to the main character of Wordsworth's poem. The character's sickliness and poverty contrast markedly with the leisurely ease of the Romantic walk. As a result of the encounter, room three serves as a place for Wordsworthian reflection in tranquility where the player is given a series of questions by which to reflect upon the events of the MOO interaction.

Programming MOO versions of poem space is the first step in digital interpretation. The next and more elaborate element is entering the space as a visiting player character. The visiting player finds himself in the poem space. He may move around freely in the space, interact with objects, and talk to other players. Each action and conversation in the MOO space becomes the visiting player's commentary upon the various levels of MOO space, poem, and initial experience of landscape. Play in the space becomes interpretation.

While most scholarly inquires follow an essay format with its singular and unified argument from a point of view outside of the object of study, the MOO allows players to work from within the text itself and adopt several perspectives (even contradictory views). Movement through space for the visiting player is performance and interpretation. What one chooses to look at, pick up, and interact with become acts that create meaning for the player in the space. These actions as interpretations can then be folded back upon the earlier layers of the "landscape" from MOO space to poem to bodies in the land (figure 2). The result of play in remediated space is a new means of interpreting poetic space and the experience which occasioned the poem.

Player movement through MOO space works much like Deleuze's schizophrenic stroll. As the player investigates various digital objects, his performance in the space creates meaning. The visiting player cobbles together new relations and creates temporary associations as he explores and attempts to understand the MOO site. Such immersion in space differs from the work done by the picturesque observer characterized by the Wordsworthian stroll. For Wordsworth, the walker keeps a critical distance from the objects he observes. The digital MOO stroll does not allow the player to maintain such distance. He must pick up objects, investigate them, and activate verbs in an attempt to orient himself in space and make sense of his relation to the environment.

A parallel can be made to the heuristic rules of critical analysis of poetic texts. Critical interpretation normally distances itself from the object of study, forms a "picture" of the work, and adopts a singular and unified argument from a point of view outside of the literary text. The critic plants his sticks in the ground and marks his path through the textual landscape. Yet, the ground upon which such criticism stands is itself never brought into question. It is this fundamental problem of finding a ground to authorize a reading which gets taken up in the MOO stroll. In the digital stroll, there is no outside space, no Archimedan point from which to leverage an objective reading. In response to the problem of grounding meaning, MOO play allows the readers to work from within the literary texts to produce their own actions and conversations as commentaries. These, in turn, become part of the playing field inside the MOO space for other players in the space to take up and interact with alongside the MOO space as literary object. As Jerome McGann explains in his justification for critical gaming and his Ivanhoe Game, "Its central object is to make explicit the assumptions about critical practice and textual interpretation that often lie unacknowledged, or at least irregularly explored, in a conventional approach to interpretational practice. . . . 'The Ivanhoe Game' is not a video game to be bested but a difference engine for stimulation self-reflection through interactive role-playing" (218-19, 222). By walking through a MOO space, the MOO player becomes the aleatory point or "difference engine" for production of meaning. The literary critic might retreat to the interior space of his mind but the Deleuzian stroll works by surfaces alone—a body without organs, without a retreat to a privileged interiority as a safe distance for observation and commentary. Working with surfaces alone, the walker affects the space and is infected by it. His actions in the space alter the MOO textual space and actions in the space can effect the player character.

While the goal of this article has been theorizing literary MOO spaces, it will be useful to consider some examples. All of these examples come from work I have done with students at Georgia Tech in the Villa Diodati MOO.[3] The goal of these spaces has been to create an immersive textuality where players work within the textual object of study. Each example shows increasing complexity in programming and immersive play from the Grazing Pasture where players milk cows to Frankenstein's lab where one role plays characters from the novel to WeatherFlash where aspects of real and virtual weather change the dynamics on the screen.

The Grazing Pasture was designed to discuss the growth of cattle breeding in the Romantic period.[4] The site begins with the visiting player entering a grazing pasture. There are several cattle standing in the field including the "Picturesque Cow" and "Bessy." The first is an exemplary cow in a painterly field. Interaction with the cow shows how the animal was used for paintings during the period. It is with the second cow that game play begins. Players are invited to "milk" Bessy. Typing the words "milk Bessy" in the MOO's command lines begins a series of steps toward getting the cow to give up its milk, thus allowing the "naturally" docile animal to yield nature's bounty for man. The irony of all this happening on a computer screen is later built into the site as the player progresses through the MOO space discovering how the animal has become a machine built to service human needs. Once the player has milked the cow, he is prompted to go to the Paybox to receive a shilling for his labors. The player has literally become invested in the role of cattle in the 18th century. Rather than being an innocent observer, the player is a participant in the economy of cattle breeding. With the shilling, the player can then advance to the London Fair room where the 1804 London fair is recreated. Paying the entry fee of one shilling allows the player to see the Lincolnshire Ox—one of the bulkiest British cattle of the period, which toured the kingdom as an example in advancements in the nation's agriculture. After a series of educational displays and opportunities to breed cattle, the site ends with 21st century cows—both the ones we love, such as Ben & Jerry's cows—and the more corporeal beasts that begin showing signs of hoof and mouth disease and BSE. The player travels from simply milking Bessy to deciding the economic feasibility of admitting some of the player's livestock have mad cow disease. Decisions made by the player affect the game play and how the player interacts in the space.

In the example of Frankenstein's lab, the interaction is a bit more complex. Before entering the lab, the player dawns a costume of Victor, the monster, or Elizabeth from *Frankenstein*.[5] Doing so changes the player's name, icon, and description to the chosen character. The player *is* the character. Entering Frankenstein's lab, the player sees the room from the perspective of that character. So, if the player is Victor, he sees aneatly organized lab with a variety of technical equipment. If the player is Elizabeth, the room looks like a gothic slaughterhouse, and from the monster's perspective it is the chaotic place of his birth. To each character, not only is the room image and description different but also the objects available for interaction change. For example, the scientist sees, and can interact with, a galvanic battery that to the other characters simply looks like a nightmarish device with no clear purpose. Three different players can be in the room at the same time—one as Victor, another as Elizabeth, and the third as the monster. While they occupy the same MOO space, each sees something slightly different. Consequently, their interactions with one another become complex assemblages of their surroundings and their personalities in the novel. As Deleuzian assemblages, each character is literally hooked up to different machines: Victor and the battery, Elizabeth and the (doctor's) sowing kit, and the monster and the decaying human and animal remains. How they work with their instruments and each other becomes the interpretive event of this MOO space. Words become actions,and our bodily typing as well as textual commitments made by our screen character take on an event structure, causing things to happen and changing our relation to the visual/ textual landscape of the MOO. MOOs vividly display how meaning changes as we are connected to new surroundings. Meaning is occasioned by coupling player with object and environment. In the MOO, visual and textual shifts in meaning effect the player's avatar and effect what the player typing thinks while at his computer.

The final example is a space still under construction, WeatherFlash. The WeatherFlash room shows Turner's painting *Tintern Abbey* but is digitally modified according to the time of day, season, and weather at the University of Maryland where the Villa Diodati MOO is housed. A one minute Flash movie of clouds blowing across the sky or the sun rising slowly or the sun setting plays according to the variables time of day, season and weather. Additionally, randomly wandering clouds set loose in the Villa can enter the Abbey space and effect weather changes. Players in the space participate in folds between a telepresent real world weather and MOO weather.

This site has a variety of dynamics at play. Foremost is the question of what sort of weather one is experiencing. The MOO is broadcasting real weather by grabbing the forecast for temperature, sun, rain, and clouds from online weather services. It may or may not coincide with the weather that the person playing experiences in his own physical environment. Of course, since most of us MOO while in an artificially regulated environment of heated or cooled office or home spaces, we don't really experience the external weather. Rather, just like the WeatherFlash MOO program, we go online to check our weather outside. The uncanny relationship between the player in the MOO space and the typing person in the office space is hightlighted by this action. Both the online self and the typing self experience weather through online filters mediating the outside world. The typing person is not at a safe remove from his online MOO player avatar. Rather, we are already within machines. WeatherFlash simply feeds these machines to us in new ways. Wordsworth's observer at a distance gets disturbed by the notion that we are already hooked up and immersed in a variety of mediated environments.

The site also plays with the variables of the picturesque as selected by 18th century painter Alexander Cozen. His instructions for painting in *The Various Species of Landscapes* delineates ten different times of day to demarcate in painting and thirteen types of weather along with four seasons (Sloan 54). These variables along with different couplings of objects in a scene make for a variety of paintings. They also point to the impossibility of accounting for all the variables within nature, be it in Cozen's categories or online weather forecasts. Both mediations select elements of the real to translate into linguistic signs so that weather is intelligible and has meaning for us, be it aesthetic or meteorological meaning. As Deleuze asks with his concept of the assemblage, what are we hooked up to and what are we hooking up to nature?

By the way the MOO is built as a new media application, it offers a new and different sort of engagement with literary texts. This essay has sought to develop several untapped areas of exploration: the divide between typing screen and typist, the role of language in MOOing, and the use of objects in object oriented programming of MOOs. MOOs are designed for communicating at a distance. So, programmers can make use of the divided self, the screen self and the typing self. Much has been done with identity in MOOs—am I who I say I am online? Yet, there are many more complex structures left for further exploration, as is evident in the mediated meteorology of the MOO space and the player's typing environment of office or home. By typing in order to communicate at a distance, the MOO relies on words to convey meaning. Anyone who has played in MOOs is familiar with the word play, puns, and quick one-liners in MOO conversations. More than in just conversations, words have an important role in describing locations and influencing player interactions. Players think and talk differently in a space called "The Library" from a space called "The Circus." Words invoke environments and moods that get coupled to players' interests and desires to produce player interaction. The MOOers conversation in the space and interaction with objects in the space is both a commentary on the space itself and a production that begets further comments and actions. As words beget actions, which are themselves more words, MOOing serve as a powerful means of thinking about how language mediates. Finally, the environment itself is object oriented programming. As such, the very nature of the computer language forces player-programmers to think about what counts as objects, descriptors, and verbs for their spaces. The dynamics of player-typist,

MOO word play, and object oriented programming serve as tools for a new heuristics for the literary text. The text becomes a textual and textured environment where players work from within the literary object itself. Inside the text, players orient themselves by creating paths of meaning with steps and missteps, dead ends and long rambling journeys. Each walk is an event and each event offers new possible couplings, assemblages, and roads for thinking about literature.

Notes

1. So much has been written as introduction to MOOs, I am assuming some familiarity with this computer environment. For an introduction or refresher on MOOs see http://lingua.utdallas.edu/ . EnCore developed out of the work in LinguaMOO which remains the foremost site for creative MOOing and gathering of educational-MOO developers.

2. For further explanation of this space see http://www.lcc.gatech.edu/~broglio/mooworlds.html .

3. The Villa takes its name from the house in the Swiss village of Cologny, with a splendid view of Lake Leman, that Lord Byron rented in the legendary summer of 1816. It was, of course, a famous story-telling contest held at the Villa that served as the impetus for Mary Shelley's *Frankenstein*. To enter the Villa MOO go to http://www.rc.umd.edu and click on the *RC MOO* button or go to http://www.rc.umd.edu:7000.

4. To get to the Grazing Pasture, once in the Villa type @go Grazing Pasture or @go #3055.

5. To enter this space in the Villa MOO, type @go Costume Closet or @go #2668.

Works Cited

Bogue, Ronald. *Deleuze on Literature*. New York: Routledge, 2003.

Broglio, Ron. 27 May 2005. "MOO-Poems: Exploring Poems. <http://www.lcc.gatech.edu/~broglio/mooworlds.html,>.

Broglio, Ron and Carl Stahmer. *Romantic Circles Villa Diodati*. <http://www.rc.umd.edu:7000>.

Burnett, D. Graham. *Masters of All They Surveyed*. Chicago: U of Chicago P, 2001.

Deleuze, Gilles. *Difference and Repetition*. New York: Columbia UP, 1994.

Deleuze, Gilles, and Guattari, Felix. *Anti-Oedipus*. Trans. Brian Massumi. Minneapolis: U of Minnesota P, 1983.

—. *Kafka: Toward a Minor Literature*. Minneapolis: U of Minnesota P, 1986.

Gilpin, William. *Observations on the Mountains and Lakes of Cumberland and Westmoreland.* 1786. Vol. 1. New York: Woodstock Books, 1996.

Haynes, Cynthia and Jan Rune Holmevik. *LinguaMOO.* 27 May 2005. <http://lingua.utdallas.edu/>.

Heidegger, Martin. "The Question Concerning Technology." *Basic Writings.* Trans. David Farrell Krell. San Francisco: HarperCollins, 1993. 311-41.

Keats, John. Letter to Richard Woodhouse, 27 October 1818. *Complete Poems and Selected Letters of John Keats.* New York: Modern Library, 2001.

Massumi, Brian. "Introduction." *A Thousand Plateaus.* Gilles Deleuze and Felix Guattari. Trans. Brian Massumi. Minneapolis: U of Minnesota P, 1993. xiii.

McGann, Jerome. *Radiant Textuality: Literature after the World Wide Web.* New York: Palgrave, 2001.

Sloan, Kim. Cozen. Alexander and Robert Cozen. New Haven: Yale UP, 1987.

Vitanza, Victor J. "Of MOOs, Folds, and Non-reactionary Virtual Communities" *High Wired.* Ann Arbor: U of Michigan P, 1998. 286-310.

West, Thomas. *A Guide to the Lakes in Cumberland, Westmorland, and Lancashire.* 1784. Oxford: Woodstock Books, 1989.

Wordsworth, William. Advertisement for *The Prelude. The Poetic Works of William Wordsworth.* New York: Oxford UP, 1971.

—. "I wander lonely as a cloud" *The Lyrical Ballads, and Other Poems, 1797–1800.* Ed. James Butler and Karen Green. Ithaca, NY: Cornell UP, 1992.

11 Funkcomp

Jeff Rice

Welcome to station WEFUNK, better known as We-Funk,
Or deeper still, the Mothership Connection.
Home of the extraterrestrial brothers,
Dealers of funky music.

—P.Funk, uncut funk, The Bomb—"P Funk (Wants to Get Funked Up)"

The Funky Writer, Part I

Funk is not just a feeling. Funk, as Rickey Vincent writes in his classic breakdown of the music genre, "is the extremes of everything . . . Funk is a way out, and a way in. Funk all over the place" (3). Funk, in the lyrics and music of George Clinton (bandleader of both Parliament and Funkadelic) is about the "one." The essential beat driving funk through its emphasis on non-traditional popular music rhythm counts, the one is a collaborative process. In funk, "all participate as part of a greater whole. A locked, happening rhythm brings everybody together grooving as one" (Vincent 37). Parliament's "Everything is on the One" stresses this feeling through the repeated mantra:

Everything is on the one today y'all, now hit it
Everything is on the one today y'all, and don't forget it.

Funk, Gregory Ulmer explains, belongs within the rhetorical principles electracy creates towards developing a hyperrhetoric. Electracy, Ulmer's definition of the shift from literacy to electronic meaning making, depends on mood in order to sustain narrative. Funk, Ulmer claims, creates the necessary mood for electronic writing. "A crucial moment in the invention of literacy," Ulmer writes, "was Aristotle's formulation of the 'thing' in the practice of definition. Now the *thang* is similarly important to electracy" (*Internet Invention* 316).

As an instructor of writing, my question regarding Ulmer's observation is: What might be the *thang* for a composition pedagogy which funkifies rhetorical instruction? I want to extend Ulmer's proposition that electronic rhetoric operates according to a *thang* principle by locating the *thang* funk teaches in a specific electronic writing practice I will invent for new media work. Such a task involves imagining writing outside the restrictions of print-based literacy (as Ulmer suggests). The conceptualization of language as referent to actual "thing," Jack Goody writes, prompted the invention of literacy.

> Writing, and more especially alphabetic literacy, made it possible to scrutinize discourse in a different kind of way by giving oral communication a semi-permanent form; this scrutiny favored the increase in scope of critical activity, and hence of rationality, skepticism, and logic. (Goody 37)

In the conventional writing classroom, whose focus typically is the teaching of literacy, the ability to name a concept or pinpoint an idea materializes in the demand that students write topic sentences. The topic sentence represents a permanent idea, a "thing" which can be named and referred to. Literacy's contribution to classroom practice has been to emphasize the topic sentence as central to writing pedagogy. To be literate, composition studies teaches students, a writing's purpose is emphasized in this pivotal sentence.

In order to be electrate, on the other hand, contemporary writing students need to shift away from thinking in terms of the thing (i.e. the topic sentence) and must identify the importance of the thang, the central mood in funk. The thang indicates doing something "one's own way" as in the expression popularized in The Isley Brothers' song of the same name: "It's your thang, do what you want to do" and noted in Parliament's "One of Those Funky Thangs."

> I just heard it's gonna be one of those funky thangs
> We're the freaks that we freakin' to

Thang also refers to an overall feeling that is outrageous and non-conformist, a feeling that cannot be named, that is allusive yet meaningful, that does not depend on logic or rationality, and that cannot be declared in one specific sentence situated strategically in an opening paragraph. To help students understand the relevancy of this feeling to electracy, I propose another analogy. What rationality and logic were to literacy's need for definition and classification, outrageousness is to electracy's usage of funk.

In the literate model, the book (and eventually, the textbook) serves as a tool for disseminating literacy. In electracy, funk teaches students how to write with mood, yet mood does not serve as a category or definition but rather an overall feeling. Its place of expression does not require the permanence literacy demands. The pedagogical challenge for me is to work with students in order to flesh out the analogy and create an actual digital writing which is funky. Instead of proposing music as the tool to teach electracy, I propose the Web, what I understand as the funkiest of all new media forms for how it displaces text, image, and code in both familiar and unfamiliar ways.

If I am to develop a funky writing practice, I also need to consider an appropriate apparatus which will support such writing. Particular to my interests is the discipline of composition studies, the field I work in. In composition studies, the textbook plays a primary pedagogical role in producing literate citizens. How can I create a new electrate practice for a discipline still using the tools of literacy? "Powerful, alternative formal possibilities are now key genres of public discourse," Geoffrey Sirc notes, "and kids understand them, and Composition Studies could care less" ("Virtual Urbanism" 14). Sirc recognizes that popular media forms, like the Web, generate alternative places for expression, but that composition studies is slow to respond. In particular, Sirc directs me towards funk as one type of public discourse worth further pedagogical exploration. "Funk now becomes a key index of compositional authority," he writes ("Stagolee"). Accordingly, I will use not just the mood funk to teach digital writing, as Ulmer instructs, but the musical genre itself as guide.

Take It to The Bridge

To invent a funky writing practice, I continue with Sirc and focus on his work with the Happening. Recognizing composition's need to challenge conventions (whether in writing or in instruction), Sirc argues that the Happening offers an appropriate media-oriented model for writing instruction. Sirc proposes its role in composition studies as "pedagogy as dare" (*English Composition as a Happening* 8). The model dares both teachers and students to consider alternative forms of expression.

> An enthusiasm has been lost, particularly among those entering the profession. Even the newest technologies for composition are rapidly succumbing to this lull—witness collections on what makes writing good in the digital age, taxonomies of email, or standards for evaluating web pages. The cause of our current stasis? Doubtless the major influence has been Composition's Professionalization, its self-tormented quest for disciplinary stature. The price we have paid for our increased credibility as an academic field has been a narrowing of the bandwidth of what used to pass for composition. In figuring out our place among the disciplines, we have made the notion of disciplines paramount—what we talk about when we talk about writing is writing-in-the-academy or "real world" writing that reflects (legitimates) academic departments. (*English Composition as a Happening* 24–25)

Sirc's critique allows me to ask if funk can be the element which restores enthusiasm lost in student writing (and consequently, the teaching of writing). "Funkiness," Vincent writes, "[i]s an aesthetic of deliberate confusion, of uninhibited, soulful behavior that remains viable because of a faith in instinct, a joy of self, and a joy of life" (4). Following these concerns, I work from funk's "enthusiasm" for outrageous behavior and hard backbeats in order to propose a new composition practice tentatively titled Funkcomp.

The principles of Funkcomp come from a different form of *composition* than that typically emphasized in the writing classroom: musical composition. Too often, composition studies limits the definition of composition to "student writing." In doing so, it creates a circular pedagogy. We teach students to write as students write. In turn, other forms of writing, and in particular, other forms of writing charged with emotion, remain ignored. When composition does look to alternative forms of discourse like advertising, film, video, or the Web, it does so in order to teach students how to read these forms as texts (i.e. hermeneutics), not how to learn from these forms rhetorical instructions. By shifting focus to musical composition, my purpose is to get composition studies to pay attention to the rhetoric of funk in order to teach students the role of the funky writer. Consequently, I might say that the theme for this essay is taken from Funkadelic's statement "Who says a Funk Band Can't Play Rock?" The analogy for composition is "Who says composition can't be funky?"

The Funky Writer, Part II

It is too easy to begin my project by declaring how unfunky composition has been throughout its roughly one-hundred-and-twenty-year existence. Yet, in order to describe the funky writer, I must draw some attention to composition's unfunky practices. The opposite of funk is the literate composition textbook. As example, I choose for its wide scale usage, and not to cast blame on one particular text, the popular *The St. Martin's Guide to Writing* and its opening advice to student writers.

> As writers we learn how to order and present our thoughts in language patterns that readers can recognize and follow. If you are writing a position paper, for example, you need to know that readers expect claims to be supported by relevant reasons and evidence. (Axelrod and Cooper 5)

Reading through this passage, I cannot argue with the advice because it makes sense. The authors' choice of "order," "relevant," and "reason" as keywords in the writing process stresses the importance of logic and clarity to writing. If you aren't relevant, or if you don't embrace order, your work will go misunderstood. Yet the very relevancy *The St. Martin's Guide* argues for quickly translates as commonplace assumptions and expectations which students rely upon as they attempt to make their work "relevant" for instructors. Expectation, as the student understands it, means familiarity, and familiarity means the obvious. My concern with guidance like that of *The St. Martin's Guide* is how students interpret the instruction of relevancy to mean "give the teacher what she wants." In the early 1960s, Ken Macrorie complained that this emphasis on relevance creates Engfish, the uninspired and bland types of writings students believe teachers expect them to produce. In *Uptaught,* Macrorie critiques Engfish as the unmotivated, yet relevant, school language, what I understand as nothing more than unfunky writing:

> Such language could only be learned in school; no one anywhere else would hear it in the bones of his ear. Key university words are there: *process, experience, role, tend, knowledge, proficiency, participate,* and *important* twice. But nothing is said worth listening to. (16)

Funk is not the language of school. School language derives from, among other places, the textbook. The textbook teaches an unfunky language, one which, because of its goal to produce an uncomplicated citizen who can follow the rules of the university and eventually of society, produces a standardized discourse void of meaning or insight. As early as Edwin Woolley's 1907 *Handbook of Composition,* we find such teaching. Proper English must make sense.

> English discourse employing words generally approved by good usage, and employing them in the sense and in the grammatical functions and combinations generally approved by good usage, is called good English. (qtd. in Brereton 360)

Good usage implies complicity in language and thought. How, then, do we negotiate Woolley's remarks with George Clinton urging fellow funksters to get onboard the Mothership (the place where all composing takes place) and take risks in life?

> All right, all right, Starchild here
> Put a glide in your stride and a dip in your hip
> And come on up to the Mothership.
> Loose Booty, doin' the bump. Hustle on over here.
> ("Mothership Connection")

Funk is "out there"; it does the bump; it hustles, it puts a "dip in your hip." Because of its willingness to take chances with movement and expression, therefore, funk is anything but obvious. The obvious form of writing, the cliché or generalized statement dominant in many first-year writings, motivated Macrorie to question why educational goals don't challenge students to take chances.

> I had devoted most of my career to teaching Freshman Composition because I wanted every college student to write with clarity and pezazz [sic]. Sometimes attending my class, students became worse writers, their sentences infected with more and more phoniness, and eventually stiffening in *rigor mortis.* (Macrorie 16)

Although Macrorie made this complaint almost forty years ago, I find its meaning relevant today. I want to encourage students to get beyond this phoniness of "inventing the university," what Sirc calls "an endless stream of *Ways of Reading* knock-offs" and "how the middle-brow samey-sounding essays result in their own perfect approximation" (Re-Interview). I want to get students to be funky, but I want them to do so in the digital sphere.

Funketelechy

In order to fashion a digital writing which is funky, I choose to work primarily with George Clinton's work in the bands Funkadelic and Parliament. Clinton proves an exceptional model for digital writing because of his fascination with outer space, his belief that funk emerges from the juxtaposition of technology and science (funketelechy).

> Funk upon a time in the days of the Funkapus
> The concept of specially-designed Afronauts capable
> of funkatizing galaxies
> Was first laid on man-child ("Prelude")

My appropriation of funk for the purpose of digital writing responds to what I understand as a very unfunky approach to electronic writing currently practiced, a pedagogy largely inherited from the examples I presented above. Whereas Clinton challenges the electronic with new "funkatizing" concepts, composition's foray into the digital has, for the most part, relied on non-digital methods of expression, practices put in place long before digital writing and applied as if digital writing is non-existent.[1] Thus, it is not uncommon to find textbooks geared toward electronic writing repeating the same kinds of lessons dominant in textbooks prior to either the PC revolution of the early 1980s or the proliferation of the World Wide Web after 1993. Beth Kolko, Alison Regan, and Susan Romano's *Writing in an Electronic World,* for instance, displays student writing that, for all purposes, is not representative of an electronic world, but could appear (and does appear) in an unfunky, print world. The textbook's "Writers Using Technology" sections are narratives about using technology, not narratives which reflect usage of technology (i.e., their narrative structure is print-based, not electronic). Indeed, in the "electronic world" the authors promise, we find the very unfunky instructions prominent in many other textbooks, like James McCrimmon's canonical *Writing With a Purpose.* In McCrimmon's work, we read that writers

> Must therefore always begin with a clear sense of purpose. The means that before he starts to write he must think carefully about two related questions: "What precisely do I want to do?" and "How can I best do it?" Answering these questions clearly is the first step toward writing well. (McCrimmon 3)

And in *Writing in an Electronic World,* we read that "it's a good idea to begin your invention activities by thinking about the rhetorical triangle and about writing and *purpose*" (56 emphasis mine).

> While there is nothing wrong with having "purpose," purpose in itself is not an electronic writing strategy, nor is it an unfamiliar position to the student. In fact, the question of purpose has been internalized by students into the very unfunky concept of the topic sentence ("this is what I will write about"). Instead of asking student writers to identify topic sentences in their work or have purpose, Funkcomp asks students to "make it funky!"

Tear the Roof Off

How, then, do we make it funky? Because funk is a mood, my claim for the practice of Funkcomp is that composition must involve emotion. Such was Macrorie's contention that the only way to get around Englishwas to encourage students to write about personal experience. Instead of opting for an expressivist pedagogy as Macrorie did, however, I want to turn to funk itself for lessons regarding how to use personal experience and emotion in digital writing.[2] The first thing I learn from funk involves the role persona plays in writing. Adopting a wide range of personas, George Clinton, funk's most important figure, has renamed himself from record to record, depending on the funky mood he wishes to convey. In turn, Clinton's persona, his writerly voice, has been Dr. Funkenstein, Mr. Wiggles, Starchild, and the evil Sir Nose D'Voidoffunk. These personalities emerge from the complex intersection of race, culture, place, and class played out in Parliament's music.

The rationale for extending one's persona (or altering it) stems from the digital user's need to juxtapose identity and mythology as she struggles to fashion a relationship with technology. Identity and digital writing, Jay David Bolter writes, are intertwined in complex ways so that their cultural foundations lead to mythological associations.

> We employ media in defining both our personal and our cultural identities. Because media are simultaneously technical analogs and social expressions of our identity, we become simultaneously both the subject and object of our contemporary media. (Bolter 17)

John Corbett writes that, in Clinton's case, the need to construct a mythological identity is a reaction to standardized non-technology based mythologies the white, dominant culture creates in order to limit African-American self-expression or the role of African-Americans in American culture. "Consider Parliament's Clone Funk Afro-nauts, a mythological, mechanized-but-funky bunch also known as the 'children of production'" (Corbett 19). The Afro-nauts bear little resemblance to mythological stereotypes and expectations in cultural circulation, stereotypes often dependent on racist assumptions (such as African-American lack of interest in technology). Clinton uses the alter ego (Dr. Funkenstein) to defamiliarize such stereotypes and to forge new claims. The defamiliarization of old mythological identities and the creation of new ones is an important lesson Clinton teaches in Funkcomp. Mythologies, Roland Barthes wrote in his 1957 text of the same name, indicate meanings assumed to be "natural" because of their proliferation and mass-acceptance, but which are latent with ideological meanings. Myths, Barthes states, spring from individual perceptions of identity.

> Myth has an imperative, buttonholing character: stemming from an historical concept, directly springing from contingency (a Latin class, at threatened Empire), it is *I* whom it has come to seek. It is turned towards me, I am subjected to its intentional force, it summons me to receive its expansive ambiguity. (Barthes 124)

Thus, I can expand from the racial myths Clinton exposes to composition's formulation of a mythological student identity, and consequently, mythological student writing. These myths include the role of organization, clarity, and coherence popular in writing instruction. These myths structure a student writer accordingly, asking her to think of herself as a unified, clear, and coherent being whose writing reflects rationality and reason. Even the seemingly chaotic advice of Peter Elbow's freewriting and brainstorming, for instance, intends to reach a rational conclusion. "When I go get writing, I discover that much of the preparation time was a waste of time. The important things happen during writing; after a first draft; trying to clean it up or reconcile contradictions" (*Writing Without Teachers* 31). Clarity, Funkcomp declares, is an ideological construction.

Learning from Clinton's dislocated personas, Funkcomp asks students no longer to think of themselves as "clear and coherent" when they write, but to adopt the funk model which prompts writers to create an alter ego as precursor to invention. Thus, Funkcomp writers reject clarity as means towards freeing their minds to new discursive possibilities.

> Swift lippin,' and ego trippin,' and body snatchin,'
> Dr. Funkenstein, you are really out of sight
> (Yeah, hit me one time, one time!) ("Dr. Funkenstein")

Through this process, Funkcomp asks students to think of themselves not as the product of textbook culture (whose emphasis on the commonplace assumption of clarity often prohibits inventive work), but instead as media creations. "Commonplaces," David Bartholomae writes, "are the 'controlling ideas' of our composition textbooks, textbooks that not only insist on a set form for expository writing, but a set view of public life" (77). This view, I contend, insists students identify themselves as student writers and not as *writers* whose identities are tied to media. The commonplace identity of student writer limits student expression to the kind of writing Macrorie vehemently critiqued as meaningless. Because the student identifies herself as a student writer, her work becomes internalized as school work, and not writing. School work involves commonplace ideas (due dates, appearance, grades, pre-set topics). Funkcomp, on the other hand, requires students to construct and adopt the alter ego as motive to defamiliarize the commonplace. Instead of being a "student," the Funkcompositionist adopts a funky identity.

The rationale for adopting a funky identity is to get students outside of commonplace expectations (accepted by both the student and the composition course), which deny the student the space to truly "invent." Despite claims that writing leads to self-discovery, much of composition's expectations of the student are not conducive to invention. "We teach students how writing discovers the self and shares it with others" Erika Lindemann writes in a *Rhetoric for Writing Teachers* (7). "Through writing," *The St Martin's Guide* notes, "we learn to reflect deeply on our personal experience and to examine critically our most basic assumptions. Thus writing enables us to understand ourselves better" (Axelrod and Cooper). The unfunky methods taught towards such discovery have only re-enforced previously constructed ideas regarding self; these methods teach students to cling to clichés and expectations regarding selfhood, not to challenge their expectation of self.

To actualize *The St. Martin's Guide's* claim, then, Funkcomp asks students to adopt an alter ego as first step towards challenging their "basic assumptions" regarding personal experience and rhetoric. A simple, personal reflexive paper won't do that because self-reflexion on its own does not challenge assumptions; it supports them by causing a writer to consider the first thing that comes to mind (which is a basic assumption). The construction of an alter ego precludes a second assignment, which allows a writer to take this new alter ego and go beyond the cliché, thus denying expectation. This second assignment must make students, and consequently, the audiences for their work, say "What the. ." when they write through these alter egos. Audiences say "What the . . ." as they express initial bafflement and confusion because expectation has not been met. Thus, to do all of this, students must first say "What the. ." about themselves. The alter ego, the funky identity I've been outlining, becomes the basis for such a funky writing assignment.

What the . . .

How, then, does Funkcomp translate as pedagogical practice? I offer one sequence of assignments which speaks to the spirit of Funkcomp and teaches students a method for producing digital work. One of Funkcomp's concerns stems from the legacy of Strunk and White's *Elements of Style,* a canonical text which has created a very specific (and popular) expectation of writing.[3] Amid their numerous stylistic rules and regulations regarding usage of "that" and "which" or "can" and "may," the authors instruct writers to "prefer the standard to the offbeat" (81). Writers, they argue, should emphasize accepted stylistic norms as opposed to inventing new forms or adopting temporal usage into their work. Using a musical metaphor, Strunk and White dissuade students from writing that is exciting or from coming "under the spell of these unsettling drums" (81): By the time this paragraph sees print, *uptight, ripoff, rap, dude, vibes, copout,* and *funky* will be the words of yesteryear, and we will be fielding more recent ones that have come bouncing into our speech" (82). Inadvertently, Strunk and White's warning names Funkcomp. Instead of utilizing their conservative writing agenda, I borrow Strunk and White's funky exclamation as recognition that funk is not a passing fad but, in fact, a form of digital writing.

As my outlining of Funkcomp so far demonstrates, in funk, the offbeat is preferred to the standard. Funk's basic notion of composition, the one, stresses the offbeat of the typical four/four rhythm scheme. Generalized from musical rhythm to composing, the one is a lesson for funky writers to be offbeat in their compositions as they work to produce ideas. Creating "offbeat" work is not typically the focus of writing instruction. Thus, when David Bartholomae examines student placement exams written on the topic of "creativity," he struggles to find writing which creatively approaches the topic. Instead, the writing marks "a set of conventional rituals and gestures" (75); the writings Bartholomae reads, in fact, are standard, not offbeat.

In order to perform the offbeat, Funkcomp's response to standard writing is to use the *ethos* already constructed in the funky alter ego position in order to create the "What the . . ." writing assignment. An extension of the whatever assignment I have proposed elsewhere,[4]

What the . . . deals with "whatever's" ambiguity and allusiveness, but reflects a greater sense of the shock implicit in exclaiming, "What the hell." Unlike a typical composition assignment, which demands clarity and purpose from the writer in order to create immediate audience understanding, What the . . . assumes a different context for writing, one which challenges first impressions by creating work which cannot be easily understood at first, which does not begin with the expectation of a topic sentence explaining "this is what I mean." In *The St. Martin's Handbook,* Andrea Lunsford advises writers that audience expectation serves a primary purpose in good writing.

> Readers expect that a piece of writing will make one or more points clearly and illustrate or support those points with ample evidence—good reasons, examples, or other details. Effective use of such evidence helps readers understand a point, makes abstract concepts concrete, and offers proof that what you are saying is sensible and worthy of attention. (Lunsford 5)

Like the position emphasized by the unfunky writer noted earlier in this essay, it is hard to disagree with such sensible instruction. In order to defamiliarize expectation, however, Funkcomp must teach otherwise by asking students to adopt the unclear, insensible George Clinton remark, best represented at the end of "Prelude": "May I frighten you?" ("Prelude"). A What the . . . assignment uses the rhetoric of the offbeat in order to present information to an audience so that it is, in some aspects, almost frightening in place of being clear.

The What the . . . assignment may be contexualized in any number of ways as long as it takes place on the Web. Students may be asked to write about themselves, a given social issue, a local community problem, a national issue, etc., as long as they approach the argument from the rhetorical methodology of Funkcomp. Thus, Funkcomp, like Clinton's music, is not dependent on the topic of funk. Funk serves as the model for this specific kind of digital writing. The form and content of the writing should be based on a sense of outrageousness, a mood not unlike many of the Parliament-Funkadelic examples scattered throughout this essay.

The What the . . . element funk teaches is modeled after Clinton's concept of Funketelechy, the idea of "The Promentalshitbackwashpsychosis":

> The doo doo chasers, friends of roto-rooter
> Music to clean your shit by. (Promentalshitback-
> washpsychosis Enema Squad, The Doo-Doo Chasers)

The outrageousness of such writing may, at first, appear silly or inconsequential. Its social commentary regarding consumption, however, echoes Kenneth Burke's well known statement in *A Grammar of Motives,* "what we want is *not terms that avoid ambiguity,* but *terms that clearly reveal the strategic spots at which ambiguities necessarily arise*" (xviii). In Funkcomp, ambiguity is further enhanced by technology itself, the application of HTML-related scripts made available to writers who are not programmers (through online libraries of cut and paste scripts). The final step towards creating a What the . . . assignment, then, is to work with code (Code in a writing course? Outrageous!) as writing itself (thus, challenging further writing expectations). Merging technology with content, funky writers use web-based scripts rhetorically to present an outrageous argument. Javascripts, DHTML, HTML, CSS, and even Flash may be used in non-print ways. As Clinton challenges expectation in his juxtaposition of alter ego, technology, African-American culture, and music, so does the student experiment with a variety of forms and media and, in turn, challenge how we view and use code to shape egos and writing. A summary of the assignment as given is as follows:

1. Identity. Adopt a funky identity that reflects a specific attitude you want to espouse. Demonstrate that identity on a website by actively using HTML, javascript, and related scripts so that you don't tell a narrative but rather demonstrate your identity through technology.

2. What the . . . Use that identity to make a claim about a specific issue. Readers of your What the . . . should not be able to recognize its purpose immediately. Your What the . . . should be ambiguous enough as to attract attention and interest; readers must ponder what its purpose is by reconciling your content, identity, and usage of technology.

Funkcomp teaches digital invention by asking students to locate the *thang* of discourse, the ambiguous merger of technology and expression. Simultaneously, it challenges composition pedagogy to better comprehend the demands new media creates for writing instruction. Clinging to coherence and rationality in light of electracy's emphasis of a different kind of rhetoric prevents the teaching of digital writing. Clinton's concept of funketelechy, represented in the thang principle of electracy, updates Aristotle's literate conception of "entelechy" described by Kenneth Burke as "the individual's potentialities for becoming a fully representative member of its class" (Burke 27). Media beings (as we all are) represent more than permanent classes or categories. Ambiguity created through alter ego and through allusive meaning reshapes our understandings of how explanation and argument are constructed in new media. Funkcomp marks one such place where we and our students can consider the one, the offbeat, and the outrageous as principles of digital composition.

Notes

1. I am referring to the practice of uploading print-based papers to the Web, the over-emphasis on rhetorical analysis of websites instead of the production of websites, and the ideological belief that the conventions of print we have become accustomed to apply easily and directly to all new media work (topic sentences, paragraph structure, etc.).

2. My usage of the terms "personal experience" and "emotion" (and even my usage of Macrorie's work) does not parallel expressivist pedagogy which, too, relies on these terms. Instead, I am drawing from the question of the alter ego and mood, which have nothing in common with expressivism.

3. Even if composition studies does not teach *The Elements of Style* any more on a regular basis, it is still a popular text with non-academic and academic audiences.

4. See "The 1963 Hip-Hop Machine: Hip-Hop Pedagogy As Composition." College Composition and Communication. 54.3 (2003): 453-71.

Works Cited

Axelrod, Rise B. and Charles R. Cooper. *The St. Martin's Guide to Writing.* 5th ed.. New York: St. Martin's Press, 1997.

Barthes, Roland. *Mythologies.* New York: Hill and Wang, 1972.

Bartholomae, David. "Inventing the University" *Teaching Composition: Background Readings.* Boston, MA: Bedford St. Martin's, 2002.

Brereton, John. *The Origins of Composition Studies in the American College, 1875–1925: A Documentary History.* Pittsburgh: U of Pittsburgh P, 1995.

Burke, Kenneth. *A Grammar of Motives.* Berkeley: U of California P, 1974.

Corbett, John. *Extended Play: Sounding Off From John Cage to Dr. Funkenstein.* Durham, NC: Duke UP, 1994.

Funkadelic. "Promentalshitbackwashpsychosis Enema Squad (The Doo-Doo Chasers)" *One Nation Under a Groove.* Capitol Records, 2002.

Goody, Jack. *The Domestication of the Savage Mind.* Cambridge: Cambridge UP, 1995.

Lindemann, Erika. *A Rhetoric for Writing Teachers.* New York: Oxford UP, 2001.

Lunsford, Andrea. *The St. Martin's Handbook.* Boston, MA: Bedford/St. Martin's, 2003.

Macrorie, Ken. *Uptaught.* Portsmouth, NH: Boynton/Cook Heinemann, 1996.

McCrimmon, James. *Writing With A Purpose.* Boston: Houghton Mifflin Company, 1963.

Parliament. "Aqua Boogie (A Psychoalphadiscobetabioaquadooloop)." *Motor Booty Affair.* Polygram Records, 1978.

—. "Dr. Funkenstein." *The Clones of Dr. Funkenstein.* Polygram Records, 1976.

—. "Mothership Connection (Starchild)." *Mothership Connection.* Universal, 1975

—. "One of Those Funky Thangs." *Motor Booty Affair.* Polygram Records, 1978.

—. "Prelude." *The Clones of Dr. Funkenstein.* Polygram Records, 1976.

Sirc, Geoffrey. *English Composition as a Happening.* Logan: Utah State P, 2002.

—. "Pre-Text Re-Interview with Geoff Sirc." Online posting. 8 Nov. 2002, Pre-Text Discussion List.

—."Stagolee as Writing Instructor." *Enculturation.* 4.2, Fall 2002.

—. "Virtual Urbanism." *Computers and Composition.* 18(1) 2001 11–19.

Strunk William and E.B. White. *The Elements of Style.* New York: Mac-Millan Publishing, 1979.

Ulmer, Gregory L. *Internet Invention: From Literacy to Electracy.* New York: Longman, 2003.

Contributors

Ron Broglio received his PhD in English Literature at the University of Florida in 1999. He has taught at Georgia Tech since 2000. His research focuses on how philosophy and aesthetics can help us rethink the relationship between humans and the environment. His book *Technologies of the Picturesque: British Art, Poetry, and Instruments 1750-1830* covers technology in the British landscape aesthetic. He is beginning a second project on animals in contemporary art called *On the Surface*. Meanwhile, Broglio continues publishing on the visionary poet William Blake and writes occasional essays on digital humanities. He has received fellowships at the Huntington Library and Yale Center for British Art. He is associate editor of *Romantic Circles* and book review editor of *Configurations*. Broglio's essays appear or are forthcoming in *Journal of Visual Culture, New Formations, The Wordsworth Circle, Praxis, TEXT Technology, AI and Society*, and *Visible Language*.

Elizabeth Coffman is an associate professor of communication at Loyola University Chicago. She teaches documentary production and film studies. Her articles have been published in the journals *Camera Obscura* and *Paradoxa*. Her film work includes both experimental and documentary projects that have screened at film festivals, been installed in museums, and broadcast on internationally. She has co-produced a documentary on nation-building in Bosnia and is currently working on a documentary about the wetlands in Louisiana.

Denise K. Cummings is an assistant professor of critical media and cultural studies at Rollins College in Winter Park, Florida, and has lived in Florida since 1997. She received her PhD from the University of Florida, where she pursued film studies and twentieth century studies in the Department of English. Her areas of teaching and research interest include film history, theory, and criticism; American Indian literatures and film; American literature; modernism; and cultural studies. At Rollins, she teaches courses in film and media studies, literature, and composition while also increasingly working with students in service-related projects in the Central Florida community.

Bradley Dilger is an associate professor at Western Illinois University, where he teaches composition studies, new media, and professional writing. His research centers on the influence ease bears on culture and technology, from nineteenth-century composition classrooms, to technical communication, to networked computing.

Michelle Glaros is an assistant professor of communication at Centenary College of Louisiana, where she teaches digital video production and media studies. Her research interests include experimental film and video, new media arts, and academic labor studies. She has published in *frAme: Journal of Culture and Technology, Kairos: A Journal of Rhetoric, Technology, and Pedagogy*, and *Academe*. Currently, she is in post-production on an experimental documentary about the cultural identity of Shreveport, Louisiana.

Michael Jarrett is professor of English at Penn State University, York Campus. He is the author of *Sound Tracks: A Musical ABC* (Temple University Press) and Drifting on a Read: Jazz as a Model for Writing (SUNY Press).

Barry Jason Mauer earned his doctorate in cultural studies from the University of Florida's English Department in 1999. Both Gregory Ulmer and Robert Ray served on his dissertation committee, with Ulmer chairing. Since 1999, Mauer has been an assistant professor (now associate) at the University of Central Florida in Orlando. His primary responsibility at UCF is to the Texts and Technology PhD program, which is housed in the English department. In addition to his work as a teacher and researcher, Mauer also writes and records music. His CDs are available through CDBaby and Amazon.

Marcel O'Gorman is an associate professor in the Department of English at the University of Waterloo and Director of the Critical Media Lab. His published research, including *E-Crit: Digital Media,*

Critical Theory and the Humanities (University of Toronto Press, 2006) is concerned primarily with the fate of the humanities in a digital culture. O'Gorman's most recent work investigates the "collusion of death and technology," a concept that he calls "necromedia." O'Gorman is also a practicing artist, working primarily with physical computing inventions and architectural installations. Samples of his work may be viewed at http://marcelogorman.net.

Robert Ray is a professor of English at the University of Florida. He is the author *of A Certain Tendency of the Hollywood Cinema, 1930–1980* (Princeton University Press); *The Avant-Garde Finds Andy Hardy* (Harvard University Press); and *How a Film Theory Got Lost, and Other Mysteries in Cultural Studies* (Indiana University Press). He is also a member of the Vulgar Boatmen, whose records include *You and Your Sister*, *Please Panic*, *Opposite Sex*, and *Wide Awake*.

Jeff Rice is an assistant professor of English and Director, Campus Writing Program, at the University of Missouri-Columbia. He is the author of *The Rhetoric of Cool: Composition Studies and New Media* (Southern Illinois University Press) and the textbook *Writing About Cool: Hypertext and Cultural Studies in the Computer Classroom* (Longman) as well as numerous essays on new media and writing. He blogs at Yellow Dog (http://www.ydog.net).

Craig Saper, professor of English at the University of Central Florida, is the author of *Artificial Mythologies: A Guide to Cultural Invention* (1997) and *Networked Art* (2001). His recent publications appear in *At A Distance: Precursors to Art and Activism on the Internet, Performance Research, and Rhizomes*. He is the media editor of *HyperRhiz: New Media Cultures* and co-directs the folkvine.org site.

Gregory L. Ulmer, professor of English and media studies at the University of Florida, is the author of *Electronic Monuments* (Minnesota, 2005); *Internet Invention: From Literacy to Electracy*, (Longman, 2003); *Heuretics: The Logic of Invention* (Johns Hopkins, 1994); *Teletheory: Grammatology in the Age of Video* (Routledge, 1989); *Applied Grammatology: Post(e)-Pedagogy from Jacques Derrida to Joseph Beuys* (Johns Hopkins, 1985). In addition, Ulmer has authored some fifty articles and chapters exploring the shift in the apparatus of language from literacy to electracy. His media work includes two video tapes in distribution (one with Paper Tiger Television, the other with the Critical Art Ensemble). He has given invited addresses at international media arts conferences in Helsinki, Sydney, Hamburg, Halifax and Nottingham, as well as at many sites in the United States. He teaches in the media and communications program of the European Graduate School, Saas-Fee, Switzerland. Ulmer's Internet experiments are organized around the problematic of the Internet as a fifth estate, for which he is developing a deconstructive consulting practice—the EmerAgency. Ulmer teaches in the Networked Writing Environment (NWE) at the University of Florida, featuring Web design as the medium of learning. His current project is "Miami Virtue," a psychogeography of the city of Miami, in collaboration with the Florida Research Ensemble.

Index

Printed in the United States
120683LV00004B/166-213/P

9 781602 350632